ATTACHMENTS:
Poltergeist of Washington State Part 2

By
Keith Linder

Once is happenstance. Twice is coincidence. The third time it's enemy action

~ Wild Things

Glossary of Terms

Word	Meaning
Apparition	Ghost-like. A supernatural appearance of a person or thing. Generally viewed as startling.
Demon	An evil spirit gone rogue from its collective to bring about mental, spiritual, and physical destruction of human beings. Operates from multiple tier levels.
Demons in Seattle	Title of the *Ghost Adventures* (Travel Channel) episode that originally aired February 28th, 2015. Viewed by many as a gross depiction of the events happening in the Bothell house.
Demons in Seattle Uncovered	A documentary cataloging Steve Mera's and Don Phillip's two – and-a-half week investigation of the Bothell home. The documentary is an antithesis to *Ghost Adventures* claim of the house not being active.
EMF	Electromagnetic field
EVP	Electronic voice phenomena
Intelligent Haunting	A spirit that interacts with environments or occupants.
IT	Information Technology — the technology involving the development, maintenance, and use of computer systems, software, and networks.
IT Project Manager	IT project managers plan, organize, and integrate cross-functional IT projects that are significant in scope and impact
Minions	Evil spirits with a group mind to bring about mental, spiritual,

	physical destruction of human beings. Vile and opportunistic.
Nikki (Nicole) Novelle	Paranormal researcher – assembled a US team to investigate the Bothell house. Their findings debunk *Ghost Adventures'* claim of the house not being active.
<u>Poltergeist</u>	A poltergeist (/ˈpoʊltərˌɡaɪst/; German for "noisy ghost" or "noisy spirit") is a type of ghost or spirit that is responsible for physical disturbances, such as loud noises and objects being moved or destroyed.
Residual Haunting	Energy or spirit trapped at a location due to a traumatic event.
R.S.P.K - Recurrent Spontaneous Psychokinesis	A view held by many in the paranormal world as being the root cause of poltergeist phenomena. 'Living agent' unbeknownst to the occupants in the home is the one that's creating the activity.
Sleep Paralysis	Is a feeling of being unable to move, either at the onset of sleep or upon awakening? The individual's senses and awareness are intact, but they may feel as if there is pressure on them, or as if they are choking. Hallucinations and intense fear may accompany it.
The Bothell Hell House	A book detailing the horrors Keith Linder and his ex-girlfriend Tina Davis experienced in 2012 to 2016 in a recently built home outside Seattle, WA.

Keith Linder

TABLE OF CONTENTS

INTRODUCTION

February 16th, 2016, I received an email from parapsychologists Steve Mera. I have to admit Steve's email was a shock to me. You'd be surprised how many paranormal teams have told Tina and me that they'd stay in touch and guess what? They didn't. Tina and I would never hear from them. These were the same teams that called us daily before they came to our house. 'Keith, are you telling us a majority of paranormal teams stopped communicating with you after gathering evidence?' The answer is yes. So, when parapsychologists Steve Mera told me in late January that he would be staying in touch with me quite honestly, I didn't give it much thought. Steve's email read: *Hi Keith, one of the initial things we* (him and Don Philips) *do on arriving at properties is to take a three or four- second video and then an immediate photograph, taken around the properties. We had recently checked our mobile phone footage, and it was discovered. The analysis shows the shadow not to fall in with the characteristics of standard shadows and angles, quite odd.* Steve's email to me included one photograph and one twenty-four second video. I watched Steve's video and almost dropped the glass of wine I had been sipping.

The shadows I've seen in our house come in all shapes and sizes. A majority of them aren't human form. They're too small to be human. Think miniature gargoyle. That's what the majority of the shadows I see look like. How tall are they? One foot, give or take. I call them minions. Not to be confused with the Universal Studios movie with the same name that came out in 2015. No, the term minion was around way before that movie. What's a minion? According to <u>Webster's</u> dictionary, a minion is *a servile dependent, follower, or underling. A subordinate.* I'm going to talk a lot about them in this book. They're the ones creating a majority of the havoc; therefore, it's important that I talk about them. The minions are not the only shadows in the house. There are human silhouettes that pop up now and then.

1

The ones I have seen have primarily been female. How do I know that? Let's just say they're well defined (see book cover). Strangely these female silhouettes appear and move in the same manner as the minions.

The movement I've seen has been right to left. Left to right and almost always out the corner of my eye. Occasionally, and this has happened only once, I'll see them dead ahead in front of me. Spring 2013 - I was sitting on my couch watching TV. A shadow emerged from behind the TV. A silhouette of a woman walking sideways. This silhouette moved from the direction of the chimney to behind the entertainment center. The way it moved would suggest someone was behind me. What's behind me? The kitchen. Ladies and gentlemen Tina was not in the kitchen – she was upstairs. I spun around thinking *did Tina come downstairs. Did I not see her?* The answer to my question was no. I turn around and see no one there. I turned back towards the television. Not surprisingly, the shadow was gone.

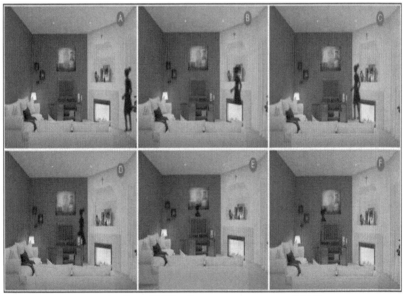

A thru F Shadow movement – 2013

Shadow (Reenactment)
https://www.youtube.com/watch?v=cDhoveM05nE

The picture and video Steve just sent me (see next page) reminded me of what I saw back in 2013. This is the room Tina, and I were in when we heard a kid 'cough.' I was not expecting anyone to capture this. But I shouldn't be totally surprised. Medium Karissa Fleck captured a similar shadow a few days ago in the upstairs hallway. What Steve found interesting (his word not mine) was the angle and characteristics of the shadow. Interesting how the shadow appears on the picture shot and not on the video shot. Notice how the shadow appears flat behind the table (see next page). I noticed a similar characteristic in the shadow that I saw in 2013. The shadow I saw moving that night outlined the wall of the den. It moved behind the entertainment center. Suggesting those objects don't exist in their reality.

Stephen Mera   2/14/16
to me

Hi Keith, one of the initial things we do on arriving at properties is to take a three or 4 second video and then an immediate photograph, taken around the properties. We had recently checked our mobile phone footage and it was discovered. Analysis shows the shadow not to fall in with the characteristics of standard shadows and angles, quite odd. Also such paranormal phenomena seems to often manifest in the vicinity of Don as he is a catalyst. Very interesting...

Steve.

Steve's email 2/14/2016

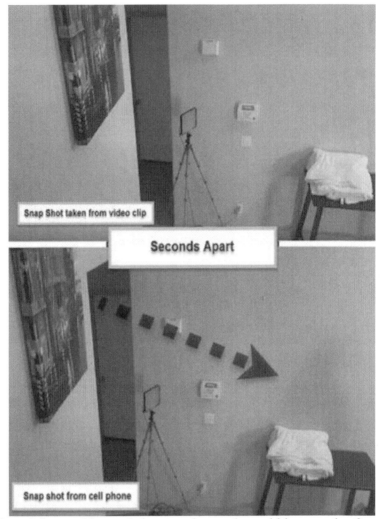

Steve Mera – video and photograph are taken within seconds of each other yield different results.

More Shadow Videos
https://www.youtube.com/watch?v=pTzB7pWLJ3M
esp. at 1:13

If you were to ask five people what their definition of an attachment is, it wouldn't shock me if you got five different answers. One of the things I've learned about paranormal research is you have to avoid painting yourself (intellectually) into a corner. Remove the idea in your head that "Geist" hauntings all exist within a certain confine. We're talking about the paranormal. Nothing is as it seems. This book is a perfect example of that. If your definition of evidence is 'that which reinforces my world view' then you've bought the wrong book. Seriously you should stop reading now! The spirits in the Bothell house wouldn't pause their machinations one second to learn about your worldview. They could care less about what you and I refer to as paranormal. This notion researchers have of 'nothing is real until I've seen it with my own eyes,' is the result of a level of fear settling in within the paranormal community. The fear of being pranked. Or it's pure ego. Want to be an atheist? Fine. Want to be an agnostic? That's fine too. It's not my place to tell you what to believe and what not to believe. That's not why I'm here. I'm here to tell you the truth. The truth, as I saw it. As I lived it. Every human on this planet suffers from what is known as "confirmation bias." "The tendency people have to embrace information that supports their beliefs and reject information that contradicts them." If you suffer from a severe case of *confirmation bias* – you will not like this book. It's best you stop reading.

Attachments: Poltergeist of Washington State picks up right where *The Bothell Hell House: Poltergeist of Washington State* left off. That book ended with the announcement by two competent paranormal research teams. Nicole (Nikki) Novelle led the United States' team. Parapsychologists Steve Mera led the United Kingdom's team. It's important to note that both teams worked independently from the other. That was by my design.

If you haven't read my book, *The Bothell Hell House,* my advice is you should. Everything you're about to learn here began in that book. And I do mean everything. One of the questions people asked me before I moved out was, "do you think the spirits will follow you?" If you read *The Bothell Hell House*, you probably already know the answer to that question. The things that happened to me while I was away on business and the attacks, I received at my job suggest I already have attachments.

The term "being followed" doesn't quite describe what an attachment is. At least not for me. We're going to talk about that on every page of this book. Did the spirits want me to move? Did they view my move as a negative? Was the activity showing signs of escalating? Keep in mind one of the things you do before you move out of a rental home plagued with poltergeist activity is make renovations. Walls have to be painted over. Holes in the walls have to be plugged. Furniture has to be moved out. Stuff you no longer need have to be donated or sold. Are the spirits agitated by that? You're damn right they are. Who do they attack as a result of being agitated? Keith Linder.

What happened after I moved? What happened the day of the move? What happened on day two of me living in the new place? Am I still being poked and prodded? What does that mean? Short answer – being poked and prodded is a horror I experienced in the Bothell house, which started in 2014. It's still happening. That's explained with a lot of evidence in my book *The Bothell Hell House*. Did any of the missing items ever come back? Did Tina and I ever reconcile? What were the markings on the wall (inside my office) made out of? Those answers are in this book.

There was no way I could get everything about the Bothell house. About what happened afterward in one book. I tried. It was impossible to do. The reason I choose to self-publish my story is that I wanted to keep creative control of the story. A lot of publishing houses wanted this story. They wanted it on their terms though. No way. No how. That's what the publishers told me. 'Can you condense the story?' 'Can you remove certain subjects?' Can you combine certain events?' My answer, I will not. Putting everything in one book would have forced me to leave certain things out. I refuse to do that. There's no insignificant information about this case.

Yes, three Bibles did catch fire in the home or were burned I should say. That's horrifying. I get that. But so is hearing a heartbeat from inside your pillowcase - from within your mattress. I have to ask that you set aside what you think you know about the paranormal. Suspend all forms of prejudice for the duration of this book. My advice is what Master Yoda once said:

"Unlearn what you have learned." I'm talking about the paranormal. Most of what you think you know will not make sense here. You think you have a grasp of what creates a poltergeist? You don't. There's no organization out there with all the answers. No experts. Paranormal researchers love to say that, but do they believe it? You can't say there are "no experts in the field" when you, yourself are glued to a world view. That world view being your own. Everyone's offering up the same thing. A theory. A theory based on the data they collected. Well, guess what? Theories evolve or should evolve at the advent of new data. Dear world that new data has just arrived.

Three of the biggest questions surrounding the Bothell house have been the makeup of the wall markings (see Chapter 18, 28, 30 of my book *The Bothell Hell House*), and the heartbeats within the bed mattress and the biggest question of all: why was our house haunted? Those questions and more will be answered in this book. Can you think of any other paranormal book where the house occupant (not the researchers themselves) through use of his wherewithal was able to uncover facts about the house that up until now had remained unknown? The opportunity of figuring out why this house was haunted was always there. It goes back to what I was saying earlier about unlearning what we've learned. The best evidence to be obtained doesn't come from handheld tech devices. It comes from research. There's no way you can grasp the gargantuan amount of information that's inside this book the first time around. To do so would be extremely difficult. People (the world over) loved how interactive my first book, *The Bothell Hell House*, was. Mixing in evidence, photos, audio, video, emails, etc. within the time frame, in which they occurred per chapter was beneficial. I've applied the same formula with this book. So, what's the best way to read this book? Honestly, the best way to read this book the first time is to read it straight through. The links you see here. A majority of them take you to my YouTube Channel - others take you elsewhere. The crucial component to this book, like all books for that matter is the story. The story from start to finish. There is an end here. Not a Hollywood ending but an ending non-the-less. The second time you read the book which you will have to do because it's just so much information. So, much story. Regardless of which format you have. Kindle or Paperback version – now is the time (if you want) to start viewing links. I can't think of any other book where the reader pays this low of a dollar figure and in return receives countless hours of video footage. All free mind you. I can't think of any other paranormal book where the evidence is put at the reader's fingertips for viewing. Wait a minute I can think of another book like that? It's called *The Bothell Hell House*. The third time you read this book, which is what I strongly recommend (because that's how the book was written, to be read three times) is where it all comes together. Hopefully, by this point, you would have viewed all the footage, listened to all the witness provided testimony, watched parapsychologists Steve Mera's hour and a half lecture about him and Don Philips findings. Hopefully, by that point, you would have gone to all the links I've provided. Articles, videos, audios, etc. and in doing so, walked away with a deeper understanding of how everybody (especially Tina and myself) were in over our heads. Do not gloss over the links I've provided! My true story notwithstanding. The links and pictures (please study) in this book are my gifts to you for purchasing this book. Don't forget about them. Four words worth remembering for the rest of your life. **Bone Black** and **Dippel's Oil**. Understand something. I'm not a writer. I'm an information technology professional. If you told me one day, I would be writing two books about my encounter with a poltergeist I'd laugh at you.

Why I'm doing this reminds me of something my dad used to say. "It has to be done." Me and Tina's four-year ordeal is a story that deserves to be told. It should be told. That's where I come in. If you're one of those people who habitually corrects or criticizes the method and manner in which a story is told versus understanding what's being revealed, you might have a hard time finishing this book. I'm not an author. I'm a storyteller. What you hold in your hand is a non-watered-down version of everything that happened. I wish I could say that my book is the icing on the cake for everything related to this case. It's not. Once again, the icing on the cake is the various links throughout the book – including the hour and twenty-eight-minute documentary by chief researcher Don Phillips. Enjoy!

CHAPTER 1
Substantiated

"Many that live deserve death. And some that die deserve life.
Can you give it to them? Then do not be too eager to deal
out death in judgment"
~ Gandalf.

This horror when it started was never supposed to be about substantiating me and Tina's claims. It was supposed to be about making a newly built house located thirty minutes outside of Seattle safe enough to live in. It was supposed to be about answering one question and one question only: why is this house haunted? My reason for staying changed as a result of the fallout from the "Demons in Seattle" *Ghost Adventures* episode that aired on the Travel Channel. 'Tina and Keith made it up. They had to. Zak and his team always find stuff' was the response from many who watched the episode. Correct me if I'm wrong but don't you have to be a witness to someone hoaxing before you can claim that there's hoaxing? *Ghost Adventures* for the short period they were here didn't find anything. Where did this hoaxing notion come from? You'll be surprised to know there are a lot of paranormal organizations out there that believe 'if *Ghost Adventures* can't find anything, no one can.' It gets worse! Paranormal television shows have created the perception that every paranormal investigation yields results. It's incorrect to believe that a house as active as ours was is going to be equally active when an investigative team arrives. The horrors house occupants experience come in waves and spikes. Ghost Adventures would have done a huge service to their audience had they told them the odds of their team getting substantial evidence is pretty much next to zero. But they didn't.

That's where the paranormal community is at right now. One team determines what's real and what's not. Then came Nicole (Nikki) Novelle and her team. Then came parapsychologists Steve Mera and his assistant Don Philips. Both teams did something no other team ever thought to do. Get ready for it. Here it comes. They lived in the house.

You might find this hard to believe, but the paranormal teams in and around Seattle never asked Tina and me if they could live in the house. Neither did *Ghost Adventures*. That question never came up. Here came Nikki and Steve who after a period of vetting and research, took it upon themselves to fly to Seattle. That ladies and gentlemen, this is how they got their evidence. And boy did they get it. Talk about cup runneth over. Those familiar with this story, pardon me for a second as I give a quick synopsis to those not already familiar with this case.

In 2012, my girlfriend and I took up residence in a suburban neighborhood outside Seattle, Washington. What we saw and experienced within weeks of moving in, changed our lives forever. Everything that wasn't tied down got thrown in our house. Everything! Loud bangs. Phantom footsteps. Phantom voices and spontaneous fires. In between each of those things I've just mentioned were door slams, water puddles, missing objects, shadow figures, and one unexplained phenomena that caused some people to doubt our claims outright. Wall writings! That and the Bible burnings are what angered some people the most. People thought we did it. They thought we were the ones setting fires and writing on walls. That became an albatross for Tina and me. People wanted to see these feats captured on video. "There's no way a house could be this active, and there not be a video of some of the events being reported." "Nothing's real until it's captured on video." We heard that over and over. Thank God I ignored those naysayers. You wouldn't be reading this book now had I chose to believe them more than my own eyes.

My girlfriend and I spent two years looking for help. And we found it. Or so we thought. I found out the hard way that help and good help are two separate things. I said in my introduction that this book would be a continuation of my first book *The Bothell*

Hell House. Paranormal researcher Nikki Novelle and Parapsychologists Steve Mera have just concluded that the claims Tina and I have been reporting are the works of a poltergeist. A poltergeist-like no other. An armada of minions for reasons we've yet to figure out have taken over this house. Before I go into detail about who these minions are, I want to first talk about something I hear all the time from cynics and skeptics: "extraordinary claims require extraordinary evidence." You'd think skeptics invented that quote themselves. That's how often skeptics throw it out there. Most skeptics I've talked to reference that quote incorrectly. Now I'm not one to debate Carl Sagan. It's his quote, by the way. Carl Sagan was right "extraordinary claims do require extraordinary evidence." But you can't obtain extraordinary evidence without first acquiring extraordinary investigators. You have to have competent researchers. Investigators with the know-how and experience. That's what Nikki brought with her when she came to the house. That's what Steve Mera brought when he descended on the house the first time. One US team. One UK team. Two teams working in parallel (weeks apart) without the other team's knowledge. Both came up with extraordinary results. Most of what they found is in *The Bothell Hell House* book. Before we get into the details of what happened two months before I moved out of the Bothell home, I want you to understand something. The claims Tina and I made about what was happening in our house should have never been viewed as being "extraordinary." Not within the paranormal community. Poltergeists have been throwing objects, setting fires, writing on walls (in languages no one can understand), and leaving cabinet doors open for centuries. Every culture on every continent has experienced what I just described. The only thing that might separate our case from previous poltergeist cases is the level of targeting taking place. What does targeting mean? Targeting is when a spirit decides to pick on one person more than the other (see *The Bothell Hell House*).

It sounds weird to say this, but it's true. Our case got famous for all the wrong reasons. You should see the look on people's faces when I tell them that. Most of them don't understand what I'm talking about. They don't understand that the word poltergeist as Claude LeCouteux cleverly states was "originally written as two words *polter* and *geyst*, and then as one word once the meaning was established. The term is composed of the root of the verb *poltern*, to make noise, to tap, and Geist, spirit, which can designate both the devil and demons as well as ghosts and other beings." Most paranormal researchers who came to our house don't even know that the term *polter geist* is rooted back to the year 1540. These paranormal investigators never took the time to study the phenomena up close. If they did, they would know that poltergeist have been burning Bibles and writing on walls for quite some time. These types of spirits are famous for throwing things. They're famous for evading investigators. Tina and I had malevolent spirits living with us – an elusive poltergeist - *several poltergeists*. That's right multiple poltergeist. Might as well break you in abruptly on what this book contains. An intelligent haunting, as Steve Mera likes to phrase it. Are poltergeist intelligent? You bet your bottom dollar they are. Not only that but they're extremely dangerous. Of course, I didn't know this when I first moved in. That knowledge came later. What makes them dangerous? Everything I've just mentioned. The easiest thing to overlook where poltergeist is concerned is their ability to manipulate the individuals, they're haunting. Out of all the horrors Tina and I experienced, manipulation was the one that did us in. That scheming component combined with my ex-girlfriend's ill-portrayal on *Ghost Adventures* "Demons in Seattle" episode and my belief that I can best these spirits with modern technology is what led to me and Tina's breakup.

One of the first things Nikki and her team, did when they returned to the east coast was report their findings. They informed the paranormal community about the EVPs they caught. The house noises. The heartbeats they felt inside the mattress. The doll experiment they conducted. The tripwire experiment and pages from one of my burnt Bibles turning by itself. The evidence I speak of is in my previous book. The Scientific Establishment of Parapsychology administrator Steve Mera did something a little bit more formal. His organization released press releases before their trip to Seattle, and they released press releases after they left Seattle. S.E.P was determined to tell the world about what happened or what didn't happen while they were at the house. If they found nothing – they would report nothing. Steve and Don didn't witness any fakery;

 Release Outlets

https://drive.google.com/file/d/0ByUXMaBHOgPLU01rNjdKRGp ZaHc/view

https://www.itv.com/news/central/2016-01-17/midlands-ghostbuster-to-help-seattle-couple-living-in-a-haunted-house/

http://www.americas-most-haunted.com/2016/03/18/washington-poltergeist-case-psychic-attorney-mark-anthony-hours-amamericas-haunted-radio/

therefore, they can't report fakery. Instead, they found something and therefore, are releasing it publicly. People responded from all over the world. The majority of the responses were positive. The response I kept hearing were, "Oh I remember that house, it was featured on Ghost Adventures, I thought it was made up." Or, "I remember that house on TV. I guess they were telling the truth after all." Those were the types of emails I got after both teams went public with their findings. I said in my book *The Bothell Hell House,* that a lie always travels faster than the truth. The lie is people saying, "Tina and Keith made all of that up." We didn't make any of this up. People are starting to realize that. This is great. The good news here (for those interested in the paranormal) is something is going on in this house "after all." Keith and Tina weren't lying. It took three years to get this point. Three years before my claims finally become substantiated. Guess what got lost during those three years? Evidence. I'm not talking about the evidence that was finally acquired. I'm talking about the evidence that was lost due to the paranormal community's lack of readiness and preparedness. Like I said earlier a lot of the activity we experienced came in spurts. The spirits that gave me and my girlfriend hell are not in the business of waiting. The amount of evidence Steve and Nikki captured when they were here in early 2016 pales in comparison to the amount of evidence teams could have captured had they arrived in 2014.

Do you want to know how you can tell if someone is in a particular field for the sole purpose of advancing that field versus advancing themselves? You release a press release about what was found at a location and watch the reaction from those that were there previously. As siloed as the paranormal community is within itself news still travels fast. When you think about Twitter and Facebook, it's kind of hard not to get information within seconds of it being created. Before I share with you the response Ghost Adventures gave after hearing the news that other teams found something, let me provide a few examples of what their response should have been. When I think about how Zak Bagans should have responded upon hearing the news of two teams coming in and finding something, two names come to mind: Neil's Bohr and Albert Einstein. Two of the world greatest minds occupying one of the greatest fields in science. There's not a person alive who hasn't benefited from the research of these two gentlemen. Long story short, both men had multiple conversations, i.e. debates regarding quantum mechanics. Their debates were professional, not personal. You could say both men owe a portion of their greatness to the other individual. They both advanced quantum mechanics by evaluating the other person's work. Theories? They mean nothing if they can't be tested. These men tested everything. But they're not the only scientists who did this. Scientists have been reviewing each other's work for quite some time. It's called peer review. If you have a sincere interest in advancing a particular study, then it shouldn't matter who gets to the truth first. If you're trying to help a family deal with a poltergeist problem, but the evidence doesn't appear while you're in the home, but does when other teams come in. I would think you would be congratulatory and supportive? I would think you want to know how they (Steve, Don, Nikki, Karissa, and others) came to their conclusion. What methods were used. Why reject it outright? If the goal is to advance yourself versus advancing the paranormal field (you belong to, that orthodox science scoffs at), then you might exhibit zero interests. That's exactly what Dave Schrader and Zak Bagans did.

Fig 1.1: Zak Bagans dismisses paranormal teams findings without reviewing the evidence.

Fig 1.2: Dave Schrader's Tweet

In going back to what I said about the paranormal being somewhat small. Good news or bad news, depending on your loyalty to certain TV personalities, travels fast. An individual above (not me) took it upon himself to tweet Zak Bagans after Seattle Fox 13 aired the US and UK team's assessment. I honestly don't think the individual was trying to bait Zak. I think he was trying to get Zak Bagans' intellectual response. His Neil's Bohr or Albert Einstein's response. He tweeted Zak Bagans' the Seattle Fox 13 press release. Zak's statement of "that's their proof" is the second most idiotic question he's ever asked about this case. Zak Bagans should know better than anyone else that the media synopsis is never the full synopsis.

No parapsychologists on Earth would ever state that a house is legitimately haunted based one piece of evidence. Zak knows this.

But as you can see from his tweet, Zak's response is not directed at the paranormal community. It's directed at his fans. I don't even have to ask Nikki or Steve if they received a call from Zak Bagans and Ghost Adventures because I already know the answer. The Scientific Establishment of Parapsychology didn't reveal their findings in a two-minute Fox News clip. No, they revealed their findings by releasing a series of reports. Steve and Don went on the record and said any investigative team, i.e. organization could request to see their findings. Zak's knee jerk response to the tweet above would be the second time he failed to provide a teachable moment to the community he belongs to. He could have educated his fans, i.e. his audience with the important fact that you can't always get evidence the first time around. The show could have ended with that. Don't have your audience thinking you Zak Bagans are the only one in the world that can prove a house is haunted. Don't have people thinking the house occupants are liars or publicity seekers only because you didn't find anything. Professionals like Einstein and Bohr don't feel belittled when someone in their field discovers something new. The response Zak should have given, for example:

It thrills me to know that a team after living in the home for several weeks found something. I'd like to review their findings because this case still interests me. It pleases me to know that Keith and Tina were able to get some answers. I hope that they can find peace. That, ladies and gentlemen, is the answer (or something to that effect) Zak should have given. Both men could easily have said we'd like to see the evidence. We'd like to see and talk to the investigators. One of the most horrific things I've learned about the paranormal community as a result of our haunted house is there are factions that exist within groups and teams - that quite honestly has curtailed its growth. An adolescent territorial mindset exists.

Q13 Seattle Fox 2/15/2016

https://q13fox.com/2016/02/15/bothell-home-haunted-by-poltergeists-parapsychologists-have-proven-it-resident-says/

SEP
THE SCIENTIFIC ESTABLISHMENT OF PARAPSYCHOLOGY

The Scientific Establishment of Parapsychology
Investigative Measures & Analytical Research
Case Ref: 26411

SEP have attended a location in Seattle and carried out a two-stage active investigation using rig 2 and rig 4 equipment for the duration of 6 days in an attempt to obtain credible and authentic evidence in support of reported paranormal disturbances by the house owner (Keith Linder). All preliminary test procedures and analytical questions were carried out prior to SEP arrival on January 21st, 2016. Satisfactory preliminary results were obtained leading to active investigation. Occurrences logged and post analytic evidence produced...

Logged incidents:

1. Three noted accounts of physical phenomena, i.e. physical manipulation, one account provides a digital log of the event at a time no human agencies were present in the incident location. Details of time stamp and incident recorded within the official completed documentation.

2. Three accounts of in air audible phenomena noted and heard by multiple witnesses at the time of the incidents. No rational explanations were discovered. Failed replications and incidents noted within the official completed documentation.

3. A large amount of unknown audible phenomena captured on digital recording devices and digital professional cameras during active investigation over the period of 6 days. 93% of audible incidents demonstrate possible vocal recordings. Electronic Voice Phenomena (EVP) obtained 427 recordings, 318 of those have now been categorised as Class B, 81 have been categorised as Class A and 28 have been categorised as Actual Voice Phenomena (AVP). Those vocal recordings in direct response to questions or current environmental undertakings. Three vocal in air audibles were also logged as noted in section 2. Many recordings demonstrate Irish Accents.

4. Research carried out to date: Environmental perimeters, geological and aerial survey, geomagnetic and electromagnetic measurements, magnetometer and radiation tests. Temperature and humidity analysis, electrical leakage survey, site maps and pre-build surveys (currently on-going). Stray reflective light conditions, psychoanalytic surveys and questionnaires completed. Interviews carried out with client and visiting priest.

Current diagnostic due to conclusive evidence: LIH
Localized Interactive Phenomena: Often referred to as an Intelligent Haunting.
Diminishing Possibilities: Evidence supports land locked phenomena with possible subtle decreasing incidents and passive physical occurrences continuing at low frequency/severity.

Dated: February 6th, 2016.   Documentation Overview: S. Mera
Case Ref: 26411

Mr. Stephen Mera: SEP Director
BSc.Dip.Ft.Dip.PPsy

CHAPTER 2

Homework

T he only homework Steve and Don gave me (before they left the first time) was going to the county records office. See what information (if any) I can get about the land underneath the house. No one has yet to figure out why this house is haunted. Nikki and her team through all their house monitoring and in-house investigation still couldn't ascertain why this Bothell house is behaving the way it is. The question remains: why is this house "Geist" infested? Is it the land? Could be. But that creates a serious question: Why aren't the other houses having problems? None of my neighbors have experienced anything. Remember, our goal is to erase questions off the whiteboard, not add them.

So, guess what? I'm going to the Snohomish county records office. What am I looking for? I have no idea. Whatever I'm looking for is going to have to find me. That's typically how research works. You have to put yourself in a position where the answer finds you. For some people that's boring. Not me. I love researching stuff. For me, the hunt for the truth has always been somewhat of a quest. A self- reward that's baked into whatever information you find. I walked into the county records office a few days after Steve and Don left, carrying two things: my cell phone and my twelve-ounce cup of Starbucks coffee. Why am I here now? I'm here because I feel I have support. People are working on this case now. Nikki Novelle and Steve Mera have gone on record and said this house is "haunted." The paranormal community has been presented with some startling evidence. They haven't seen anything yet. Neither have I.

If you ever decide to research your own home – the land underneath that is, it's important to go to the county website first. Call in advance and see what the rules are. Even though the information is free, there are still rules one must follow. You'd just be wasting the time you took off work by showing up unannounced. I had called in advance and in doing so had given them my house address. The clerks working there did most of the heavy lifting, and I mean literally. I had asked the clerk's office (via email) for everything they had. Everything tethered to my home address. There were fifteen to twenty boxes waiting for me when I got there. Huge boxes mind you. Time to put the content of each box through the microfilm projector. One by one. I must have been in that office five hours before I finally found something. Well, I will be damned. Look here — there was once a house where my house now sits. A cabin.

Fig 2.1: A cabin-like structure.

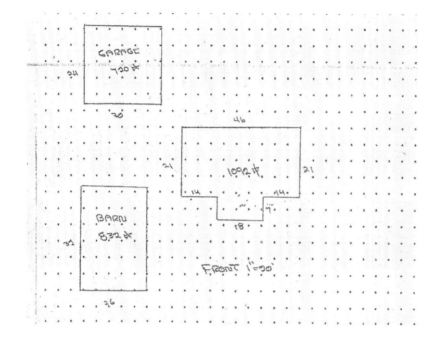

Fig 2.2: Overview of a housing unit.

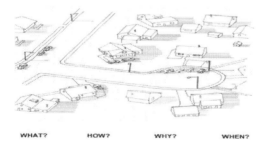

Fig 2.3: what's a REVAL?

The house was built in 1942 – built as a cabin. One story home: two bedrooms, one bath. The house was forty-nine years old at the time of its 1991 REVAL. What's a REVAL?

A revaluation is a program undertaken by a municipality to appraise all real property within the taxing district according to its full and fair value. WHAT HAS TO BE DONE DURING A REVALUATION PROGRAM? Both the interior and exterior of each property are usually physically inspected, and building dimensions are noted during the revaluation process. In addition, recent sales of properties are studied and may be adjusted to estimate the value of the property that has not been sold. Property typically purchased for revised investment purposes is analyzed in terms of its income-producing capability. In short, all information believed to influence the value of a home will be gathered, reviewed and analyzed to make a proper determination of each property's value.

https://www.state.nj.us/treasury/taxation/pdf/lpt/revaluation.pdf

The house (see Fig 2.1) was valued at forty-eight thousand, one hundred dollars at the time of its 1991 REVAL — a thirty-three percent depreciation. The land underneath the house was valued at four hundred and fifty-four thousand dollars. Interesting! None of this explains why my house was haunted. But I don't believe in coincidences. Out of the eighty plus houses around mine, none of them had houses where they currently stand. None except mine. That has to mean something. I sincerely hope so. We'll see.

When I got home the first thing, I did was email Steve Mera and Don Philips. Steve was still compiling his official report as was Don. There are still a lot of unanswered questions – we know who lived in the house. Their names are listed on the REVAL documents. I have to find them. I want to ask them questions. That's going to take some time. This REVAL was done in nineteen-ninety-one. The house I'm living in was built in two thousand and five. None of the documents I read reveal when the cabin was torn down. We're talking fifteen years at least between when the last REVAL was done and when the new house was built. That's an eternity (when trying to find someone). The hard reality is people die. Memories fade, and who wants to answer questions about demons and poltergeist? There I am sitting in my office thinking; this *is going to be a long and tedious process.*

CHAPTER 3

Wall Writings

If you need justification on why I decided to go public with our claims, this chapter is where you'll find it. I'm a firm believer that four eyes are better than one.   In our case, hundreds of eyes are better than one. More eyes mean more brains. More experience. Just because I'm at my wit's end on a majority of things happening in this house, that doesn't mean someone else has to be. I've learned a lot of things over the years in my role as an information technology specialist. The world is a lot smaller thanks to the invention of the internet. Information, ladies and gentlemen, travels at nearly half the speed of light. We're talking about 85,000 miles per second / 5.1 million miles per minute / 306 million miles per hour. That's how quickly an answer to a question you asked can come to back to you. Everybody can talk to everybody now. All you need is that person's email address. Or that person's Twitter handle or Facebook alias.

One of the questions I get from people (the world over) as a result of seeing my house on Travel Channels *Ghost Adventures* show is what is that stuff on your walls made out of? What is it? My response to them, depending on which wall marking they're referencing, is I don't know. The phenomena known as wall markings began in the summer of 2014. My girlfriend and I would come home and find our house ransacked. Couches and love seat all upside-down. Kitchen cabinet doors were wide open – all of them. The kitchen wine rack emptied of all its wine bottles. This was happening daily for about six to seven months. It's important to remind you that what I just described happening to Tina and I is typical poltergeist behavior.

Every case on record lists this type of destruction. What makes our case interesting, is what I now refer to as poltergeist 2.0. The destruction that happened in our house happened primarily while we were away. I'm talking about the ransacking of our home. Anyone who studies poltergeist phenomena will tell you the majority of the activity taken place happens when the house occupants are present. That characteristic is what gave rise to the theory known as Recurrent Spontaneous Psychokinesis often referred to as R.S.P.K. Proponents of that theory believe poltergeists are the works of an unknown human agent, typically, an adolescent child or troubled female. The events Tina and I reported throw that theory out the window – hence the muted response from individuals in the paranormal community. In my book *The Bothell Hell House*, you see me lacing the house with motion detection cameras (as instructed by relatives and paranormal teams). I was trying to catch the activity in real-time. This act of trying to catch the "Geist" or some home intruder red-handed is what led to the activity spiking. Not only that but the cameras I erected soon went missing. Others outright destroyed. I'm talking to the brinks of powder. Soon after that came the wall writings.

Fig 3.1: Normal day – camera detects missing chair.

Fig 3.2: Attack Day – after cameras were set up.

Multiple upside-down crosses were drawn on my office wall and my office carpet (Chapter 22 *The Bothell Hell House*). That's not all the poltergeist did. My office was completely trashed. It looked like Hurricane Sandy had visited me. It was easy to determine what the upside-down cross markings were made out of based on how easy it was to clean. The first markings were made out of ash. Tina and were advised to sage the house thoroughly every day. And we did. We left the sage stick (what was left of it) in one spot and one spot only— the hallway bookshelf. Well, I came home one day and resting in my office by my computer keyboard was a sage stick. It had shortened quite a bit. Don't laugh at me but I tried to duplicate what the spirit did by writing on my wall with the same sage stick and guess what? I could not write on the wall with the newly dimmed stick. Not even close. How the spirit was able to do that is beyond me. Once again, those markings were easy to clean up.

Fast forward to October 31st of that same year. One of the worst house attacks happened while Tina and I were away. We came back November 1st after midnight and found our house in a worse shape than ever before. New wall writings and, boy do I mean new wall writings. The substance this time was different than previous substances. The previous wall markings always resembled black paint like substance. We owned no paint cans whatsoever. These markings that appeared Halloween night were different and by different, I mean harder to clean up. *How am I going to get this off my walls?* I've already spent a significant amount of money to paint over the previous wall markings. We're talking hundreds of dollars. I've gotten more emails about the wall markings that appeared

November 1st, 2014 than all the other wall markings combined. Everyone always asks me what's that stuff made out of? You can look at the markings themselves and know they're not man-made. When someone say's 'it looks like spray paint' I can't help but laugh. Not only are you not looking at the markings objectively but you're also not looking at the markings closely. The spirits who did this (I'm talking about the markings that appeared Halloween night) are trying to tell us something.

Fig 3.3: Multiple markings appeared in the office Halloween 2014.

There's an unbelievable message hidden in these writings. I'm going to share with you what that is later in the book. Like I said at the beginning of this book, poltergeist have been writing on walls for centuries. It was funny to hear Zak say on the "Demons in Seattle" episode that the markings look like spray paint. Just because you think something looks like spray paint doesn't necessarily mean it's spray paint. Did it ever occur to you that the spirits do these things in such a manner to create suspicion? If you, Mr. Zak Bagans, think it looks like spray paint, then why not have the wall markings analyzed? I was shocked when I learned *Ghost Adventures* didn't take a piece of the wall markings with them. They didn't even ask us if they could. Had they asked me the answer would have been hell yeah. Take a piece of the wall with you. Your producer asked Tina and me not to paint over it weeks before you guys arrived. Why wouldn't you have it analyzed? Wait till you learn what this stuff is made out of. You're going to flip out.

March 2016 – I was sitting in my office surveying my surroundings. The walls had been painted over for quite some time. I was sitting in my office chair mentally taking in all the hell that was taking place here. The poster fire, objects being thrown, the Gray and White Lady apparitions, the shadowy figures, the Die KL, upside-down cross, and upside-down man wall writings. I was taking all that in while at the same time thinking about Tina. I was thinking about the day she was standing next to me, and the TV and stereo came on by itself. I was thinking about the time she helped me back to my office chair after that mysterious fall down the stairs. I miss her. I miss her screaming "Keith, come here" and I get up from the desk to go see what she wants and sure enough she's reporting an unexplained phenomena. I miss her walking by my office door and me saying, "Baby, come here, I want to show you something." I miss Tina walking in and leaning over my shoulder. We were both watching video footage from the previous night. Could be anything. Lights going off and on by themselves or it could an apparition gliding across the floor. I miss Tina saying, "That's different." And she's right. That which we just witnessed had never happened before. I was thinking about all of that while staring at my office door.

My eye finally rested on a portion of the closet door I don't normally see. *I missed a spot.* And there it is. A section of the door with the markings from Halloween night. The black braille-like substance. I let Nikki and Steve know I found a leftover wall substance from the Halloween house attack. Steve and Don had told me before they left that they would have loved to have gotten samples off the door and wall had there been any wall substance left. Well, guess what? There is. A few days later I came up with a Hail Mary idea. There's a paint store down the street. It's the paint store where I've been getting my paint and primer (after *Ghost Adventures* left) to repair the house. Maybe they'll know what this stuff is made out of. If I'm going to go to this paint store and ask strangers what this substance is made out of, I need to have someone with me. Who can I take with me? I know who. Patty Hale. Patty's been to the house multiple times. She's the one who picked up Steve and Don when they arrived at the airport back in January. We became friends her and I. She's seen some stuff.

Yeah, that's who I want to come with me. If the paint store finds something, she'll be the perfect witness. If I remember correctly, her husband has a truck. I'm going to need one if I'm going to do what it is, I'm thinking. And just so you understand what it is I'm about to do. I'm about to remove half of my closet door — the door that has the left-over wall markings on it. I'm going to haul it to a paint store and hopefully ask them what this braille-like substance is. This is not the actions of hoaxer. This door doesn't belong to me, it belongs to the landlord. I'm removing a piece of the property and taking it somewhere else. This door could easily break as a result of me moving it. If it does, I'll have to buy a new one. That's two hundred and fifty dollars. That's how much Costco said a door like this cost. What I'm about to do is extremely dangerous. And I don't mean dangerous like crab fishing in the Berlin Straights. No, I mean dangerous like walking across a tight rope over a den of sleeping lions. This type of research has the potential of conjuring up the activity again.

The activity in the house has been relatively quiet since Steve and Don left. It's a level one right now. What's a level one? In this house, a level one activity is loud bangs, wall knockings, and phantom footsteps. That's what I mean by level one activity. When you remove a piece of the property from a house, you're changing the environment. There could be negative consequences for doing that. It's going to sound weird, but there's evidence to support this (my case included) of spirits objecting to loud noises. It sounds hypocritical but it's true. Poltergeist who are experts at creating loud noise actually abhor it. I can tell you from my experience alone this theory is one hundred percent true. Some of the deadliest objects to be thrown while living in this house came seconds after me and Tina arguing. Our friends saw one of Tina's flowerpots fly across the room while attending a housewarming party. Noise raises activity – it did in our house. Weirdly - a local paranormal team advised us to scream and chant out loud whenever we got the feeling of being watched. Scream to the top of your lungs the words GET OUT OF MY HOUSE! LEAVE THE HOUSE NOW! Did the activity die down? Nope, it increased. That level one stuff I just told you about, who do you think is behind that? Where do you think these spirits live? They live here. The minions in this home are always observing. Always listening. They know I'm having thoughts about taking the office door down. They know why I want to take it to the paint store. That's what I mean by staring into the abyss. Taking the closet door down and driving it to the paint store is nothing short of giving them attention. These spirits love attention. They relish in it. I may also be violating something. Some law I'm not aware of. This door I'm attempting to move is probably as old as the house itself. Removing it from this office, let alone this house is enough to anger some minions. Oh, they couldn't care less about the door. Screw the door! The spirits might be thinking 'Keith, you're investigating again. You're creating noise.' Everyone who knows my story knows the day I bought cameras into the home was the night the activity spiked. I changed the environment within the house itself when I did that. Me removing a door in my office might not be the same as putting up cameras (see *The Bothell Hell House*). But then again maybe it is. I'm reminded of Carl Sagan's quote "extraordinary claims, requires extraordinary evidence." Guess what? Extraordinary evidence doesn't create itself. It requires extraordinary actions. There I am sitting in the office — the markings on the door are staring dead at me. I'm thinking, *someone out there has to know what this substance is made out of*. Ding! I looked down at my phone and saw Patty's response. She said "yes." Patty knows as I do. The only way to make an omelet is to crack a few eggs. The spirits are not going to tell you what this stuff is made out of. That's not their job. Before I tell you, what happened as a result of me taking the door to the paint store, let me go back a few weeks to when Steve, Don, and Nikki's paranormal press release went viral on the internet.

Seventeen million people watched the Seattle Q13 Fox News story about the Bothell house. It was creating quite a controversy. A percentage of *Ghost Adventures*' fans were up in arms about the latest update. This update Steve and Nikki had released contradicted what Zak and crew said about the house. The paranormal community at the time of this press release was going through what I call a civil war. It was during Spring 2016 that the term 'Para unity' was being popularized. Sounds childish, right? But it's true. While Tina and I were going through hell inside the Bothell house, the paranormal community was at war with itself. Individuals were basing their loyalty on which paranormal TV shows were most successful. Ghost hunting had gone mainstream as a result of so many paranormal shows hitting the cable networks. The Scientific Establishment of Parapsychology and Nikki Novelle's findings came right amid all that politics. Tina and I could care less about the politics within the paranormal community. While these individuals were eating themselves alive on social media over whose dust particle is the best there was a scientific awakening happening at the house in Bothell, Washington. That corner of the United States no one cares to think about where "Geist" activity is concerned is about turn the paranormal community upon its head. You all can fight it all you want. The truth is coming.

Sunday, March 20th - Patty arrived with her husband's truck. Let's do this! I unhinged the door from whatever device it was resting on and walked it downstairs. I wish you could see me. I was tiptoeing down the stairs with this closet door under my arm. I was praying to God that the spirits don't see me. Most all that they don't hear me. *I know deep down they can.* It could've taken no more than five minutes for us to get to the store. The man behind the counter knows me already. I've asked him numerous times how I can paint over the wall writings in my house. I never told them what caused the wall writings for fear of them thinking I was some loon. But today was different. My face had been blasted on local television multiple times. People walk up to me and refer to me in a joking manner as "that demon guy" when I'm out in about running errands, I'm bombarded with questions.

Patty and I were in the paint store for maybe twenty minutes. The guys working there could not explain what the substance was, nor could they explain how it was applied. Their words, not mine: "we don't know what this is." I remember looking at Patty and her looking at me. The expression on our faces said, *dammit we've reached a dead end. We've hauled this door from my house to this store and we've come up empty-handed. It was a long shot to begin with, but dammit I was hoping they could tell me something. Give me a clue or something.* Unfortunately, that's easier said than done. The guys behind the counter gave it their best. Them not knowing what type of paint this is speaks volumes. Them not knowing how the paint was applied speaks even louder. My mentality then was, no harm is done. I wasn't butthurt coming home from the store. *Never get upset about taking the initiative.* That's what my dad taught me. I had an idea and I ran with it. How many paranormal teams (after seeing my office) came up with the idea to do this? Zero! Not even *Ghost Adventures*. If you don't learn anything else from this book, learn this. The spirits in this house are <u>always</u> watching. I will be reiterating that fact a lot in this book. You'll be surprised how many paranormal teams have yet to grasp what that means. What does it mean? It means paranormal investigators are being monitored the second they walk into a house. In my opinion hiding motion cameras and other monitoring devices (as suggested) in a "Geist" infested home is one of the most ridiculous plan of actions imaginable.

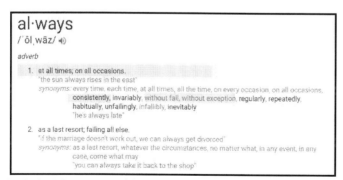

Fig 3.4: Always – without fail, at all times; on all occasions.

What's the difference between a supernatural event and a paranormal event? In short, the paranormal is something that's not understood by current scientific knowledge. The explanation is beyond our current understanding of things. The keyword here is current. Science may one day be able to explain the unknown voices coming through on multiple devices: voice recorder and video recorder. Things considered to be supernatural can never be explained by science. How can a television play music when it's not even plugged in? How can a television channel play the same song for fifteen minutes? I'm talking about the same verse over and over (see The Bothell Hell Chapter 13). How about localized stench? Localized sound? How can one electronic device pick up noise in the room it's in and a different device cannot? Both devices are sitting side by side. Science can't explain that. Science can't explain dimes raining from the hall ceiling. If science can't explain how those things occurred, then I know they're not going to be able to explain the next story I'm about to tell you.

When Patty and I pulled up to my driveway, the first thing we did was raise the truck cover off the truck bed. *I can't believe I'm sneaking a door back into my own house hoping I don't get detected.* Within seconds of me pulling out the door, Patty says, "Keith, wait a second. There's something on the truck." Patty's deadly serious – something's on the truck. I laid the door back down in the bed of the truck and joined Patty in surveying the ceiling of truck cover. She's right. It was covered with black markings. I'm talking about the ceiling of her husband's truck cover. These markings Patty and I were looking at look identical to the black markings on the office door. This is nuts. This is the same braille raised coloring I painted over months back. The same black substance that's on the office door now. The only difference between these markings and the ones that appeared in the Bothell home back in 2014 is these markings haven't formed words yet. There's no 666 this time. No upside- down man. No 'Die KL.'

 Poltergeist – Back from the paint store
https://www.youtube.com/watch?v=u-UTd37duCQ

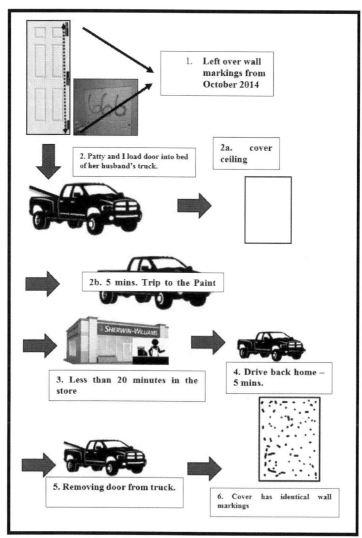

Fig 3.5: trip to the paint store

Fig 3.6: Truck after returning from the paint store – March 2016

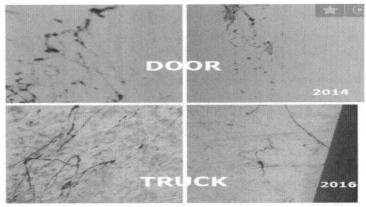

Fig 3.7: Marking comparison October 2014 vs. March 2016

Remember what I said earlier about the spirits always watching. Always listening? We now have a truck with markings on it. Identical to the markings that were on my office wall Halloween night. To whoever is reading this right now. Do you know what this means? Whatever reason you had for buying this book, I want you to know that you've come to the right place. By right place, I mean the real paranormal. The real supernatural. This is it. You have no idea the amount of truth that's coming your way. My first experience with the paranormal was a phantom kid 'cough.' That incident and the other ten-thousand crazy things have altered my life forever. It's about to start all over again. Now watch the video again – pay special to time stamp 6:35. Wear headsets if possible ⌒. A 'Hey' is heard in the middle of me and Patty's conversation. Sounds like a female.

The drive to the paint store could've been no longer than five minutes. Patty and I spent less than twenty minutes in the paint store. The drive back to my house was an equal five minutes. The question we have to ask ourselves is when did these markings begin appearing? Based on the other phenomena's I've seen in the house I'm going to have say these markings appeared instantly. If you pause the video where the markings are shown in the video, you'll see an interesting symmetry forming on the ceiling of the truck cover. It suggests equal distribution. Every marking you see on the ceiling of the truck I think appeared instantly. It fits perfectly with everything else that's happened in this house. Did these markings appear while the door was in the truck or while the door was in the paint store? We'll never know.

Patty's husband confirmed to Patty that the markings were not there before. He didn't get upset about what had happened. I'm glad he didn't. You never know what people's reaction will be to the paranormal. I'm so glad he didn't take the approach some friends and family members have taken which is disassociation. I've lost family and friends over less weirder things than this. People I loved. It hurts. Damn it hurts. Still hurts. I was not thinking about the weird markings on Patty's husband's truck the following Monday at work. All I remember that morning was me wanting coffee. Good ole Starbucks coffee. I got to the coffee machine in our break room and immediately begin pressing buttons. Seconds into me making coffee, Wyeth, a co- worker from another team, walked up to me (empty coffee mug in his hand) and said, "Dude, I didn't know you lived in a haunted house." I turned from the Starbucks coffee machine and looked at him. Wyeth saw the look on my face and realized how shocked I was that he knew my house was haunted. And he was right. I was shocked. There are people at work who know that my house is haunted. They've seen me race home after seeing videos of my house being attacked. So, my co-worker standing in front of me quickly says, "I saw you on Fox News the other night. Wow, that's trippy stuff." I turned sheepishly away from Wyeth and smirked. Yeah, our house is the house from hell. He replied, "Sorry to hear about you and your girlfriend breaking up. I saw those pictures of the burnt Bibles, of the wall markings. That's some crazy shit." I was thinking to myself *uh huh... yep, all of that is true*. I can tell you right now everyone who knows me. That knows Tina(including co-workers). Know this is not something Tina and I would make up. Seventeen million people saw the Seattle Fox 13 news piece about my house. It never occurred to me till now that in that seventeen million number were fellow employees of mine.

Wyeth and I were standing by the coffee machine, and the question finally got asked. "Did the UK team and you figure out what that stuff was made out of?" I told Wyeth that I painted over the office wall writings with the hopes of squashing the activity. But I wasn't completely thorough. There was a piece of the closet door that still had wall markings. My friend Patty and I took that door to the paint store over the weekend with the hopes of them telling us what the substance was. They didn't know. Wyeth said, "I'd be happy to test the door for you, why don't you bring it in?" I swear to God I almost dropped my coffee mug. What do you mean you can test the door? Wyeth's face lit up. "Yeah, we have a lab upstairs, I'm pretty sure I can find out what that substance is made out of."

I've known Wyeth going on two years. He works for the quality manufacturing division of my company. I work for the global logistics side. We report to different managers – but we work very close proximity. Hence the reason for us talking at the coffee machine. Funny how you can work alongside someone for a little over two years and still not know exactly what it is they do. Wyeth told me that he has a lab upstairs. I wasn't aware we had a lab in the building. An analysis lab at that. One of the things Wyeth does is test paint. He's "pretty sure" he can find out what the wall substance is made out of. And why can he do that? One of his roles and responsibilities here is testing paint for quality assurance and legal purposes. His job, i.e. the department he works under is to make sure our vendors use nothing illegal (un-authorized materials) on our company's products. I wasn't aware that certain paint ingredients are banned in certain countries. I'm talking about metals inside. Every country, according to Wyeth, has its own rules and procedures as to what can come in. If customs find an illegal ingredient on our products, that's a huge fine. We're talking millions of dollars. That's what the lab upstairs is for.

I texted Patty a few hours after Wyeth and I talked. I learned from watching other paranormal teams in action that you should always have a witness around when you're attempting to gather evidence. What I'm talking about specifically is me going home and chiseling off a piece of the office door. I admit it's not as sexy as dressing up in blue jeans and a black t-shirt, running around house basements with a K2 looking for dust particles. This is a little bit more scientific. This involves multiple people. People who have no interests in the paranormal. Wyeth couldn't care less what this stuff is made out of. He's doing this as a favor to me. If Keith Linder says a poltergeist (whatever the fuck that is) wrote on his wall, you best believe one did. That's what everyone's thinking at work lately. "Wow, Keith's house is trippy." "Keith's house is hell." "Keith's house is fascinating." No one and I mean no one (at work) have said, "That stuff looks like someone spray painted on the wall." IT professionals don't think that way. Our profession demands that we think outside the box twenty-four seven.

Occam's Razor? Sorry. That outdated concept doesn't work here. I got home that night and did exactly what I said I was going to do. I took the door back off the hinges (with Patty present) and sawed a piece of it off. The next morning, I walked over to Wyeth's desk and said here it is. Wyeth turned around, took off his Beats by Dre earphones, and said, "Follow me."

Fig 3.8: March 2016 - chiseling off a piece of the office door.

CHAPTER 4

Bone Black

"W hat's bone black?" That's what the paint store employee said when I asked if I could buy some bone black. The clerk paused a little bit and asked, "Come again, what are you looking for?" I'm looking for bone black, I repeated. Do you have some? Every paint store I called between Bothell and Seattle were clueless about what that was. Don't feel too bad if you haven't heard of the term bone black. Not too many people have. I know I didn't. Out of the ten art galleries I called in the United States only five knew what I was talking about. I was referred to those five individuals by others in their field.

You sure you want to know what the markings on the door are made out of? Here it is. Bone black aka *"Bone char (Latin: carbo animalis) is a porous, black, granular material produced by charring animal bones. It consists mainly of tricalcium phosphate (or hydroxylapatite) 57–80%, calcium carbonate 6–10% and carbon 7–10%."* It's been primarily used for pigment and the refining of sugar. The most interesting thing about bone black ironically is its ingredients. It's derived from bison — cow bones. That's important to remember. How much charring is required to turn a bison bone into bone black? 700 °C (1,292 °F) that's how much. We're talking extreme heat. *Why am I not surprised?* One of the products produced as a result of incinerating buffalo or cow bones is a substance called Dipple's Oil. Remember that!

IMPORTANT – *"Bone char is also used as a black pigment for artist's paint, printmaking,* **calligraphic,** *and drawing inks as well as other artistic applications because of its deepness of color and excellent tinting* **strength.** *Bone black and ivory black are artists' pigments which have been in use since* **historic** *times--both by old masters like Rembrandt and Velázquez, and more modern painters such as Manet and Picasso.*

It should be noted that bone black is insoluble in water as in *"incapable of being dissolved.* **Once dry,** *the paints become insoluble in water"* Synonyms: *"indissoluble, incapable of dissolving, these minerals are insoluble in water."*

Several words in the description and definition of bone black should stand out to you by now. Those words being calligraphy, buffalo, and bison. I never believed for one instance that the paranormal events taking place in my and Tina's home were random. The spirits that occupy the Bothell house are not in the coincidence business. Nothing's happenstance. If you look closer at some of the events taking place, you'll realize certain activities are a continuation of previous events. You don't use bone black unless you have a specific purpose. A specific endgame. Like I said earlier a majority of the paint stores I called had never even heard of the word bone black. We know the upside-down man drawn inside my office is a Native American symbol. We know it's a form of calligraphy. We know it means a man has died or a man is about to die. Those facts have existed online for the world to see before the Bothell house was even a blueprint.

I wrote in my book *The Bothell Hell House: Poltergeist of Washington State* how difficult it was for me to remove these writings after they appeared. It wasn't always difficult. First, it was the sage ash. That was relatively easy. Then came the harder substance that looked like black paint. We had to paint over those markings, and even that didn't always work. The markings (for reasons I can't explain) began bleeding through the layers of paint we added. That required me buying expensive primer. Sometimes it worked. Most of the time it didn't. The part about bone black being "insoluble in water" is fascinating. One of the benefits of paint is its ability to be insoluble in water. You get that. I get that.

Bone black is, however, organic as you might have surmised from the makeup of it — *tricalcium phosphate (or hydroxylapatite) 57–80%, calcium carbonate 6–10% and carbon 7–10%.* The calcium element in bone black is one component that makes it insoluble in water. In short, difficult to clean. Here are the pictures of the wall writings that appeared Halloween night 2014.

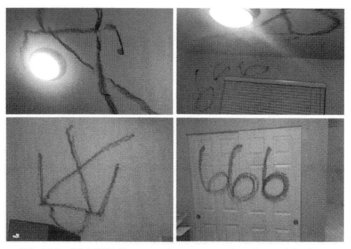

Fig 4.1: 2014 Halloween house attack – bone black

Fig 4.2: 2014 Halloween House Attack – Multiple upside-down man calligraphy-like drawings.

Observe Fig 4.1 Top Left – it's hard to tell if that's an upside-down man or a standing man. See how the arm is wrapped around the light fixture? It's as if that was done on purpose. As if to suggest it's holding something. The right arm – or right hand I should say, looks like a clenched fist. None of the other upside-down man stick figures have hands (please study the pictures). They have arms hanging down by the side. This drawing (Fig 4.1) has a knot at the end of its arm. The knot is facing inward. The same direction your hand would be if it were clinched. Not to be overlooked are the elbows. Look at all the other upside-down man wall photos. No elbows. The arms are straight. Not Fig 4.1, 4.3. The man's arms are bent. I'm sure this means something. If you have an idea – please let me know.

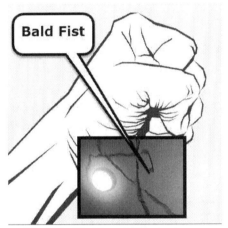

Fig 4.3: Fist/hand illustration

How did my co-worker and I conclude that the wall stuff from the Halloween attack was made up of bone black? My co-worker with a piece of the office door in his hand told me to follow him to his lab. Minutes later that's where we were – his lab room. Wow! It's a lab room alright. Not a chemistry lab. No, this was an engineering lab. There were big machines, and there were small machines. Everywhere I look there was a workstation. Numerous equipment and tools were lying around. Ah, there's something I recognize from my days at Dell computer. Multiple electrostatic wrist bands. Yep, this is a tech lab alright.   So, my co-worker motions me over to this table where there are multiple pieces of equipment lying around. I've never seen items like this before. They look like something you'd see in a Star Trek movie. On the table were these ray guns - these are called XRF/XRD analyzers. "XRF/XRD analyzers provide fast, easy, accurate, and non-destructive alloy identification and elemental analysis from Mg to U. Used on location for immediate results" as described on multiple internet sites. "XRD is a technology developed for NASA's Mars Curiosity Rover, ... these unique devices are offered in both benchtop and field-portable versions. The device allows the engineer (that would be my co-worker) ultra-fast analysis for full compound identification of major, minor, and trace components." *My co-worker wasn't bullshitting me. He really can help me.*

So, what did my co-worker do? Well, it was quite simple. Wyeth laid the piece of the closet door down and placed the nose of the gun on top of the black braille-like substance. On the opposite side of that nose was a mini screen. My co-worker squeezed the trigger, and there began a series of beeps and pings. The screen lit up, and that was it. Now the gun is not going to utter the words bone black. That part comes later. What the screen is going to show is the materials it picked up. And let me tell you the words out of my co-worker's mouth were basically: "wow, this is weird; there's no metal or paint-like substance." My co-worker did a second stab with the gun (just to be sure) within seconds he blurted out a.) High concentrates of phosphate b.) We got calcium carbonate 6–10% and c.) Low percentages of activated carbon +/- 7%. These are things you don't normally find in 21st-century paintings. Or any paint for that matter.

My co-worker finished. He did several zaps with these expensive gun(s) and got the same reading: 80% or higher of phosphate. The results are almost identical to the makeup of bone black. Of course, we don't know that yet. My co-worker gave me the notes he had written down and said he doesn't know what the black stuff is made out of except to say it's not a well-known paint substance. I introduced Wyeth's findings to one of the local paranormal teams in the area. One I had been maintaining communications with. The leader of the group (like me) found the wall writings in my house extremely interesting. "Why an upside-down, man? Why write 'Die KL? Where did that black stuff come from?" Those were the questions she and others were asking. Going to her with my co-worker's notes seemed like the logical thing to do. It didn't take long for her to respond.

A few art galleries in Seattle and elsewhere told the investigator based on the pictures they've seen, and the results given to them from the test Wyeth conducted, they were ninety percent sure it was bone black. What the hell is bone black? *Let's see what the internet says.* My mouth got wider and wider with each website I went to. That's how taken aback I was — charred bison bones? *Where do bison bones come from?* They come from dead bison. I know enough about the United States to know bison were never inhabitants of the State of Washington. Specifically, the Pacific Northwest. I need to research this further. The quickest way to confirm or debunk this being bone black is by calling multiple art galleries. I started calling several art galleries in and around the Puget Sound area. I got some interesting responses. One person at the Seattle art gallery said they were pretty sure the substance was bone black. The results we got off the wooden door in my co- worker's lab suggests that's exactly what it is. Bone black has distinguishable chemical makeups.

As I'm going through the motion of calling these art galleries, I know not to mention the word bone black. I'm only giving them what my co-worker gave me. That and the pictures of wall writings from the Halloween house attack is the only thing I'm giving them. Truth be told. The majority of the people I talked to didn't know what it was. What I found more interesting than that was them not having an alternative as to what it could be. No one said spray paint. I suddenly realized you either knew what it was, or you didn't. Those who knew it was bone black knew because of their interests in ancient forms of paint. I decided to go a step further with my questioning by asking them how confident they were with the analysis I gave them. Is it really bone black?

Everyone I talked to said they were ninety-to ninety- five percent sure the substance was Bone black. Their words, not mine: "The results you got from the XRF/XRD guns you used makes it easy to reach that conclusion. We have devices like that in our facility. We test stuff every day." Bone black, ladies, and gentlemen. You really can't make this up. One of the things that are frustrating about paranormal research is every answer you get creates new questions. Can I find something that answers all the questions Tina and I have? Can I find something that answers every question you have? Two steps forward are starting to feel like twenty steps backward. You can tell I've been an IT project manager too long. We make our living based on the why factor. Why are we doing this project? Why is the project behind schedule? Why are we over budget? Why is the maintenance window being canceled? Why do you need more time? Why? Why? Why? That's what projects managers do every day. We ask a lot of why questions. Not knowing what the root cause is what keeps us up at night. Law students are taught never to ask a question you don't already know the answer to. In project management, it's the opposite. You keep asking questions to avoid being blindsided. Project managers (I included) make our living by removing unknowns for many equations as possible. The unknown for me right now is why bone black? Why bone char? Bone black often referred to as bone char, is not a substance you can easily find. Doubt me? Call your paint store right now. Ask for a can of bone black. Better yet. Ask for some bone char. Call Home Depot. Call Wal- Mart. Call your local art gallery. See what kind of response you get. We're going to revisit bone black, Dippel's oil (what that is exactly) later in the book. Where are we right now? It's mid -March 2016. I've been keeping both US and UK teams up to date on the findings of the house. Everyone's astonished. That astonishment is about to be out done by something else. The spirits aren't done haunting Keith Linder.

Bone Black
https://youtu.be/97CLbvpa-0I
Length 1 hour and 9 minutes

CHAPTER 5

New Wall Markings

Do me a favor. I want you to pause for a few seconds. Create a movie in your mind of you driving home from work. Can you see yourself? Can you see your hands on the steering wheel? Can you see life happening around you? If you're like me, you're probably thinking what am I going to cook for dinner tonight? What do I feel like eating? Did the trash man come to pick up the trash today? Has the mailman run? You're in your neighborhood. You've just turned on the street that you live on. You're five houses away from your home. You can see your house. All of a sudden, your garage door goes up. Wait a minute, you haven't yet touched the garage door remote above your sun visor? The thought of reaching for the remote device hasn't even occurred. It's like someone inside your house saw your car coming up the street and in doing so, raised the garage door by hitting the panel inside the garage. How considerate of them. Wait a minute, you live alone? There's a period in my book *The Bothell Hell House*, where Tina and I were hardly talking to each other. We're not lovers anymore. We're roommates. Tina, when she leaves the house to go to work, will from time to time march back in and find me and say, "Your car door is open." Her and our next-door neighbor did that from time to time. Nothing's been removed from my car. It doesn't matter if I come home from work or if I come home after a night partying with friends. My garage door will inexplicably go up the minute my car reaches the street I live on. But it gets worse than that. It's morning now. You've grabbed your car keys (car fob), coffee mug, purse or laptop bag. You're ready to leave the house. You get to the door that leads to the garage.

You open it and all of a sudden — wow! My garage door is up? It's important to remember that the activity in my house doesn't stop once a paranormal team leaves my location.

What I just described was happening before both teams arrived. It's still happening. Let me be clear. Objects are not being thrown anymore. Doors are not being slammed. Fires are not erupting. The last wall writing was in December 2014. I'm glad those things have stopped happening. I'll take a win any way possible. But the house is still active. I still hear pitter-patter footsteps. The pinging noises I spoke about in my first book. The loud snap, crackle, and pop sounds. That hasn't slowed down. When you see your garage, door raise on its own (day or night doesn't matter) while turning on the street you live on – and then go down on its own the second you park inside your garage. That redefines the term targeting.

March 28th, 2016 - I walk through my front door. I pause and take a deep breath. I exhale and immediately listen for the pitter-patter footsteps. Sigh. There isn't any. Two years of dealing with the paranormal your muscle memory sort of takes a life on a life of its own. One of the things I'm trying to avoid while living in this house alone is not overreacting. It's important that I don't go looking for the activity, which let me tell you, is pretty easy to do. Poltergeists are experts at bringing the activity to you. That's what makes them so frightening. They know how to get attention. Truth be told, I think Tina and I did a good job of not overreacting. To a fault actually. People who experience malevolent hauntings are often accused of attention seeking. 'It's all a publicity stunt.' That accusation never made any sense to me. The world didn't know of the Bothell house till 2014. We had been experiencing nearly two years of activity by then. Imagine coming home from work and finding your furniture rearranged. I'm talking about all of it.

Upstairs, downstairs, it doesn't matter – everything's been turned upside down, inside out. The ADT alarm system is still in 'system armed' mode. Suffice to say there's nothing unusual to report. Not yet anyway.

If you had lived with me, you would know right away that I'm a creature of habit. My office upstairs is where you would find me normally. That's where I was when Tina lived here. Today was different. Today I thought since I'm down here already, I might as well watch television down here. I was an hour into my program when I began to notice something strange. Right underneath the wall picture above the entertainment center were three streaks of liquid substance. I could tell my subconscious was ignoring it at first because the streaks I was seeing had traveled significantly far. I was sitting in the den. The same room where the plant levitated in front of Tina and me. As soon as I saw the streaks, I knew right away this was the poltergeist. There's something about living in a home infested with minions that forces one to recognize the unreal from the real. By unreal I mean the paranormal. Now I've seen enough crazy things in my house to know my next response has the potential of making the situation worse or keeping the situation as is. It's time to apply the rules I've created for myself. Rule #1 don't panic. Panicking could potentially lead to more instances like this. I know that's easier said than done but trust me, the less you panic, the better.

Rule #2 embrace your common sense. Forget what other people tell you. You're smart. Your common-sense gene will help you if you let it. I've been living in this house going on four years now. There's nothing behind that wall (no pipes, no plumbing) that could have caused this. There was a paranormal event unfolding right in front of my very eyes. So, what do I do? I do what any normal person would do. I rose from the couch and walked a few steps toward the painting. I lifted the painting off the wall and confirmed what I already knew. The streaks were real. Not only that but they were getting longer. We're talking six to eight inches now. Three streaks mind you. I can see (with the picture off the wall now) three streaks - each about half an inch wide. I pressed the tip of my forefinger onto one of the streaks. *I'll be dammed. It's oily.* It's not water. That's what I *said* after rubbing my finger across the wall. Rule #3 when unexplained phenomena break out inside your home, call someone you know and trust. I called Patty. *She needs to see this.* The streaks were still streaming down the wall when Patty arrived.

Yes, this was a new wall marking. The first wall markings to ever appear were on the first floor. The spirits, i.e. minions wanted to get my attention. They got it (on my terms). They wanted to see my reaction. They got that too. Once again, on my terms. I'm not running to Best Buy to get more cameras. I'm not going to scream fuck you spirit, this is my house, get the fuck out! I've learned from my past mistakes. The best thing I can do is take pictures and continue documenting.

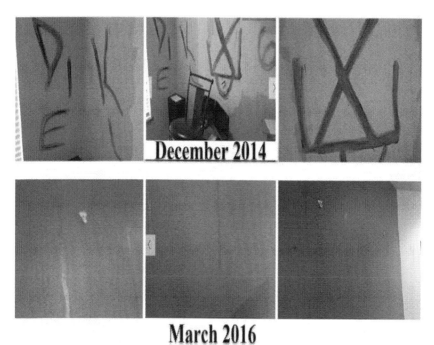

Fig 5.1: A new oily like substance began appearing on the living room wall March 28th, 2016. Two months after the US and UK's live-in investigation.

Fig 5.2: March 28th, 2016 - a translucent oily substance streaming down the wall.

Weird Stuff on Walls ☐ Inbox x   🗑 🖨 ▣

Ma_____pr@_____   3/29/16 ☆ ↰ ▾
to Don, Steve ▾

Synopsis: came home from work last night. Never made it upstairs. Had dinner from the couch and watched TV. About an hour or so of being home I noticed liquid tracks, trails if yo will descending from my picture.

Very odd I got up and moved the picture and found these 3 things. There is no plumbing behind this wall. The liquid appears oily. Almost like a vegetable Oil, Olive Oil, Incense based solution.

No stench, no smell, no odor. Clear in color when dampened on a napkin

i called Patty over to be a witness of the event. She arrived 20 minutes later

Fig 5.3: Email to Scientific Establishment of Parapsychology – March 29, 2016

CHAPTER 6

Nick Kyle

Parapsychologists Steve Mera informed me early April 2016 that he and Don were returning to conduct a second investigation. That made sense to me. Look what had happened since they left. We were ninety-five percent sure the wall markings on the office closet door came from incinerated bison bones. I told Steve about the oil incident and I sent him the pictures (see Fig 5.1). Steve found the three streaks of oily-like substance very interesting. But that's not why he and Don chose to come back. Steve and Don are seasoned investigators. Both men know a house as active as this comes around maybe once every fifty years if not longer. One of the reasons why poltergeists are so hard to troubleshoot is the activity comes and goes. They are the lightning in a Leyden jar. The Bothell, house (albeit it a level one) is active right now. There's evidence to be obtained.

If you're going to dedicate time, money, and energy to a field many find repulsive, then you have to be able to recognize what I refer to as the now moment. Recognizing the now applies to everything you do in life. Let me give you one example. Have you ever left a job interview where you felt everything went so perfectly? You answered every question given to you. The vibe between you and the person interviewing you was amazing. You could feel the pulse of the interview. Of the company. You're high fiving yourself as you make your way to the parking lot. Hot damn! You feel terrific. A few days later you get an email from the employer saying they found someone else. You're like what the hell? What went wrong? I thought I had this job in the bag. There's no way in heaven I failed this interview. That happened to me once. There was a job I wanted. I studied for two weeks. The interview was supposed to be for an hour. It ended up being two hours. The person that interviewed me asked me if I could stay a little while longer. He wanted his boss to meet me. That's how great the interview went. A few days later I got a letter saying I didn't get the job. I was floored. I was depressed. What the hell went wrong? I found out later on that the reason why I didn't get the job was because I didn't ask for it. This is what the recruiter told me. "They loved you, Keith. They thought you were spot on." Both managers were eagerly waiting for you to ask, can I have the job. They wanted to offer the job to you on the spot. You never asked for it. Management thought you weren't a hundred percent sure about wanting it. The person who came after you "asked for the job." He was hired on the spot." I found out later after talking to job coaches – most companies specifically hire based on your ability to recognize the now. This house is active. It's been active for quite some time. Steve and Don know from experience that, that's not always going to be the case. The activity will cease one day. We don't know why that happens. But it does. The iron is hot right now. We have oily substances streaking down a wall. We have black markings identical to the markings that were in the office appearing on Patty's husband's truck. We're in unchartered territory, ladies and gentlemen. The paranormal community has never encountered this type of phenomena before. Have you ever seen the look on a child's face as he's leaving Disney Land? That's how Steve and Don looked when they left my house back in January. And I get it. They're trying to exploit this now moment. And you know? That's perfectly fine. There's nothing wrong with exploiting a case if the exploitation is genuine. Hitting the iron while it's hot doesn't make you an opportunist. That's what a researcher is supposed to do. When *Ghost Adventures* came to our house in the winter of 2014, I was certain they would live in the house for a couple of days. Zak Bagans and his team didn't recognize the now moment they were currently occupying. They spent only five hours investigating.

Steve asked me if Nick Kyle could accompany him and Don. Nick Kyle (at the time) was the president of the Scottish Society for Psychical Research (SSPR). I was familiar with the SPR organization based in London. Nick's organization, it would appear, was its own independent psychical organization. I thought to myself *hmmm, Steve and Don are bringing in the big guns. An independent verifier. Their colleagues must think some of what they've gathered is too good to be true.* I know the feeling. Steve Mera told me part of their evidence review involves the sharing of information. It's called peer review. I understand the concept.

My job as a project manager involves information sharing. The data I compiled during the duration of a project goes into a repository for other project managers to review should they ever have a similar project to run. I can see why Steve wants Nick Kyle on onboard. Many of their colleagues were flabbergasted by what was being reported. No one goes into a location and gets four hundred EVPs. That's never been done.

Back track to November 2014 – the homeowner sent me an email stating I was to be in charge of all investigations happening in the house. It was never a debate between him and me as to who was in charge. You have an IT project manager who's been documenting from beginning to end him and his girlfriend's experience while living in the house. Obviously, I'm not overly frightened because look at me I'm still here. But guess what? I am frightened. I'm terrified. I'm here because of two things. No one can live in this house the way it is now. This is the mindset I adopted after the poster caught fire in spring 2014. My second reason for being here has to do with the "Demons in Seattle" episode. Had I moved out after the episode had aired? The epitaph on this case would have forever been, "zero evidence." People in the paranormal community thought Tina and I were faking it. We weren't. How a person can equate zero evidence to hoaxing is beyond me. But that's what I was dealing with after the episode aired. Obviously, the homeowner didn't think Tina and I were faking things. He was the one that greenlighted the house being investigated. He gave the OK. I wonder why?

Steve, Don, and a gentleman by the name of Nick Kyle are coming. They're going to live in the house for eight days. Since they've elected to have Nick Kyle (the president of the SSPR) with them this time, I decided to do something I've never done before. I'm going to mirror what they do. What does that mean? It means I'm going to have listening equipment already situated in every room prior to their arrival. One of the things Steve and Don did when they were here before that I admired a great deal was, they set up audio equipment (in plain sight) everywhere in the house. I'm not talking about their hand-held devices. I'm talking about listening devices. Very expensive pieces of equipment. That's probably how they obtained four hundred EVPs. I doubt I'll get four hundred EVPs. That's not my reason for doing this. My reason for doing this has to do with my YouTube channel. That's where the majority of the evidence ends up. Paranormal researchers often tell you (before they arrive of course) that every piece of evidence they capture belongs to you (that's what they've told me). That has never happened. *No Bull Paranormal* was the first paranormal to enter the Bothell house. One of the things they captured on video was white mist coming from the hallway floor. I asked for this footage and was given the runaround. I later learned that person responsible for the team's evidence storage had left the group. He took all the evidence from the Bothell house with him. Several paranormal teams have found stuff and not given it to me. I want to prevent that from happening again. The best way to prevent that is to set up my equipment. Why a YouTube channel? YouTube is the premier cloud video-sharing service. It's one of the largest free databases in the world. Think about it. What do you need to watch YouTube? Don't say computer. Years ago, you could have said that and been correct. YouTube can now be accessed through a multitude of different devices. I'm talking smartphone. I'm talking tablet PC. I'm talking touch-screen monitor. Smart TV, household appliance, Kindle, gaming console, and a slew of other things. The only thing you need to access YouTube now is the internet.

CHAPTER 7

Master Bedroom

S teve Mera, Don Philips, and Nick Kyle are about to uncover evidence that, in my opinion, trumps what Don and Steve gathered the first time. Oh, it's not even close. Don't get me wrong, the guys compiled a lot of data their first trip. Seriously, they got an inordinate amount of evidence. As did Nikki and her team. This second investigation confirms their previous investigation that something is here. But not only that. It confirms what Tina and I have been reporting from day one of us moving in. The spirits in this house are not shy. They love giving up data, i.e. evidence. Think of it as an onion that's about to be peeled. The more you peel away, the more there is to see. Keep that in mind as you go through the remainder of this book.

April 13th, 2016 – Steve, Don, and Nick Kyle walked in the Bothell house and immediately started working. Steve and Don already know they're not in Kansas anymore. Nick Kyle is about to find out. The last time Steve and Don were here, they walked around the house sort of nonchalantly. I could tell they were thinking 'there might be something going on here, but it's not to the degree Keith's been specifying.' The expression on both men's face especially Steve Mera's to the environment he was in was 'impress me.' Well, guess what? The spirits impressed them. You don't travel six thousand miles across the ocean two times in less than three months for nothing.

One of the rooms Steve and Don never got around to investigating when they were here last time was the master bedroom. There was just not enough time. The men spent the majority of their time analyzing the hallway and downstairs areas.

The poking and prodding that started back in spring 2014 had increased as of late. As soon as I lie down to go to sleep here, they come. It feels like someone's laying invisible sandbags over your legs and arms. I hate to admit this, but I'm used to it now. This is my reality now. This is what I view as being acceptable. What can I do? I'm powerless. How do we stop that? Steve told me before him, and Don arrived that he planned to spend a lot more time in the master bedroom. There are only but a handful of documented cases that shed light on what I've been reporting.

April 14th, 09:00 AM two weeks before moving out day — One of the first things the guys did after everyone ate breakfast was unpack their gear. The conversation over breakfast could be summed up in two words: "Keith's bedroom." The experiment Steve wanted to conduct with his colleague's present involved sealing off the master bedroom. Lace the room with motion sensors – particularly around the mattress of the bed. The men got up from the kitchen table and started working. It took them about an hour to get everything situated.

11:30 AM — motion sensors started going off in the bathroom located inside the master bedroom. The three men went upstairs together. They removed the do-not-cross tape and entered the room with the alarms still wailing. But something very peculiar happened within seconds of us walking in. No more alarms ringing. I'm talking about an abrupt stop. I've seen this happen before when Karissa Fleck and Rich Schleifer were here earlier this year (see it here). The room is exactly how we left it. Nothing's been moved. Nothing was out of place. No one knows why these alarms are going off. Steve makes a note in his notepad of what just happened. Everyone agrees that the bedroom should be resealed.

I don't think we were downstairs for more than five minutes when suddenly we received another disturbance call. The siren sounds were coming from the bedroom this time. The bed I sleep in. Steve, Nick, and Don marched upstairs again.

https://www.youtube.com/watch?v=b9pVNMyUG58&t=9s

Nikki, Karissa Fleck and Rich Schleifer investigation

I thought to myself, *this alarm sounds different than the previous one we heard. Sounds extremely loud.* I'll soon know why. Don, Nick, and Steve unsealed the master bedroom door and walked in. Everyone sees the same thing at the same time. *Wow!* One of the motion detection devices Steve inserted <u>under</u> the mattress is now lying on the floor. A considerable distance from where it was originally placed. *That's why it sounded loud — the device was resting near the bedroom door.*

We all were standing behind Steve when he put the motion sensor under the mattress earlier. Nick and Don approved its position prior to them sealing off the room. This was eerily similar to what Nikki experienced when she was here a few months ago. February 2016 - I was in my bed (the same bed Steve put the device under) trying to take a nap when all of a sudden, it started. The movement and pulsation I feel from inside the mattress – near the foot of the bed. What I do next, I'm very proud of. I scream for Nikki and Karissa to join me upstairs. The ladies dart upstairs not knowing what to expect. Talk about shock and awe. That's the response Nikki gave. Something along the lines of "oh my god, I can feel it." She and Karissa both could feel what I've been claiming for quite some time. Pulsating and phantom heartbeats underneath the mattress. Not the covers, the actual mattress.

I want you to imagine something. Imagine you're sleeping next to a construction site. We all know the sounds associated with a house being built. Constant knocking, constant hammering, the sound of four-by-fours being thrown around. That's what I hear when I go to bed at night. That sound is right outside my bedroom door. It's like I'm living right underneath a billiard hall or something. The constant breaking of billiard balls. But I'm not finished. While that's happening outside my bedroom and try to understand when I say outside my bedroom door that doesn't mean I know where the sound is coming from. The sound (everything I just described) comes from everywhere. Tina and I would get up in the middle of the night and go looking for where we thought the noise was coming from. We never found it.

The heartbeats coming through the mattress underneath my pillow is a daily occurrence. You're going to learn through the course of this book that moving is not a simple as it seems. Spirits can follow you. I've already experienced attacks while traveling on business. Sheets yanked off me in the middle of me sleeping. Lights going off and on. Intermittent problems with the hotel's Wi-Fi system. My room only. The heartbeats? Yes, I've experienced them too while traveling. I'm so glad Steve, Don, and Nick Kyle were witness to this. This was their experiment. But they're not done. The baseline EMF reading in the bed before the alarm going off was one 1-2 milligauss. Steve and Don took a reading near the foot of the bed where the object once was and a reading where the device now rested. They got a reading of nine milligauss.

An empty spot on the floor maintaining a nine milligauss reading for three hours? Steve, Don, and Nick could not explain it. Nine milligauss? That's the amount of energy a television puts out. This is great evidence.

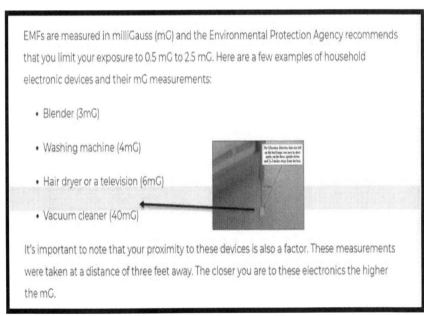

EMFs are measured in milliGauss (mG) and the Environmental Protection Agency recommends that you limit your exposure to 0.5 mG to 2.5 mG. Here are a few examples of household electronic devices and their mG measurements:

- Blender (3mG)

- Washing machine (4mG)

- Hair dryer or a television (6mG)

- Vacuum cleaner (40mG)

It's important to note that your proximity to these devices is also a factor. These measurements were taken at a distance of three feet away. The closer you are to these electronics the higher the mG.

Fig 7.1: Milligauss (mG)

RECAP - The sensor Steve put underneath my mattress is lying on the floor. The resting spot gave off a reading of nine milligauss. It held that reading for <u>three</u> hours. That's the length of time it takes for a person to drive from Seattle to Portland. Let that sink in for a bit.

It doesn't take common sense to realize that something moved the motion sensor from its original location. How exactly it happened is not important. The fact that it happened is. We live in a world of laws, ladies and gentlemen. Logic tells us if you place an object underneath a mattress and seal the room to where no one can get in, that object should remain there until it's time for to you come back for it. If it's been moved. Moved significantly in a room that's sealed off. Tripwires laced throughout the immediate area. Those trips were going off. That by definition is paranormal. Something tripped the tripwires. An object was moved. It can't be explained any simpler than that. But you see the evidence I just explained is even greater than you realize. I've been telling multiple people for over several years that I feel something in the bed with me when I go to sleep at night. I feel what I describe as paw prints. Mattress vibrations, tapping sounds coming from behind the headboard. I'm poked and prodded within seconds of lying down. Nikki and Karissa both put their hand over the area of the mattress and felt the heartbeat themselves (see link below). Two teams oblivious to what the other team is doing or better yet what the other team has found can substantiate the claims my girlfriend and I were making. I can't tell you which discovery was better. Nikki touching the bed mattress with her hand earlier this year and feeling a heartbeat herself or the UK guy's walking into my bedroom after the alarms went off and finding Steve's motion sensor resting on the floor.

<u>https://www.youtube.com/watch?v=whsHPreL</u>
<u>IZ4</u> esp. at 48:11

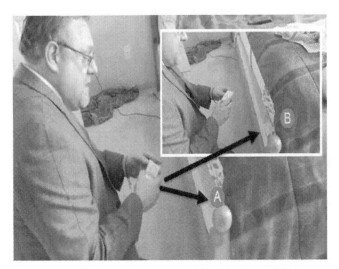

Fig 7.2: April - 2016 Parapsychologists Steve Mera sets up motion sensors underneath the master bedroom mattress.

Fig 7.3: April - 2016 - Steve Mera and Don Philips sealed off the master bedroom multiple times while trying to investigate my claims of bed phenomena.

Fig 7.4: April - 2016 paranormal researcher Don Philips places a voice recorder over the master bedroom door prior to the room being sealed off.

CHAPTER 8

Ray

E VP (electronic voice phenomena) as it is commonly called is regarded by many in the paranormal field as being the strongest pieces of evidence one finds while investigating the paranormal. It's the belief that "sounds found on electronic recordings that are interpreted as spirit voices that have been either unintentionally recorded or intentionally requested" and therefore recorded. Enthusiasts consider these voices paranormal. Orthodox science does not. Auditory pareidolia? Perhaps both parties are right. As you might already know, not all electronic voice phenomena are created equal. What some call an EVP can actually be ambient background noise. What you want is intelligence. Intelligent speech. You would think in this day and age there would be some sort of universal standard surrounding EVP gathering. I was shocked to learn that there isn't. In my project management field, we have multiple methodologies we adhere to in order to complete a project successfully. I'm talking about Waterfall or Agile methodologies. Waterfall methodology states that progress from software design "flows from the top to the bottom, like a cascading waterfall." A newer project model the one that gains popularity say ten years ago when this book was written is Agile. Agile uses incremental, iterative work sequences that are commonly known as sprints. It's way more inclusive than Waterfall. Both methodologies can exist inside the same company. Depending on a company's size and culture both typically do. The first thing that should come to your mind when thinking about project management is best practice. Those two words I've yet to hear in the paranormal field.

All projects have a beginning and an end. That's why we call them projects. There are several models that an organization uses to make sure those projects get completed.

The most recognized project management institution in the world is an organization known as the <u>Project Management Institute</u> (PMI). That organization by itself has over six standardization i.e. credentials that help you complete a project successfully. You need to be overly familiar with these guidelines in order to obtain certification.

Credentials:

- Certified Associate in Project Management (CAPM)
- **Project Management Professional (PMP)**
- Program Management Professional (PgMP)
- Portfolio Management Professional (PfMP)
- PMI Agile Certified Practitioner (PMI-ACP)
- PMI Risk Management Professional (PMI-RMP)
- PMI Scheduling Professional (PMI-SP)
- PMI Professional in Business Analysis (PMI-PBA) Certification:
- PMI Certified OPM3 Professional*

My company would not have hired me had I not acquired some of these credentials. I can imagine the look on my manager's face had I told him. I do my own thing. I don't need any models. Processes? The hell with processes. No one would take me seriously in my field if that's the mindset I had. And rightfully so. The majority of the teams that came to my house when Tina and I were still together didn't have any type of standardization on how to gather evidence. No standardization around how to protect it. No vetting mechanism was ever applied. If you ask ten different paranormal teams what an EVP is, I promise you; you'll get twenty different answers.

There's no governing committee overseeing the vast residential investigations taking place around the world. It's for that reason I chose to monitor Steve, Don, and Nick while they were in my house conducting their investigation. For me, it's not a question of looking over someone's shoulder. Not for me, it isn't. Think about it. There's really nothing for a house occupant to do except maybe stay out of the way. That's fine. I can do that easy. But! There has to be something else for me to do other than order pizza and make coffee. And there is. It's called watch and learn. Steve and Don might not have a name for their investigative methodology, but they definitely are applying something. I can see it. I've been attached to over three hundred projects in my career. I know when a methodology is being applied. Those who make it up as they go. Their projects always crash and burn. One of Steve and Don's method for obtaining electronic voice phenomena was lacing the entire house with sound listening devices. One device they used often was the Tascam DR-60DmkII 4-Channel Portable Audio Recorder. It was pretty much running the whole time while Steve and Don were here. I said I was going to shadow Steve and Don during their second visit to my house. By shadow, I mean to lay out my video and audio equipment – in plain sight. I don't have the Tascam DR-60DmkII 4-Channel Portable Audio Recorder. *Wish I did.* I had the portable Tascam DR-05 Portable Digital and portable Zoom ZH1 H1 Handy Portable Digital Voice Recorder. My proof of concept is simple. Can I obtain EVPs by doing what Steve and Don did in January? The paranormal community likes to say EVP. I prefer unexplained voices – unexplained conversations. The men captured a lot of unexplained voices on their last trip. Can we do it again? I think we can. I got one!

NOTE: *The voices you are about to hear where obtained by me. It came off my equipment. They have been vetted and reviewed by Parapsychologists Steve Mera, Don Philips, and Nick Kyle – President (then of the) SSPR. What's happening? Steve and Don are in the bathroom (master bedroom) responding to the motion sensors that recently went off.*

Listen with headsets

Keith Linder Audio Capture – Ray	Audio/Video
EVP Image Detector	https://youtu.be/3xOswSf9qX

Table 8.1: April 2016 – Steve, Nick, and Don are in the bathroom (master bedroom) reconfiguring motion sensors that recently went off.

Voice1: 'Ray… (Audible).'
Voice2: '…just dropping some cable…'
Voice1: '…Image detector … it's the only way it can be powered like that. **Go and lift one of these.'**

Who is Ray? If we listen again (feel free to), we can clearly tell the voices on here are not Steve and Don's. The fact that Steve and Don are Englishmen with very distinct accents forces me to appreciate this audio even more. All three men's accents (including Nick Kyle of Scotland) are easily recognizable. No one uses the term 'image detector.' Google it and see what you come up with. These voices sound similar to the voices Steve and Don found the first time they were here (see Table 8.2).

 Listen with headsets

Upstairs Hallway – January 2016	https://youtu.be/0O_1_vEomBk listen at 1:11, 1:14, 1:23, 1:25

Table 8.2: January 2016 Steve and Don visit.

Voice(s): 'It's a camera, it's a camera… tat tat… nite cam.'

You can tell from listening to the audio that the spirits here are trying to determine what type of equipment is being used. A voice says, 'dropping some cable.' It's obviously referring to what the men are doing. 'Go lift one of these.' That's a very profound capture right there. That sentence alone confirms what researchers have been saying for quite some time about poltergeists. They remove belongings. One of the first things Tina and I experienced when we moved into the house was missing objects. Car keys, jewelry, silverware, CDs, cash, coins, Bibles, cameras, iPod. You name it they took it.

I know a lot of paranormal investigators. None of them refer to their night vision equipment as 'nite cam' or as 'image detector.' Those who read my book *The Bothell Hell House,* know I lost a lot of video equipment as a result of trying to chase these minions down. None of my cameras have ever resurfaced. You can see how a spirit would come up with the term 'image detector.' For two and a half years they've watched me bring in all sorts of cameras. Ninety-nine percent of them were infrared motion sensors. 'Go and lift one of these.' One of the definitions listed in Webster's dictionary for the word 'lift' is to steal something.

The interesting thing about both captures (see Table 8.1 and Table 8.2) is none of us can hear the conversation while we're in the room. That's why EVPs are held in such high regard. The only thing we should hear on our recording devices is our conversations. The fact that we have other voices (conversations) makes these captures paranormal. The fact that the voices are "appropriate to the circumstances," i.e., fit the context of what's going on in the room - backs up my theory of poltergeist being observant.

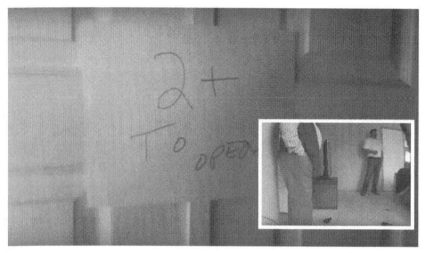

Fig 8.1: Steve, Don, and Nick Kyle spent the majority of their time conducting experiments in the master bedroom.

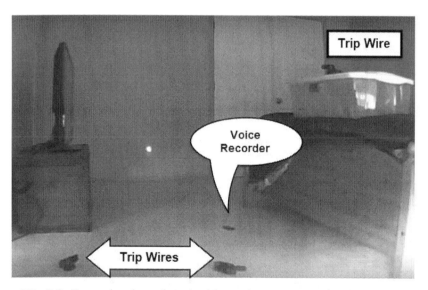

Fig 8.2: Room has been laced with motion sensors, tripwires, and voice recorder.

Keith
Linder's -
voice
recorder -

Fig 8.3: The men respond to the alarms going off. Multiple voices captured on video.

Something was going on with the tripwires that day. All we did for the next few hours was respond to motion sensors going off. If I had to guess I'd say the spirits were setting off Steve and Don's devices as a means of toying with us. Imagine if all you had to do to get people's attention was ring the dinner bell. You ring it, and people come running. That's what was happening now with Steve, Don, and Nick. Which forces me to ask the question: *who's investigating who?*

CHAPTER 9

The Woods

April 18th, 2016 - one of the things Don Philips wanted to do when he was here back in January, but couldn't because time constraints, was to venture into the wooded area behind my house. The men were told the first time they were here that my house (and the other houses nearby) were all built on Native American land. Were there vengeful Native American spirits bothering Tina and me? Maybe. The upside-down man wall markings being composed of incinerated bison bones have to mean something. I've yet to find another poltergeist case where that symbol was drawn. I've searched a lot of paranormal websites. A lot of parapsychology websites. We're talking thousands upon thousands of poltergeist cases. Nothing whatsoever about upside-down man wall writings. Interesting. Don did get the word 'longhouse' on one of his voice recorders when he was under the house last time. To appreciate the unexplained 'longhouse' Don captured on his voice recorder back in January, we need to do some research on the city of Bothell.

Fig 9.1: Bothell WA, 1909

69

"The earliest known residents of the Sammamish River and what would become Bothell were a Native American tribe that called themselves s-tsah-PAHBSH or willow people. These were members of a larger group called hah-chu-AHBSH or people of the lake and the Duwamish Tribe. The Willow People built a permanent settlement of cedar **longhouses** they called tlah-WAH-dees along a river the Americans would call Squak and Sammamish at the north end of Lake Washington." About seven miles from where the Bothell house is today.

http://www.historylink.org/File/4190
Bothell — Thumbnail History

https://en.wikipedia.org/wiki/Sammamish_people

"The Sammamish people were a Coast Salish Native American tribe in the Sammamish River Valley in central King County, Washington. Their name is variously translated as ("meander dwellers," a group residing around Bothell)." I'm not sure how *Ghost Adventures* missed all this information about tribes living in and around Bothell, but they did. If you think I have an ax to grind with *Ghost Adventures*, I don't. I'm doing what I hope every researcher has done in situations like this. I'm verifying. I found this information online relatively easily. Seriously! We're talking two or three clicks at the most. This incorrect information *Ghost Adventures*, gave during the episode had to be a result of no standardization existing around their research practices - Native Americans lived throughout Bothell – throughout Puget Sound.

Steve and Don have been working side by side for a majority of the time they've been here. That's about to change. With that many trees and foliage, there's no need for two men to go down into the woods. The men discussed Don's format before him entering the creek. Don will be taking several video and audio devices with them. Normally Steve would be the one supervising Don. Not this time. Steve had bestowed that responsibility to Nick Kyle, Patty, and me. Reason being he had his experiment to conduct. I had to admit I was kind of excited. There was a lot happening right now.

Lots of configuration going on with various types of equipment. I know these spirits. They salivate when this much people activity is taking place. We (all of us) have no idea what's about to happen. Steve Mera was about to conduct a saccade and optokinetic test. He had his laptop, his voice recorder, a small black box I later learned was a strobe device. He was juggling a lot of things right now. Both men were in full investigative mode. My excitement quickly turned into apprehensiveness based on what Don was about to do. Regardless of how far these men flew to assist me, I was still responsible for what happens to them. Don Philips was going into the woods. He was about fifty yards from my house. The last thing I needed right now was someone calling the police about a prowler roaming through the wooded area. I can picture one my neighbors now with their windows open hearing what they believe to be a man with a British accent. They look through their window towards the source of the noise and see dots of light waving from the creek. Oh, my neighbors would call the cops immediately.

It was two o'clock in the morning. All Don had on him was a flashlight. A few hand-held voice recorders and a walkie-talkie. That's it.

Electronic Voice Phenomena (EVP) as defined online.

Class A - This type of EVP is loud, clear, and of very high quality. The voice is easily understandable and does not need enhancement or amplification. Ex. Angelic Voice 'I hear spring/rings/**things**' **https://soundcloud.com/user-423872078/evp-raw-i-hear-springsmp3-** Jan 2016 captured by Steve Mera/Don Philips – Bothell House.

Class B - This is the most common type of EVP. This type of EVP is of somewhat lower quality and clarity than a Class A EVP but still very audible. Class B EVPs often do need some amount of enhancement or amplification to be heard clearly. The voice may not be clear enough to be totally understood or there may be disagreement as to what it is saying.

Class C - This is the lowest quality EVP. With a Class C EVP, even the best enhancement and amplification may not be sufficient to make the voice audible or clear. There may even be debated whether or not an EVP is actually present.

Actual Voice Phenomena (AVP). Recorded responses are extremely, clear and of very high quality as if a person was speaking at the time. The voice is easily understandable, and no enhancement or amplification is required. Tested and played back immediately. **AVP is also direct responses to questions.**

Direct Voice Phenomena (DVP). Incidents in which vocal speech is heard manifesting **from the air**, heard, identified and/or recorded. These are clear and of high quality. Ex. Kid 'cough' Tina and I heard May 2012

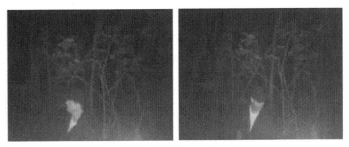

Fig 9.2: 2:00 AM. Wooded area behind my house.

 Poltergeist of Washington State
https://www.youtube.com/watch?v=xXKdMi3H9wM

Don's Question	Time Stamp	Answer
No question asked	4:09; Repeat 4X at 4:19	'Hey'
Are we talking about tribal burial?	7:49; Repeat 5X at 7:59	'Yeah'
Of this burial. Don't know if it's related…?	8:52; Repeat 4X at 9:39	'Yes'

Table 9.1

Poltergeist of Washington State
https://youtu.be/pjfiztxn27Y

Don's Question	Time Stamp	Answer
A first name would be good.	8:44; Repeat at 8:52, 8:57 (Don rewinds, listens, and confirms the name Ray is heard)	'Ray'

Table 9.2

If you didn't watch the movies above yet (Table 9.1 and 9.2), Don asks a series of questions. One specific question was: "can you tell us your name?" A male voice responded with the word 'Ray.' This is the first time we've heard the word 'Ray' being mentioned. Hold up, Keith. I thought the 'Ray' obtained in the bathroom a few days prior was the first Ray? Correct. Calendar-wise it was the first Ray to ever be captured. Don, Steve, Nick, and I didn't discover that EVP until it was near time for the guys to head back to England. They confirmed it was, in fact, an EVP. The 'Ray' Don picked up in the forest was discussed the same night it was picked up. None of us was aware that there are other unexplained 'Ray' voices on other voice recorders. Not yet anyways. Trust me, we've not heard the last of Ray. His name, his voice, and the voice of someone telling him what to do will be captured again and again in the remaining weeks of me living in the house. And SPOILER where I move to next.

Don asked a direct question, and he got a direct answer. It's impossible to know if these spirits are telling the truth for the simple fact that they're spirits. We shouldn't lose track of the simple fact that these voices Don and Steve have captured (on multiple devices, mind you) shouldn't be there at all. If we are to believe that spirits and demons don't exist, then we have a serious problem right now. A serious question: where are these voices coming from? Don't tell me they're coming from the air above? Don't tell me it's background noise or it's the neighbor's house. Don asked a direct question and got a specific response. The response was 'Ray.' The spirits in the bathroom weren't talking

73

to Steve, Don, Nick, and me. They were talking among themselves. One of the spirits called the other spirit 'Ray.' The way they were carrying on their conversation suggests they have no clue their voices were being captured on digital devices. It's either that or they don't care. It's obvious that they see us. Hell, they can hear us. We can't hear them. Not with the naked ear. Not this type of EVP we can't. But there's another bombshell EVP on the same video that can't be ignored either. On the same video you hear Don ask, "Of this burial. Don't know if it's related," before Don can finish his sentence a male voice utters 'yes.' Very deliberately I might add.

Don is asking if the area he's standing on – the area my house is built on is native land. He gets a strong 'yes' response. Another direct answer to another direct question. We've now captured an unexplained voice saying 'Ray' outside the house and an unexplained voice saying 'Ray' inside the house. We now have a voice saying 'yes' to the Native American question. We're getting very close to the truth. Ask yourself how many EVPs are you aware of that corroborate each other in the manner in which these EVPs corroborate each other? I'm talking about the EVPs in this book and the EVPs in my previous book.

Fig 9.3: Don spent a considerable amount of time in the wooded area back of the house. An interesting observation was the direction the old house was facing. Opposite to what the house is now.

CHAPTER 10
Shadowy Figures

N̲ot too long after Don went into the woods Parapsychologists, Steve Mera decided to conduct an experiment of his own. This would involve the use of motion cameras, laptops, and a stroboscopic device. Every team that's entered my home has, for the most part, conducted similar experiments using the same gear – gear as in K2 meters, EMF readers, cameras, infrared gear, etc. I can only think of one other instance where an experiment was conducted that involved a device, I was not already familiar with. That was the tripwires Steve used when he was here the last time. Now Steve is whipping out something new. He's got a laptop with a built-in camera – motion sensor software installed and a strobe light device. Where will all of this equipment be set up at? In the upstairs hallway.

Steve said something prophetic before going upstairs. He uttered the words "nothing ventured, nothing gained." The minute he said that I knew something spectacular was about to happen. "Nothing ventured, nothing gained" That's the mindset Nikki Novelle had adopted minutes before her infamous doll experiment (see Chapter 52 - *The Bothell Hell House*). Nikki knew, and it seems Steve also does. Evidence gathering is all about percentages. You have to increase the probability of the spirits interacting with you. Repetitive experiments run the risk of repressing the activity you're there to uncover. The spirits in this house have shown us on more than one occasion their willingness to engage when researchers think outside the box. Their fascination with new equipment is uncanny. Soon as Steve came back downstairs and began writing in his journal. We're talking less than sixty seconds when the motion cameras started going off. Not Steve's. Mine. I was sitting at the kitchen table with my laptop – monitoring the master bedroom.

Steve had just come back downstairs. He completed his setup in the hallway and was now sitting at the kitchen counter. The first thing I did upon hearing my alarms go off (in my headset) was tell Steve. Steve's back was turned to me at the moment. He couldn't hear the series of beeps coming through my laptop due to my headset being plugged in. I know these beeps all too well. These were the same beeps I heard when I had my house set up like Fort Knox back in 2014. The beeps let me know motion is being detected in whatever room the camera is in. These are the cameras I set up before the three guys arrived.

I unplug my headset so Steve can hear the beeps. I must reiterate these beeps are not from the equipment Steve setup. No. Steve's equipment is running on the hallway landing area – right outside the master bedroom. The only thing separating his equipment from my equipment is the bedroom door which is closed (See Fig 10.1).

Fig 10.1: My inbox is piling up with email alerts saying motion detected. Steve's equipment outside my bedroom door (see above) at this moment is capturing shadow figures. Why are the tripwires going off in my bedroom?

The first thing Steve Mera said after hearing the beeps himself was, "They don't like that; they don't like the strobe lighting." It would appear Steve was right. The alarms in my bedroom started sounding off within seconds of Steve Mera's strobe experiment. I said it once before, and I'll say it again. I don't believe in coincidences. Something was happening upstairs. We won't know what that something is for about another hour or so. That's how long Steve's experiment was.

The reader should understand at this very moment there are two investigations underway. Remember, Don is the woods right now. He's been out there for thirty minutes. He's within minutes of capturing some awesome EVPs – one of them being the word 'Ray.' Don is championing his thought experiment of the woods being linked to the house. Steve is conducting his experiment in the hallway. The most active area in my house. The first Bible to catch fire was in the hallway. The most dangerous object to ever be thrown was a chef knife. It was thrown right outside my office door. Both female sightings happened in the hallway.

What kind of house occupant would I be if I didn't have a video of what I'm about to describe? I told myself if I'm going to write a book about what Tina and I lived through, then it has to be a book that rewards the reader. This is the information sharing age we're living in. What makes information sharing easy nowadays is something known as (Iot). "The **Internet of things** is the extension of internet connectivity into physical devices and everyday objects. Kindle, smartphones, PC, laptop, Tesla cars, other smart cars, that LED screen in the elevator you're going up in while on vacation, the recent refrigerator you just purchased all have the ability to access the internet. Your reward for buying my book is all the links therein. Think about it. You have the opportunity to view these videos through multiple smart devices. In high definition, I might add. You do yourself a huge service by clicking on each link I've provided. Blow them up on your smart TV. Increase the screen size on your tablet device. You have that capability if you're bought the digital version of the book. My paperback readers – don't shortchange yourself. You can do the same thing. It's a little more mundane, but you can do it. What you're going to watch and hear through the remainder of this book survived a mirage of technical difficulty.

Oh yes, it was difficult to get some of this stuff on here. I've seen and fixed more computer and network problems in my twenty-year career as an IT specialist than I care to remember. The technical difficulties I've encountered while writing both books have dwarfed everything I've ever encountered. I'm talking about the hardware and software that helped me write this book. The operating system has been altered. I tell you the editors of my first book went nuts trying to figure why their recommended changes, i.e. proofreading was always altered.

One of the things that Rhonda (may she RIP) told me back in summer 2014 was that her son saw shadowy figures when they lived here. He saw them all the time. I knew she was telling me the truth. I know because I've seen them. I'm not talking about shadow men. No, these are not humanoid shadows. The shadows I've seen are about the size of a small dog. Think oversized rodent. They walk upright. Why do I call them shadowy figures? Well for starters they're jet black. They hover around the dark corners of the house. How they move reminds me of those old stop-motion movies. When Microsoft had their engineers at my house in 2013 to test out of their Xbox prototype, one of the things they picked up while they were in my house were these weird shadow images - hovering black masses through the kitchen and den area (see Appendix D). The guys at Microsoft headquarters told the Microsoft guys at my house to pause for a second. "We're picking up weird movement. Images we can't explain." The images we saw that day were everywhere. What Steve captured in the upstairs hallway took me back to that day. Two independent parties (visiting the house three years apart) stumped by what's on their computer screen.

April 19th, 2016 - It's early morning. Don had not too long come back from the woods when Steve came back downstairs with his laptop and equipment. It was during this time I thought *Steve's strobe experiment must have unknowingly run the minions into my room. That's why the alarms were going off in the bedroom. The minions were trying to get away from those strobe lights.* I was wrong. Behold.

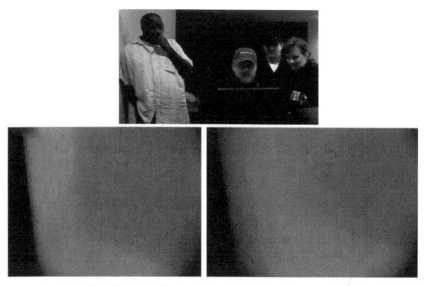

Fig 10.2: We're all watching Steve's computer screen.

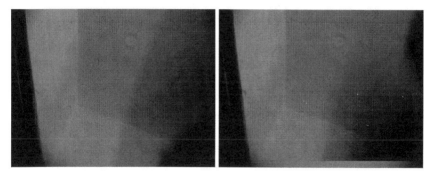

Fig 10.3

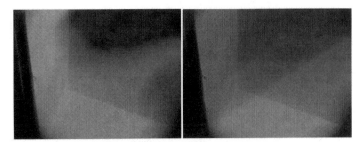

Fig 10.4

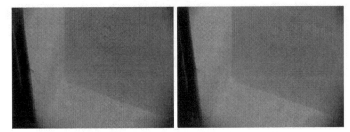

Fig 10.5: It's gone now

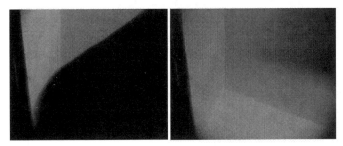

Fig 10.6: [Left] What is that? [Right] It's gone now

Fig 10.7: The cameras are almost completely covered up. Almost completely blocked out.

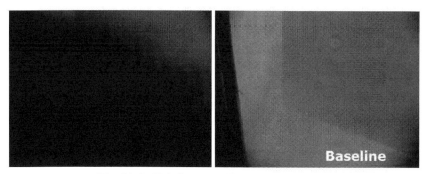

Fig 10.8: [Right] Baseline emerges again.

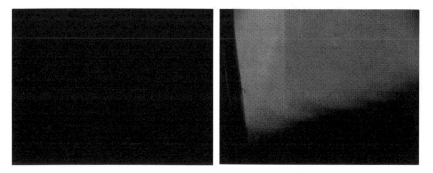

Fig 10.9: [Left] Complete black out. [Right] Furry shadow?

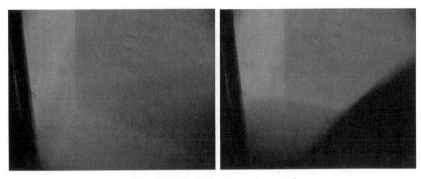

Fig 10.10: What's going on?

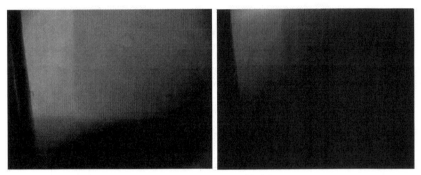

Fig 10.11: Extreme shadows

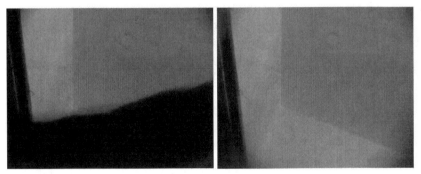

Fig 10.12: [LEFT] What is that? [RIGHT] Baseline re-appears

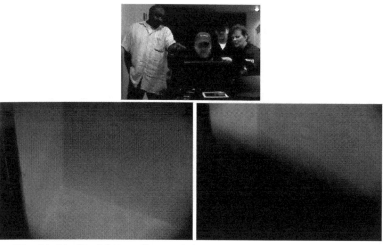

Fig 10.13: [Left] Baseline [Right] your guess is good as mine

Fig 10.14: What the hallway should like with a camera trained on it.

NOTE: There are no pets in the home.

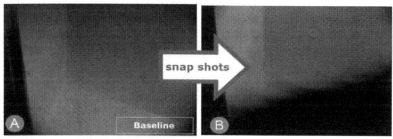

Fig 10.15: A.) A frame with nothing in its B.) Something passes the lens, triggering the motion camera.

NOTE: Frame A and Frame B should look completely identical if the hallway was truly empty.

Video version - https://youtu.be/UQxtGBUxAdk

Think of Steve Mera's camera lens as Rhonda's son. Think of it as being me. This is what I see out the corner of my eye when I'm washing dishes or when I'm watching TV. This is what's been poking and prodding me going on six years now. These are what cause the indentations in the mattress when you're trying to sleep.

These minions, as I like to call them, drew closer to Steve's equipment within seconds of him setting it down. The motion camera in my bedroom started beeping within minutes of Steve's setup. Don said it best when he said "a camera placed in an empty hallway should have nothing on it" except the empty hallway. Keep that camera going for eternity and the pictures should still be the same. Steve has just substantiated one of the biggest claims I've been making about shadowy figures lurking in and around the house. Which is this house (pardon my French) is fucked up. Like Rhonda said back in 2014, "the house is alive." That's not even debatable. What we don't know is why? We're getting close though. I promise you we're getting close.

Some researcher reading this right now might have thought I misspoke in my introduction when I said there were multiple poltergeists in our house. I'm dead serious. The evidence Steve and Don are capturing at the same in two completely different places corroborates with something I reported in my book *The Bothell Hell House*. Tina and I were both attacked – both targeted in two different locations. I'm not talking about a one-time incident. I wish it were that simple.

Who's in the hallway with Steve? If Don's is getting EVPs in the woods at the same time Steve is getting shadowy figures? How many spirits are we talking about here? I can answer that question quick, fast, and in a hurry. Lots and lots of spirits. It might not hit you now but trust me it will, by the time you get done with this book. The paranormal community has often viewed poltergeist as being something singular. That might not be accurate. We might be dealing with a fraternity of misfits – a league of extraordinary minions. Study the next picture.

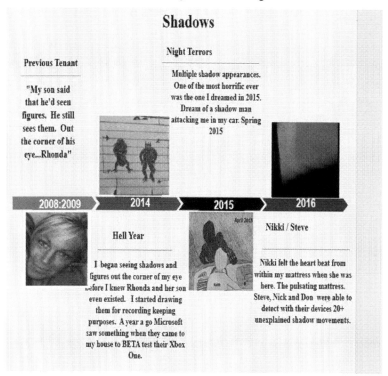

Fig 10.16: Shadow figure timeline

WHAT THE HELL IS GOING IN SEATTLE? I can tell you right now a lot is going in the suburb outside of Seattle, Washington. The interesting thing about Seattle, WA is even though it's a metro city, population eight hundred thousand, it still has a small-town vibe. Ask most people (those in the paranormal field) when it comes to Seattle. The word paranormal doesn't really cross the people's mind. Microsoft? Definitely. Home to Starbucks? Definitely. Technology city? Yeah, Seattle is a technology city. Paranormal? Hmm, whatever. Seriously, I can't tell you how many paranormal organizations — parapsychology groups included took a pass on mine and Tina's claims for the simple fact where we were located. One organization, in particular, was the American Society for Psychical Research. They said Seattle was too far for them to go. Really? You're a research organization for Pete's sake. How can something be too far? As far as the paranormal goes. Seattle doesn't exist. Look how long *Ghost Adventures* carried out their investigation. Five hours, that's it. By the time I got to the house the morning after *Ghost Adventures* lockdown, *Ghost Adventures'* crew was already en route to the airport. No one wants to stay in this part of the United States longer they have to. Seattleites know this already. So, when the UK guys announced they were coming back to my house to conduct a second investigation that created a little excitement in the Pacific Northwest. People just don't' come here out of the blue.

If you read my other book you know already, Fox News has already been to the Bothell once. They came when Don and Steve were here the first time (*The Bothell Hell House* Chapter 48). The Scientific Establishment of Parapsychology told Fox News when they were here last time that they would share their findings with them. And they did. When Steve and Don released their findings earlier this year, they never anticipated the amount of response they would get. Seventeen million viewed the Fox News clip online. That's sixteen times the amount of people that watched the "Demons in Seattle" episode.

Fig 10.17: Fox 13 News Anchor David Rose – Wall substance

Fig 10.18: David Rose interviews Don Philips about the inexplicable picture fall.

Fig 10.19: Fox News interviews Parapsychologists Steve Mera.

Fig 10.20: David Rose interviews Don Philips about the EVP experiment he conducted in the woods.

Fig 10.21: Interview

Fig 10.22: Interview with the president of SSPR –
Nick Kyle

Fig 10.23: David Rose interviews me about markings on Patty's husband truck

Fig 10.24: David Rose was very interested in the markings

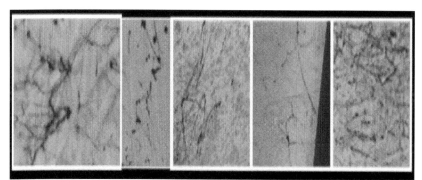

Fig 10.25: What Dave and I are looking at.

Fig 10.26: a considerable time was spent analyzing the the truck markings.

https://q13fox.com/2016/10/31/paranormal-researchers-return-to- look-into-haunted-bothell-home-again/
https://paranormalglobe.com/2016/11/08/paranormal-researchers- return-haunted-bothell-home/

CHAPTER 11

Time to Move

O ne of the phenomena's associated with poltergeist activity is the activity known as asporting. It involves the disappearing of objects. In most cases, the objects that disappear inexplicably never reappear. This captured audio (taken from my bathroom) of a voice saying: PLEASE REVIEW.

- **Voice1:** *Ray…*
- **Voice2:** *…just dropping some cable…*
- **Voice1:** *…Image detector …it's the only way it can be powered like that.* **Go and _lift_ one of these.**

Supports the idea that spirits do in fact steal objects inside people's homes. Why? Short answer: because they can. The more in-depth answer could be that spirits like humans are simply revealing a sense of curiosity. The spirits in my house have to be asking themselves, what are these small devices Keith and others keep bringing to the house? Some of you might be more familiar with the term trickster spirit or trickster ghosts than the term poltergeist. One of the acts associated with trickster spirits is the taking and rearranging of objects. It should be noted that Karissa Fleck, Patty Hale, and Don Phillips had belongings that went missing while they were living inside the Bothell house. Karissa's iPhone went missing for an entire day when she was here back in February. We spent a lot of time looking for Karissa's phone and guess what? We couldn't find it. It finally re-appeared in a place that we never thought to look. Karissa's luggage. The interesting thing about Karissa's phone disappearing was the events that happened weeks prior.

The first phenomena Karissa experienced when she entered my home happened within seconds of her walking through the front door. Karissa was sitting on the love seat in the den when all of a sudden, her iPhone shot up in the hair in a cartwheel-like manner. We're talking several feet, ladies and gentlemen. If you show a level of dependency on a certain item. Or an item becomes your number one go-to item for investigating. The spirits in my house notice stuff like that. They will zero in on that item. The spirits in my house don't necessarily limit their targeting to individuals. They focus on the items you hold dear – items we humans seem dependent on. In Karissa's case, it was her iPhone. When Karissa came to me and said her iPhone was missing, I wasn't surprised. Karissa's iPhone for the three and a half weeks she stayed with me was always in her hand. Just about everything she did she did on that iPhone. Patty had a similar instance with her hand-held device as did Don. Don, who Steve Mera describes as being a "catalyst" for paranormal activity, had an episode in my house where one of his voice recorders disappeared. Like Karissa, this voice recorder was always in Don's hand. I can see how a spirit would reach the conclusion that this device that Don keeps on his person twenty-four seven must be important. What is it? Is it a camera? Is it his lifeline? He won't let it go. You should know one of Nick Kyles' roles and responsibilities while here was inspecting Steve and Don's equipment immediately upon request. No questions asked.

The main items forever missing in my house are cameras and Bibles. Don's voice recorder (he owned several) went missing, and once again we never found it. Well, correction. We did find it. I found it. It reappeared in my new apartment. The apartment I moved into after moving out of the Bothell house. I'm not talking about underneath a couch cushion or in a box or something. I found Don's voice recorder out in the open in my new apartment. Months after I had moved. I'm a full believer (after having experienced it myself) of spirits removing objects in the home that I and others have in one way or another come dependent on. The declaration I'm making with the EVPs reveals how intelligent and observant these spirits are. But there's something more important than that I want to reveal.

More shocking. These spirits are not omniscient. Not in the electronics department they aren't. There is no such thing as an 'image detector.' No such thing as the term 'nite cam.' Steve and Don are setting up cameras in the hallway the day the 'nite cam' EVP was captured in the hallway. They were setting up a highly sensitive voice recorder. The same thing with the 'image detector' EVP. No one's laying down any cables. What's a cable? I'm pretty sure the spirit meant cord. But they're learning. By observation and by theft.

Remember I promised the reader at the beginning of this book that I would be truthful. I'm not here to promote existing world views about what this phenomenon is or isn't. Everything I've talked about and will talk about in the remaining chapters is based on what I saw. What I heard and what I felt. There are a percentage of people in the paranormal community – parapsychology community in particular that subscribe to what is known as Recurrent Spontaneous Psychokinesis (RSPK). They believe RSPK to be the root cause for poltergeist phenomena. These are the same people that say demons don't exist. I disagree. Demons do exists. And just so you understand when I use the word demon, I'm referring to malevolent entities.

Whoever was the first to say "action speaks louder than words" was correct. Actions do speak louder than words. One spirit telling another spirit to 'lift' something, to take an item that doesn't belong to you, in my opinion, falls in the category of being nefarious. Yes, the spirits are exercising their level of curiosity, but they're also exercising their right to outright steal something. If I told you to go steal something so we can review it later, you might respond by saying 'you steal something. Why are you telling me to do something, you yourself can do?' If a spirit can tell another spirit to steal something, it's safe to assume it can tell another spirit to throw something. To burn something. To scratch something. To drag someone out of bed by their ankles. To smother someone while their sleep. Actions speak louder than words. Louder than acronyms.

Are parapsychologists wrong? I don't think it's a question of parapsychologists being wrong. I think it's a question of parapsychologists putting all their eggs all in one basket. I can't tell you how many times organizations have come to Tina and me screaming what they believe this activity to be. They've not so much bought a plane ticket to Seattle to see for themselves and yet they know what it is. Steve, Nick, and Don have been here close to a week, and they're still not a hundred percent sure. The evidence they've gotten so far points to multiple culprits. No one has yet thrown out the words Recurrent Spontaneous Psychokinesis for the simple fact that the data they captured doesn't support it. Based on the evidence being captured and the claims I and the previous tenants have made it might be time for the paranormal community to revisit what causes poltergeist outbreaks.

The countdown to the UK's second departure has started. Nick Kyle made it known publicly that Steve and Don were following what Nick refers to as "paranormal best practices." The methods Steve and Don are using are methods he can approve and verify. The three men are putting their remaining two days to good use – they're documenting and backing up the evidence they've captured. From what I can tell this phase of the investigation is to many the most boring aspect of any investigation. The part where you have to catalogue everything. It's a tedious and important process. Probably the most important process of the investigation. This night, in particular, is worth sharing. Steve and Don were cataloging the evidence they'd captured. They'd forgotten that I still had equipment running. The EVP you're about to hear came from the kitchen area on one the last nights the guys were at the house — on three devices. That's right. Three devices. Two audio devices and one video recorder.

Poltergeist of Washington State	https://www.youtube.com/watch?v=o vIrMEZ-GiY 'Uuuah I thought I saw it' captured on • Voice recorder1 @ 2:07 • Voice recorder2 @ 8:28 • Video camera @ 11:26

Table 11.1: 'Uuuah I thought I saw it' EVP

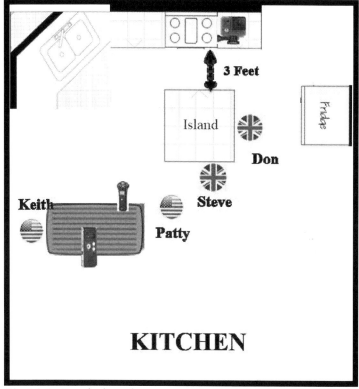

Fig 11.1: Proximity of everyone during the 'Uuuah I thought I saw it' EVP

Poltergeist of Washington State
https://www.youtube.com/watch?v=uBte7PDEmTc
'I'm a mirror' EVP

- Voice Recorder1 esp. @ 2:10,
- Video Camera esp. @ 8:26

Poltergeist of Washington State	https://www.youtube.com/watch?v=uBte7PDEmTc
@ 8:26 'I'm a mirror'	I'm configuring another device
@ 8:27	I turn towards the chimney (where the camera is located).

Table 11.2: Male voice captured (chimney area).

Can we triangulate where the 'uuuah I thought I saw it' came from? We can try. I had two voice recorders on the kitchen table recording at the time the voice came in (see Fig 11.1). Notice how the voice of 'uuuah I thought I saw it' sounds louder on those devices than it does on the GoPro. The faintness of the voice on the GoPro leads me to believe the spirit(s) had to have been near Don and me. It's impossible to know for sure, but that's what we got. What happens next is even weirder than what you just heard.

The second video (Table 11.2) did you notice how I turned toward the direction of the camera when 'I'm a mirror' was uttered? I don't remember hearing anything at that exact moment. But I must have. Look at my response. Why else would I turn towards the camera? Could it have been instinct? I don't know. All I know is I did not hear a voice. These EVPs having been discovered on audio and video devices were reviewed by The Scientific Establishment of Parapsychology and classified as unexplained.

Fig 11.2: A strange voice utters 'I'm a mirror' behind me.

That's it. That was the crux of Steve, Don, and Nick Kyles second trip. The men stayed a total of eight days. Two days longer than they did the first time. Eight days longer than *Ghost Adventures*. The thing that impressed me the most about them coming the second time was the arrival of Nick Kyle (at the time President of the SSPR.) His arrival and the capture of shadow figures, in my opinion, are the highlights of the guys' return visit. One of the things paranormal teams have to always guard against is the exaggeration of house occupants. I believe if you were to ask Steve Mera and Don Philips if any of that ever occurred, their answer would be no it did not.

I wanted Steve and Don stateside before telling them of my plans of moving out of the Bothell house. No sense in them knowing that before their arrival. I've lived in this house for four years. Four years, ladies and gentlemen. That's a long time to be living on eggshells. A long time to be poked and prodded. I've discovered recently that certain things irritate me. Certain things startle me. Example -fireworks. Fireworks on New Year's Eve or the Fourth of July – all that crackling and banging. That BOOM! I become anxious and sweaty the minute that stuff starts. I become irritable. That loud BOOM sound! I heard that for eight months in 2014. Four months in 2015. Two weeks in 2016. What's it like? Imagine someone throwing you and a pack of firecrackers inside the pressure cooker and then closing the lid. That's what it's like living a "Geist" infested home. Am I having flashbacks? It's hard to have flashbacks when you're still experiencing things. I know what you're thinking. Once again, the short answer to me staying is I wanted to leave on my terms. I'll be damned I'm going to run out of my own house. Especially by some spirits. Was I naive? I was very naive. There's not a school on Earth that teaches you how to deal with this stuff. No crash course whatsoever.

Steve, Don, and Nick Kyle were going to take these findings back to the UK. Back to their peers. They were going to tell them what they saw and what they heard. The campaign of substantiating me and Tina's claims is nowhere close to slowing down. Quite the opposite.

The Demons in Seattle Case Report

 http://online.fliphtml5.com/lglzz/nmor/

Sixty-two-page compressive report courtesy of The Scientific Establishment of Parapsychology. Contains everything they found in the house.

Analysis and further information.

Active Investigation - Stage 1: 21/01/16 - 26/01/2016	Active Investigation - Stage 2: 13/04/16 - 19/04/2016
Data Collection: 236 Gigabytes	Data Collection: 102 Gigabytes
Audio recordings - 426 obtained.	Audio recordings - 127 obtained.
EVP Class B and C discarded.	EVP Class B and C discarded.
229 EVP Class A from inside the house.	56 EVP Class A from inside and outside of house.
7 AVP (Actual Voice Phenomena)	4 AVP (Actual Voice Phenomena)
3 incidents of DVP (Direct Voice Phenomena)	Audible Disturbances throughout the house.
Audible Disturbances throughout the house.	Physical Phenomena Detected.
Physical Phenomena Observed.	Over 30 hours of video footage obtained.
Over 50 hours of video footage obtained.	211 photographs obtained and 20 anomalies.
381 photographs obtained and one anomaly.	Samples taken of unknown liquid on walls.
Aerial photography obtained.	Psychological Assessment and Profiling completed.
Interviews and documentation obtained.	Interviews and documentation obtained.

Case Ref: 26411   59

CHAPTER 12

Attack on Patty

The advice given by Steve and Don when they were here back in January for lessening the activity was an acronym I never heard before: R.E.M.A. Renovations, extensions, modifications, and alterations. This recommendation was included in one of Steve's emails. It read, '*one of the things you can do with the hopes of lessening the activity in your home is lessen the amount of home renovations. Discontinue any house modification or alterations you might have started. You definitely don't want to begin any.*' In short, try not to make the house more unsteady than it already is.

That might be hard to do. Fact number one – the house is in desperate need of repairs. Holes need filling. Walls need painting over. Carpets need shampooing. There are massive pictures that need to be taken down. Pictures that been up since I moved in. All the beds in the house need to be disassembled. Have you ever tried to disassemble an IKEA bed? Oh my god, there are so many parts to them. Those parts, mind you, have to be carefully laid out. Do you see where I'm getting at? In a normal house, these nuts and bolts would be harmless. I'm not living in a normal house. I'm living in the Bothell hell house. I've seen items smaller than the nuts and bolts I just mentioned become missiles. Everything I've just mentioned has the potential of raising the activity level. Of becoming a projectile.

I have two weeks to get this house in tip-top shape. Two weeks to get it back to how it looked when I first moved in. There is documentation (other poltergeist cases) where activity has erupted within minutes of a house being renovated. I attribute that to the noise being created. The ruckus, per se. There are tales of electricians, plumbers, painters, and construction crews experiencing weird activity in homes they've worked on. Trust me, you don't want to be on the receiving end of an object becoming airborne. Regardless of its size - you're looking at irreparable damage. I have to be careful. Here is a list of the activity that started in the middle of my restoration project:

- Loud bangs in the middle of the night
- Increased footsteps
- Fluid appearing on walls
- Coming home to pitter-patter noise
- Shaking chandelier
- Increased poking and prodding
- Increased nightmares
- Increased night terrors
    - ✓ Waking up crying

May 3rd, 2016 – I can tell you the activity does seem to elevate a bit when you begin making repairs and renovations. I've bought contractors in to repair the walls in the office. I've moved large pieces of furniture out of the house and into storage. All of this within days of the UK team leaving.

If there ever was a reason for wanting to get out of the house ASAP (once the decision had been made to move), it was the night Patty was attacked. I've seen a lot of ghastly things in this house. Things I'm still having a hard time coming to terms with. Grunting and growling noises coming from behind the wall in my bedroom and office. Pawprints on the office ceiling. When I think about those events, I can't help but wonder what kind of house did Tina and I move into? What happened here? As far as outcry goes, Patty's screams and cries are on top of the list of everything I've experienced in the house. People say, 'seeing is believing.' So is hearing. Patty had been coming over my house the last few days as a favor to me. My spider sense had been going off the last few days. Therefore, I asked Patty if she could monitor me while I was packing up things. I can't quite put my finger on it, but it felt like spirits were planning something. I could feel it. The sound of someone pacing back in forth in the upstairs hallway while I was sleeping had intensified. So has the rappings. My instincts were telling me to hurry up and get out of this house. *You've decided to move, so move dammit.* Five more days. I'll be out of this house in five more days. The thing that's keeping me up at night right now is the question I've been asking myself the last three years. Will I be followed? Do I have attachments? Poltergeist throughout history have been known to follow people. The activity has spiked when survivors moved elsewhere. These spirits know I'm moving out. How could they not? I've been making repairs and packing my belongings over the last two weeks. One night, in particular, Patty and I decided that we would have equipment recording in the background whenever she was here. That's the only reason why this audio of her attack exists.

 and LISTEN

– Patty's Attack	https://youtu.be/iNnJE71Taj0 WARNING THIS VIDEO IS SENSITIVE.

Table 12.1: Patty's Attack

If I look back on it carefully, I should have suspected Patty might be attacked. Patty, for the time period that I've known her, has been an integral part of Steve Mera's and Don Philip's investigation. Patty was the first to discover that Bothell, Washington was once robust with Irish settlers. She helped me take the wall markings on the closet door in my office to the store. Going back to what I said earlier about the phenomena known as targeting. This phenomenon like everything else has multiple levels to it. The level I want to talk about is the level I refer to as O.M.P.T. On my person targeting. It's when activity breaks out on you. This, in my opinion, is one of the deadliest forms of haunting.

Person	O.M.P.T.
Tina and Keith	2013 - Night terror campaign Jan 2nd, 2014 – fall down the stairs
Keith	Poking and prodding
Tina	2014 2015 — Inexplicable scratches her arms.
Patty Hale	Three blisters on Patty's hand.

Table 12.2: O.M.P.T. examples

Like I said, there are different types of "Geist" targeting. The one where phenomena happen in and around one individual rarely gets talked about. Example - a few days into Steve and Don's second visit Patty walked up to Steve and extended her right hand. She pointed to three lines forming on her hand. Three blisters. I remember where I was when this was happening. I was sitting at the kitchen table working off my work laptop. I could hear Patty's conversation with Steve. What surprised me more about that incident (more than the burn marks appearing) was Steve's dismissiveness of Patty's claims. Her claim, in my opinion, was not farfetched. The thing people seem to forget, and I do this a lot as do the investigators researching my home, I forget how close proximity the spirits in my house are to us. They are always present.

The spirits, regardless of us being aware, are always doing something. I went so far as to say in my previous book that my anxiety about what's going to happen next spikes when the house is quiet. The scars that appeared on Patty's hand in real-time are a perfect example of O.M.P.T (on my person targeting) as is the attack she received when she spent the night. The fact that Steve chose (who I respect a great deal) not to investigate Patty's blister issue more thoroughly points to something I noticed throughout the paranormal community. Particularly the parapsychology community. Data that challenges one's world view often gets cast aside. Most do it unconsciously, meaning they're not aware they're doing it. There comes a time (talking about my house) where you have to decide. You have to make a declaration! There are countless events Tina and I saw that point to demonic activity taking place.

I'm not talking about the 666 stuff. I'm not talking about the wall-writings. I'm talking about malicious attacks. I'm talking about the stench. The appearance of flies in the house in the middle of winter. I'm talking about the sound of a chest of drawers being dragged around, that latch swinging back in forth sound. We don't own that stuff. The marks Patty received that night. Three lines burnt into her hand LIVE as if an invisible blowtorch was performing right then and there. Naturally, we couldn't see what was causing the blisters in my opinion that's not paranormal. That's demonic. There are a lot of EVPs Steve and Don captured that haven't been made public that suggests demonic haunting.

One EVP, in particular, was a voice saying, "The demons are over there." Another response to a direct question. The other haunting EVP, the men captured was the spirits admitting to pushing me down the stars. I heard that EVP. Steve and Don played it to me. Steve and Don know I was pushed down the stairs. They know I sustained a serious injury. They've seen the medical report. The world has seen the medical report (see *The Bothell Hell House*). Why not call attention to it publicly? Why not perform some drill- down analysis on Patty's injury? Like I said earlier, the researcher's world view of what the phenomena is or isn't can at times get in the way. That and the possible ridicule from friends and colleagues – a form of professional peer pressure. It's the only way to describe it. Patty has a permanent mark on her hand. Something hot seared three lines into Patty's hand. We all watched it form in real-time. How that manifested on her hand in real-time reinforces a theory I have about how the second and third Bibles caught fire. Those Bibles caught fire close to Tina and me. That suggests some sort of black body radiation technique was enacted in the presence of Tina and me. Same thing with Patty, myself, and Steve. What is black body radiation? According to WIKI, "black-body radiation is the thermal electromagnetic radiation within or surrounding a body in thermodynamic equilibrium with its environment, emitted by a black body (an idealized opaque, non-reflective body). It has a specific spectrum and intensity that depends only on the body's temperature, which is assumed for the sake of calculations and theory to be uniform and constant. Most of the energy it radiates is infra-red and cannot be perceived by the human eye." A good example of a blackbody radiator would be anything that emits "visible light or whose radiation is used for other processes include the electric heaters, incandescent light bulbs, stoves, the sun, the stars, night vision equipment, burglar alarms, warm-blooded animals, etc." Do you understand what I'm saying? Something standing very close to Patty – emitted a spectrum of light invisible to the naked eye. It caused those burnt marks to appear on Patty's hand. In real-time. I believe the 2nd and 3rd Bible were burned in the same manner. This would explain why the fire alarms in our house never went off. Other poltergeist cases that involve inexplicable fire incidents the witness speaks about how the fire seems to erupt around them. I don't have to guess who attacked Patty. I know who attacked Patty. The same bastards that pushed me down the stairs on January 2nd, 2014. Minions. What are minions again? Minions are a league of demons working together for a common purpose. The shadows from Steve's strobe experiment? That's them. You do not. I repeat, you do not want to be in the crosshairs of these type of spirits. Patty was right not to come back to the house again. Patty said the first few words that came out of her mouth were not ever hers. Something else was speaking. Someone else was screaming. Do you understand that? It's time to go. It's time to leave this forsaken house.

CHAPTER 13

Move Out Day

"I say we take off and nuke the entire site from orbit. It's the only way to be sure."
~ **Aliens**

Picture a softball in your hand. Literally in the palm of your hand. Better yet, picture it under your pillow. Under your feet, knees, and ankles — multiple softballs. Can you feel it? Imagine it's pulsating. The softball you're holding is breathing. Rapidly! You'd swear the softball just completed a 10K marathon. That's how fast the pulsating is. It's alive. It's just you in the room right now. Remember everything I've just said. You're going to hear it for yourself later in the book. These knots I've described. Very omnipresent. Left side? Poke, poke, poke. Right side? The same thing. Try to sleep on my back? Oh, that's a huge no-no. They respond quickly when you lay on your back. Why? I don't know. How long has this been going on? Too dam long! Shamans, mediums, priests, and paranormal teams have all tried to rid the house of angry spirits. Nothing so far has worked. Now I've made the situation worse by packing up and moving. Switch rooms? That doesn't work anymore. It used to. Not anymore. The minions descend on me within seconds of my head touching the pillow. Understand that the pulsating doesn't last forever. It dissipates and reemerges at various hours of the night. Steve Mera got a glimpse of how that works during his second visit to the house.

Fig 13.1: 1.) Motion camera picks up shadowy figures on the hallway landing area. Few feet from the bed. 4.) One shadow covers up the entire screen/lens.

May 7th - I asked my friend Barbara if she could do me a favor by taking pictures of the house. I needed her to photograph all the renovations I've done. I don't know how I did it, but I got the house looking like it did when Tina and I first moved in. Let me tell, you seeing the house the way Tina and I saw it when we moved on May 1st, 2012 hit me hard emotionally. Four years ago, Tina and I were bringing in boxes. Pure excitement about the house we acquired. We had already heard the kid 'cough' by now. That didn't faze us. Neither did the missing items we began experiencing. Why not? Simple: house high! I acquired this house through years of hard work. Through goal setting. I wanted to take my relationship with Tina to the next level. I wanted to make my mom proud. I wanted to make my dad proud. I got this house because I wanted to entertain my friends and family. I'm sure you can identify with some of the reasons I just mentioned. I'm not trying to make myself look admirable. I'm just letting you know that I'm a human being. Nothing was going to interfere with my plans. I was wrong. I lost my girlfriend – a woman I loved. I doubt I'll ever get over that. I invited my friend Barbara over because I wanted pictures of the house looking normal again. Professional pictures. A lot of cynics and skeptics said, "You and Tina did all of that yourself." "You put the holes in the hallway." "You did the wall writings in the office." "You set the fires." They obviously never read the fine print inside a lease agreement. There are laws that protect a homeowner should he or she ever be in a position of seeking restitution. I'm talking about extreme damages to one's property that exceed whatever the deposit was. All of that is listed in the lease agreement. Tina and I were renters. Not homeowners. Renters. You don't bring the media in. Bring the Travel Channel in too film damage you caused. Get that through your thick head, Mr. and Mrs. Skeptic. The homeowner can sue us. He has the law on his side. What can I do? Can I subpoena a poltergeist? You'd think the spirit behind all of this would show up and testify in my favor?

Do I want my deposit back? Of course, I do. I need my rental history to remain clean. That involves receiving a good reference from the homeowner, which I'm happy to say he's given me. But that's not the only reason why Barbara's coming over. Far from it actually. No, I'm doing this because of something else. I'm trying to shed light on the phenomena the paranormal community refers to 'as the feeling of being watched.' I need for you to understand everything that <u>phenomena</u> entails. This piece of evidence that my friend Barbara and I are about to acquire is part of my hypothesis for the remaining chapters of this book. These minions are not going to go out of their way to snicker and comment if it's just me taking pictures. They've seen that multiple times already. No, I have to give the spirits something new. Something newer than Steve and Don. When you live with the spirits for as long as I have you can't help but know what they go for. These spirits in my house love technology. That's where my friend Barbara comes in. Barbara's cameras are state of the art.

See section titled **<u>Theory - Poltergeist of Washington State</u>** at the end of this book for the conclusion of the above thought experiment.

Another required listening.

Haunted House - EVPs Captured (headsets required)* **eliminate your background noise**	https://youtu.be/wDauzQr 58ro Whispers begin at: @ 2:01 'GPS.' @ 7:50 'Shit.' @ 7:59 'The girl' @ 8:01 'So unsure' @ 11:13'Yeah shit.' @18:59 '**You chickened out, you puss**'

Table 13.1: Audio Transcript Photoshoot of the house.

I would label that experiment a success for the simple fact that there shouldn't' be any voices on the audio at all. The whispers you just heard are not coming from Barbara and me. Why would we be whispering? Once again, another unexplained voice phenomena - that fits the context of what was happening.

May 8th, 2016 - I remember when the movers arrived. My first thought was *here goes nothing*. I wasn't worried about furniture flying or anything. Everything was shrink-wrapped and gone. No, I was thinking hot damn! I did it. I've survived the Bothell house. I survived the physical abuse. Now comes the mental aspect. That's going to be a lot harder to survive. History tells us that people who have lived in haunted houses like this have at times been followed. I've thought about that possibility for over three years now. Will the minions show up at my new place? What does that look like? I know what hell feels like here inside this house. I know what hell feels like in a hotel room. I know what hell feels like on an airplane – (see *The Bothell Hell House*). Should the minions follow me to the new place, what then?

Now I'm not trying to cast aspersion, but this is important. I haven't seen the homeowner in over four years. That's right. He's never come by the house in the four years Tina, and I lived here. Even after our claims went public which was October 30th, 2014, I'll repeat what I said in my book *The Bothell Hell House*. If there's anyone who deserves to be a skeptic to the claims Tina, and I are making it's the homeowner. He's the only person in a position to doubt our claims. It's his house. He has that right. But he never did. The homeowner never put Tina and me on the defensive. He never said, 'I'm going to sue you for damages.' Nor did her say 'get the fuck out of my house.' He never said anything close to that. Not even after *Ghost Adventures* left and found nothing did, he say 'you guys are hoaxers.' Maybe because he knows the absence of evidence (at the time *Ghost Adventures* left) doesn't necessarily mean the house is not haunted. Did he know? You decide. Here's a portion the email the homeowner sent me after I asked his permission to bring researchers in.

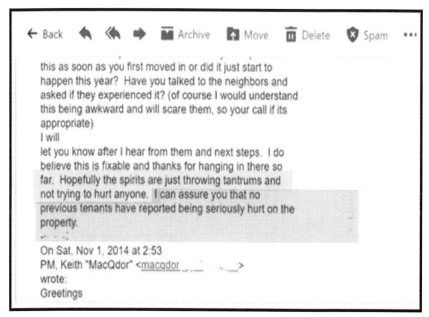

Fig 13.2: November 2014 - partial email exchange with the homeowner.

You can tell from reading the email (above) that the homeowner was supportive. Talk about being sympathetic to our situation. He even thanked Tina and me for "hanging in there." I've just explained to him *Ghost Adventures* interests in investigating the house. His house was just aired on local TV as being haunted. The fires that erupted. The damage done to the office and hallway. Most landlords would have taken offense to Tina and me going public with our claims. Not ours. As a matter of fact, he said, "Keith, you can spearhead the investigation; I approve teams coming in." But there's something else. The homeowner said, "I can assure you that no previous tenant has never reported being seriously hurt on the property." I never asked the homeowner if someone was seriously hurt. I asked him if it's OK if a research team came in. "Hopefully the spirits are just throwing tantrums." The homeowner, whether he meant to or not, just defined in the simplest way possible what a poltergeist does. They throw tantrums.

May 9th, 2016 - the homeowner came over to pick up the keys to the house. I have to say it felt kind of weird us meeting again if you consider everything's that's happened. If you consider this is the first time he's come back since Tina, and I moved in. If you consider the fact that he doesn't live in the house himself. If you consider that the woman I love is now gone, it pains me to admit this, but I have no choice. The spirits won. It's just me now. I couldn't tell you what Tina was doing right now if my life depended on it. The last time we saw each other was a week after the "Demons in Seattle" aired which was February 28, 2015.

The owner and me meeting for a second time in four years. I have to admit it was awkward. I could tell the homeowner didn't want to be here. That's understandable. You're standing in the Bothell hell house. No one wants to stay here longer than they have to – that includes my landlord. The house, for the most part, looks the same. Minus the newly painted walls in the living room and den, the house looks exactly how it did the day Tina, and I moved in. When it came time for us to view the house together – the same thing we did four years ago. We were in perfect agreement. The house was in the condition in which I found it. I got my deposit back.

CHAPTER 14

Water Puddles

May 10th, 2016 – I woke up around 5:30 AM, in my new place of residence and did something I normally don't do. I decided to check my work email. I was logging into my company's web access account when all of a sudden, I started hearing a series of tapping noises. *This is new.* I have to say, as much as I've seen and heard over the years, I still haven't gotten used to being in the spirits' crosshairs. By that I mean I'm slow to recognize at this very moment I'm being haunted. A voice inside me finally says *pay attention Keith, pay attention.* Tap, tap, tap, tap, tap – that was all I heard. I got up from the office chair and started walking toward the kitchen. Nothing. I check the bathroom. Nothing. Both faucets were completely off. I was making my way back from the kitchen, and that's when I saw it. Puddles of water. I'm talking about a huge amount of water on my kitchen table. I thought to myself, *What the fuck! I haven't been in this house twenty-four hours yet, and they're already fucking with me?* I went from feeling good about my new apartment to feeling frustrated – all within a matter of seconds.

If you ever want to understand the disconnect between a skeptic and those who experience this type of activity, all you have to do is watch *Jaws 2*. There's a scene in that movie that describes the level of obtuse skeptics have whenever claims are made. Sheriff Brody is standing in front of the city's city council. He's holding a picture in his hand of what he believes to be a shark. He knows it's a shark. He knows because he went toe-to-toe with one a few years ago. Brody's now an expert on great white sharks. He didn't ask for it. It just happened.

The look on the face of the men and women sitting on the city council as Brody waves that picture around is priceless. Everyone's looking at Sheriff Brody (the guy who killed the shark in the first *Jaws* movie) as if he's gone insane. Anyone who's encountered a malevolent spirit understands where Brody is coming from when he says, "I know what a shark looks like because I've seen one up close. And you'd better do something about this one because I don't intend to go through that hell again!" Preach, Sheriff Brody! Preach!

I can hear the snickering coming from the skeptics the second I report this water puddle incident. "I call bullshit. He's trying to milk his experience for everything it's worth. He sees shadows where there aren't any." I've experienced enough paranormal events in the last four years to know what's paranormal and what's not. The water puddles forming on my kitchen table inexplicably is a well- known poltergeist characteristic. No one knows for sure why this event occurs except to say that it does. I have two options: I can crawl under my bed and begin sucking my thumb. I'm dead serious. I should go buy up all the liquor at the liquor store. Come back home and just get wasted. I'm not going to show up to work anymore. I quit. The spirits attached to me have made it known that they are not going to go away.

When I think about that, I can't help but tear up. I'm spent! Mentally and spiritually. You want to know what's worse than walking on eggshells twenty-four seven? Being on the defensive mentally and spiritually twenty-four seven. I've forgotten what eight hours uninterrupted sleep feels like. Attachments? I'm not even sure what that means. Where I come from an attachment is file you tether to an email you're about to send. When Tina and I decided to stay in the Bothell house after the poster caught fire. The word attachment never crossed our mind. No one told us about the possibility of having attachments as a result of living in Bothell house. What protective measure (if any) should we have used?

I've been in the information technology field most of my adult life. Documentation is what we do. It's what every project manager does. *I need to call the building maintenance department. They need to see this.* That's option number two. I called the emergency after-hours phone number and left a voice mail.

The first thing the mechanic said after seeing the leak for himself was "there are no pipes up there, no plumbing whatsoever." Which he knew already – you see, he's doing the same thing I'm doing. He's using top-down logic aka deductive reasoning as means of problem-solving. I feel bad for these maintenance guys. I do. They're trying to get the bottom of this. Which is what the Bothell fire department tried to do Spring 2014, when they responded to my office catching fire. What they believe to be a leaky roof is a big deal. I'm a new tenant. The last thing the property manager wants is me getting renter's remorse. Washington State has laws in place that protect renters.

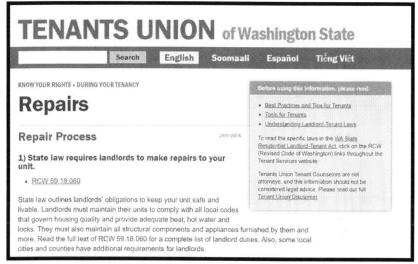

Fig 14.1: Reasons for breaking a lease

https://tenantsunion.org/en/rights/breaking-a-lease

https://tenantsunion.org/en/rights/section/repairs

The two maintenance guys walked out of my apartment to talk to the people upstairs. Maybe the water's coming from their unit. The men come back to my apartment ten minutes later with a puzzled look on their face. The firemen who responded to my poster catching fire when I was living in the Bothell house had the same facial expression. When you see an event taking place that you can't explain all you have left are the words 'what the fuck?' When it comes to poltergeist, the thing you have to understand is everything acts and behaves weirdly. Sound. Objects thrown. Apparition sightings. Phantom footsteps. Water puddles on the floor or the kitchen table are no exception. The maintenance guys made a point to mention that the ceiling they were touching was dry. How's that possible? They concluded that there were no pipes whatsoever between the first and second floor. Nothing was wrong with the apartment upstairs — no busted dishwasher. No overflowing bathtub. No overturned fish aquarium. The men couldn't ascertain where the water is coming from. Normally you would see a puddle of some sort forming around the leak itself. Some ceiling deterioration. My ceiling didn't have that. No condensation or water buildup whatsoever. That's weird. Where is the water coming from?" That's what both men said. As much as I wanted to answer them, I can't. I have to do the same thing I did when the fire department arrived at the Bothell house spring 2014. I have to act like I don't know what the hell is going on. My biggest fear at the moment was them realizing who I am. 'Hey, I know you! I saw you on Seattle Fox News 13. You're the guy with the haunted house.' I don't know how they would react if they found out I was that guy.

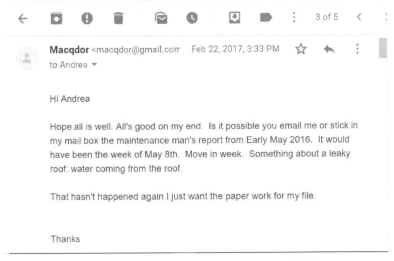

Fig 14.2: My email to property manager February 2017

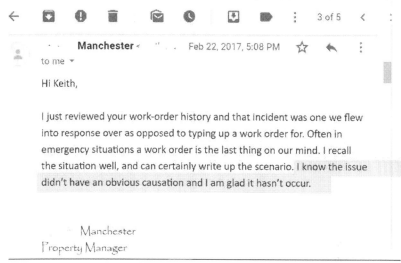

Manchester ‹ " . Feb 22, 2017, 5:08 PM ☆ ↰ ⋮

to me ▾

Hi Keith,

I just reviewed your work-order history and that incident was one we flew into response over as opposed to typing up a work order for. Often in emergency situations a work order is the last thing on our mind. I recall the situation well, and can certainly write up the scenario. I know the issue didn't have an obvious causation and I am glad it hasn't occur.

Manchester
Property Manager

Fig 14.3: Property manager's response.

February 23, 2017

Re: ******REDACTED ***** #P1
Leak from Ceiling in

On approximately **Tuesday, May 10th, 2016 Keith** reported that he had dripping coming out of his ceiling.

Zack went into P1 and discovered dripping coming out of the ceiling hallway outside of the kitchen. Found damp carpet, **no water on the laminate**. He knocked upstairs to see what had occurred above to cause this. They looked at all the suspect places under the kitchen sink, bathroom sink, and dishwasher and there was no obvious cause. Per P7 nothing happened to their knowledge! After Keith's report, he cleaned up the water, and there were no further occurrences.

Very Truly Yours,

*****REDACTED Manchester
Property Manager

Fig 14.4: Halloween 2014 / May 2016 water puddle event.

Water Puddle Event May 10th, 2016
https://youtu.be/Aj6p2FWGxtY

CHAPTER 15

Embrace the Suck

One of the things I told myself before I moved out of the Bothell house was that I need to avoid having the mindset that everything weird or unexplained happening around me is paranormal. I mean, look where I came from. I came from the Bothell house. Arguably the most active "Geist" infested house in recent memory. That's one of the things skeptics and researchers both agree on. Skeptics (not career skeptics) will say while maintaining their level of skepticism, "If your house is haunted, then it would have to be the most active house on record." Researchers who've been to the house have a more informative opinion.

Which you'll find in these documents below:

- Exhibit A. The Bothell Hell House.
- Exhibit B. The book *Fire and Whispers* by **Steve Mera** and Jenny Ashford
- Exhibit C The S.E.P case report - included inside this book.
- Exhibit D. "Demons in Seattle Uncovered documentary" by Don Philips – link included inside this book
- Exhibit E. Nicole Novelle (Nikki) and Karissa's Fleck **https://www.youtube.com/watch?v=whsHPreLIZ4** A MUST LISTEN
- Exhibit F. *A Century of Ghost Stories* by Richard Lugg
- Exhibit G. *Project Phenomena Evaluating the Paranormal* by Brian Allan
- Exhibit H. The book you're reading right now.

I've been in my apartment for less than three days and I'm already experiencing things. Yesterday it was the water puddles on my kitchen table. Today it's my car battery. I tried to start my car the next morning and guess what nothing happened? The lights wouldn't come on, and the engine wouldn't turn. Another example of how "Geist" phenomena inconveniences you. So, the roadside assistance guy arrived, and jump started my car for me, and that was it. They were off on their next emergency call. I decided to drive my car to Sears Auto shop to see what was going on with my alternator and car battery. The battery was fine. That's what the mechanic said. This is two thousand and thirteen Hyundai Sonata. It's possible the battery inside the car has had its day. *No harm in buying a new battery.* I bought a brand-new battery and went about my day. You know that's not the end of it. You would never have heard this story had it been just an isolated incident. I had three more battery instances within weeks of moving into my new place. Each was identical to the story I just told you. Those instances were equally perplexing to the mechanics at Sears as they were to me. I take that back; it wasn't perplexing to me at all. Not after the second incident. But that story pales in comparison to the story I'm about to tell.

June 8th - I sent an email to my apartment manager informing her that my dishwasher had stopped working. It was not completing its wash cycle. Before we get into the dishwasher, let me explain a few things. All the appliances in my apartment are brand new. Beautiful touch screen stainless steel appliances. If you read my previous book, you know that's not a good thing. The minions attached to me are not going to pass up an opportunity to mess with new electronic equipment. Hell, no they won't. My dishwasher for reasons I can't explain, *well actually I can, but humor me* — seems to turn itself off within minutes of me walking away. I kid you not – that's exactly what it was doing. I used to think I was imaging things (like I said I'm trying hard not to label everything paranormal). The minions are going out their way in convincing me that all of this is their doing. They want me to know they're in the house with me. Everything that's happened so far has been a classic definition of déjà vu.

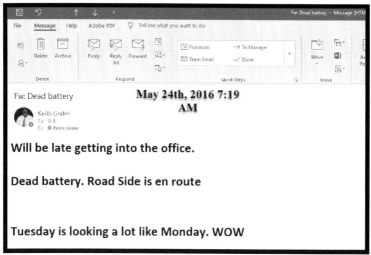

Fig 15.1: Email to my boss

When I say everything, here is brand new. I mean that. The washer and dryer in my hallway are brand new. The oven is brand new. The refrigerator is brand new. Both electrical and cable wiring is brand new. The water heater in my closet is brand new. The heating system is brand new as are the fire alarms systems. The LED panels still have plastic film protecting them. You know that thin layer of film you remove with your fingernail? You can't get more brand new than that. So why is my dishwasher on the fritz? My apartment manager said she would have the maintenance guy come by and check it out. Yes! The same maintenance guys that responded to my 911 call about water dripping from the ceiling. Guess what happened when they came over? Nothing. Absolutely nothing. I came home from work and found a work order the mechanics left resting on my kitchen table. It read 'no problem found.' Typical poltergeist behavior – make the house occupant look and feel as if he doesn't know what the hell he's talking about or in this case whatever it is he's reporting. *I guess I was imagining things. No harm. No foul.* I turned on my dishwasher again that night and guess what?

The same thing happened again. The dishwasher kept cutting off and on. Off and on, off and on. This is a brand-new dishwasher. *This is not a paranormal incident. I refuse to leap to that conclusion!* Then I thought. *Maybe the problem will correct itself. Let's wait for a few days.* So, I waited for a few things. The problem never corrected itself. I called the leasing office that following Monday to report my dishwasher was still having problems. The property manager said she would send the maintenance guys back over. I came home and found another work order on my kitchen table. It read – *we've replaced your* (brand-new dishwasher) *with another brand-new dishwasher. Contact the leasing office if you have any more problems.* When the problem came back, that's exactly what I did. I called the leasing office again!

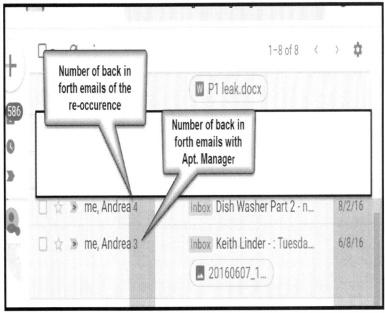

15.2: Two Month Email Exchange – Property Management

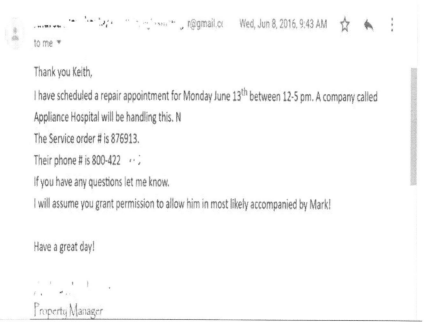

15.3: Email exchange with the apartment manager – June 8th, 2016

[Thank you, Keith,
I have scheduled a repair appointment for Monday, June 13th between 12-5 pm. A company called Appliance Hospital will be handling this.

The Service order # is 876913.

Their phone # is 800-422-****

If you have any questions, let me know....]

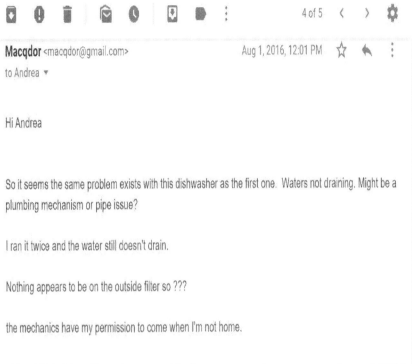

Macqdor <macqdor@gmail.com>   Aug 1, 2016, 12:01 PM

to Andrea ▼

Hi Andrea

So it seems the same problem exists with this dishwasher as the first one. Waters not draining. Might be a plumbing mechanism or pipe issue?

I ran it twice and the water still doesn't drain.

Nothing appears to be on the outside filter so ???

the mechanics have my permission to come when I'm not home.

Fig 15.4: Email exchange with the apartment manager – August 2016

Andrea .   Aug 2, 2016, 9:59 AM

to me ▼

Oh for Heaven sake,

We will get in there and dig up what is the major malfunction Keith.

Andrea
Property Manager

Fig 15.5: Email exchange with the apartment manager – August 2016

It's frustrating for the apartment manager and me. And there is the lesson: poltergeists are about inserting chaos and uncertainty into a peaceful environment. It's what they're good at doing. Albert Einstein said, "the definition of insanity is doing the same thing over and over and expecting different results." That's what the apartment manager and her repairmen have been doing. Don't get me wrong. They're doing the right thing. We're all intelligent people. The dishwashers, for reasons we can't explain, are not working properly. Not in this apartment. The appliance repair guy and the building maintenance have replaced the dishwasher three times. The problem is still there — the dishwasher keeps cutting off. Every dishwasher they bring has had the same problem as the one leaving the apartment. I know what you're thinking. Maybe the problem is not with the dishwashers. Maybe the problem is the plumbing underneath the dishwasher. Maybe the problem is the cavity under the kitchen counter where the dishwasher sits. We've already ruled that possibility out. My original dishwasher and the dishwasher after it was put in other apartments and guess what? They worked fine. I understand that form of troubleshooting.

When I worked at Dell computer (back in the 1990's) as a technician, we used to swap out parts we thought were defective. We'd put them in other chassis to see if the problem still existed. If it did, we knew we had a defective part. If it didn't, we knew the problem wasn't with the part we swopped. This is an effective form of troubleshooting. I finally had to stop reporting that the new dishwasher they gave me (and yes, all the dishwashers were brand new) was on the fritz. Because I know it's not the dishwasher. Five dishwashers having the same problem. Come on! That's not a coincidence. I know these minions personally. They won't stop. You can bring them dishwasher after dishwasher – they'll do the same thing. The only hope I had of my dishwasher working properly was to ignore the fact it was not working. I've been in this brand-new apartment a little over three months now, and in that time frame, I had three brand new car batteries. Water puddles on my kitchen table that came from the ceiling. No root cause whatsoever on what caused that. No root cause on why my car is having battery issues. Sooner or later someone in the leasing is going to put two and two together — you're the guy whose house was haunted in Bothell. 'You're the demon guy.' That's my biggest fear now. Why did I move into an apartment? Why not another house? My reason for choosing an apartment was simple. It didn't make sense to move into another house. It was just me now. My goal of living in a house of my own has evaporated. I'm done.

March 2016 - I ran into my apartment manager at a wine event in Woodinville, Washington. I was with a group of friends when all of a sudden, someone bumps me. I turned around to see who and low and behold it was my old apartment manager from the community I lived before I moved into the Bothell house. Wow, that was four years ago. There we were standing in the middle of Chateau Saint Michelle winery talking about what each of us had been doing over the last few years. I was just waiting for her to blurt out something related to the Bothell house. She told me the community I used to live in had been completely renovated. I couldn't ignore the timing of our conversation – the timing of our meetup. I'd already made up my mind about not getting another house. The question in my mind at that time was *where do I want to live afterward*? What options do I have besides crawling under a rock? The Pacific Northwest is a small area. An African American male living inside a haunted house. When has that ever happened?

Andrea asked me if I was looking for a new place to live. I told her I was. I told her I'd need a new place by May of this year. She replied, "Come by the office when you have time. I'll give you a tour of the new units we have. Everything's brand new. Even the appliances." That's how I got here. Andrea sold me on the idea of moving back to where I once lived. Everything's new now. She's right. Everything is new. Everything's marvelous. I could see how embarrassing this is to Andrea. I mean, she convinced me to move back and look at everything that's happened. She's probably thinking; I convinced this guy to move back with us and look what's going on? I want to tell Andrea so bad that it's not the appliance inside the apartment. It's not the ceiling or the plumbing for that matter. It's me. I'm the guy who resided at the Bothell house.

I can't tell her that. I can't have her regretting her decision about asking me to come back. The only thing I can do (as a favor to her) is not reporting these incidents as frequently as I've been reporting them. I need to let this phenomenon run its course. The demon responsible for sabotaging my dishwasher will eventually get bored. Let's see how long the dishwasher keeps acting up as a result of me accepting things as they are.

The military has a proverb for situations like this. It's called embracing the suck. It's a Buddhist concept that says. "When we deny what reality is giving us, what is really happening, then we create suffering. So, life is a dance between minimizing expectations and surrendering to what our lives actually reveal to us." Life has introduced me to the poltergeist. The question I have been asking myself for over four years is why me? Life quickly responds with 'why not you.' The Buddhist concept states, "by embracing our lives totally (even the stuff that sucks), we get through them." Which goes back to what I was saying earlier about what options do I have? Option number one deals with darkness and death. Isolation, depression, feeling sorry for myself, and all the stuff in between – those are negative things. Option number two is me embracing the suck. It's going to suck being a haunted person. I can already tell.

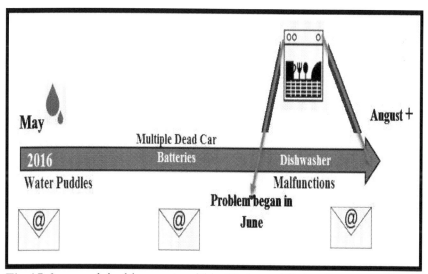

Fig 15.6: unexplainable events within 90 days of living in my new home. Vexation attempts.

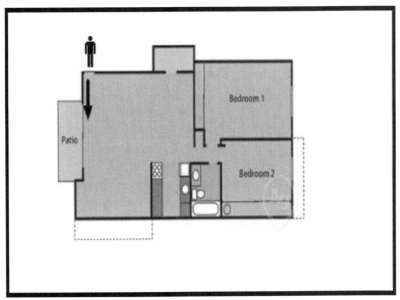

Fig 15.7: 960 Square foot – two-bedroom apartment 1st floor

CHAPTER 16

Buckle your Passenger Seat Belt

Imagine you're driving home one night. I say night because that's when this experience I'm about to tell has happened the most. I don't remember exactly where I was coming from when the phenomena first occurred. Odds are I was coming from a friend's house. I was on the highway driving home when all of a sudden, I saw something flashing on the dashboard. The passenger seat belt light was flashing on and off. As soon as I turned directly towards the flashing light, it stopped. *That's weird.* I turned my attention back toward the road in front of me and guess what? The passenger seat belt flashed on and off again. *Do I need to put my car in the shop? Is this some computer malfunction?* I started looking at the passenger seat belt light again. On and off. On and off. That's what was happening. It stopped flashing the second I looked at it.

The next morning, I was driving down the same road. I'd forgotten about the passenger seat belt incident. I was halfway to my vanpool park-in-ride when, yep, you guessed it. The passenger seat belt light started flashing on and off again. I kid you not — the passenger seat belt indicator light was going on and off, on and off. It was doing exactly what it did yesterday. Interesting how it knows when to stop flashing on and off. It only does that when I look at it.

Two weeks later – I was feeling good about a date I just had with a woman I met online when all of a sudden, my passenger seat belt light started going on/off on/off on/off on/off on/off on/off. Help me out here. A malfunction regardless of what type of malfunction it is, has no way of knowing if you're looking at it or not? A malfunction doesn't have a conscious after all it's a malfunction.

Two months later – Yes that's right, two months later. The 🚹 on/off passenger seat belt thing was still happening. But like all the other paranormal events Tina and I've experienced it has to evolve. The indicator light continues to flash even after I look at it. It wasn't doing that earlier. The passenger seat belt indicator light had been/going on and off for weeks 🚹. It was intensifying. That's the nature of malevolent hauntings. To be clear, this is, in fact, a malevolent haunting. I might not have objects flying at me from every direction. I might not have Bibles bursting in flames like I did before I moved here. Those things I just mentioned are not the only definitions of a malevolent haunting. The word malevolent means "to cause harm." Guess what? The harm comes in all shapes in sizes. Increased anxiety is harm. Increased angst or being frightened abruptly is harm. There's only one reason for a car seat belt light to be going on and off. The person sitting in the passenger seat hasn't fastened their seat belt. Cars today come with either a seat occupant sensors (sos), occupant detection systems (ods), passenger weight system (pws), or occupant classification system (ocs). These electronic sensors (key word here is electronic) are embedded in the driver and passenger seat of every car being made today.

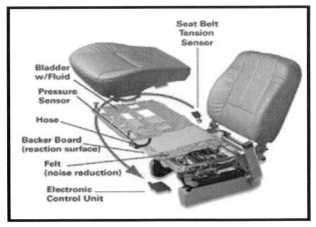

Fig 16.1: Seat belt sensors

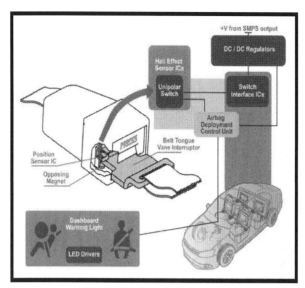

Fig 16.2: Seat belt sensors

These systems know when a seat belt is not fastened. How the computer is able to determine, this can be summed up in one word. Weight. There are two sensors in play. Sensor A is located somewhere underneath the car seat. Sensor B is located somewhere within the 🔲🔲 belt buckle itself. The sensor (including the airbag) activates or deactivates when a weight threshold is reached. Now could all of this be a malfunction? Of course, it could. We're talking about something man-made.

September/October 2016 – I went to the Hyundai website to see if there was a known recall on my make and model. There wasn't. I called the car dealership to be sure. Nope, no recall whatsoever on seatbelts. Are the minions in the car with me? That's the question I was asking myself. Some of you reading this might think that's not possible. Those who've lived through what Tina and I lived through know better. Understand, for every story, I've shared, five other stories have yet to come out. I've not released those stories because of the questions I still have. They're extremely bizarre. Too bizarre even for me. That's why I haven't shared them. This I can share. It might sound weird, but this makes sense to me. It involves computers. I told myself a while back I'm not going to lean back when events like this occur. I'm going to do the opposite. I'm going to lean in. I'm embracing the suck, ladies and gentlemen. It's obvious I have attachments. I have no clue whatsoever as to how to get rid of them. Until I do? Embrace the suck. Am I scared? Yeah, I'm scared. I'm terrified. Every one of us has ingrained in our heads, (I'm talking about our preconceived notions) of a worst-case scenario where malevolent spirits are concerned. Some we're born with. Others we get off the TV. It's a constant battle (within me) to keep these preconceived notions at bay. The one I'm fighting right now (the one that got me sweating) is the notion that my car might fly off the road. If a spirit can infiltrate my car's Occupant Classification System, what else can it do? The mechanics can't figure this thing out. They've run diagnostic tests on the car and came up empty. I'm paying for this test. The money's coming out of my pocket. Three hundred and seventy-five dollars – that's what I paid to get to the bottom of this. The other avenue I'm trying is one I've become too familiar with. Conduct an EVP session the next time the passenger seat belt light starts acting up. I know these spirits like I know my last name. If the spirits are in the car with me – they're going to talk. I've never done an EVP session before. I've seen Nikki and Karissa conduct one. I've seen Don conduct one. I think I can do it. Click the link below and hear what I found. Headsets required.

https://youtu.be/nF2X2rTiGwA

Demons in Seattle – Electrical issues

*NOTE: The video above/below demonstrates the electronic issues I experienced with both my 2008 and 2013 Hyundai Sonatas.

Fig 16.3: Passenger seat belt indicator light has been going on/off for weeks. Mechanics are dumbfounded.

Electrical Issues best with headsets on	https://youtu.be/nF2X2rTiG wA Time stamps below
Question – Is there a spirit in the car with me?	Answer: at 7:41 'sit in the chair'
Repeat	9:27 'sit in the chair'
Repeat	9:32 'sit in the chair'
Repeat	9:34 'sit in the chair'
Repeat	9:36 'sit in the chair'
Repeat	9:39 'sit in the chair'
Repeat	9:49 'sit in the chair'
Repeat	9:55 'sit in the chair'
Repeat	10:00 'sit in the chair'
Repeat	10:01 'sit in the chair'
Repeat	10:02 'sit in the chair'
Repeat	10:03 'sit in the chair'

Table 16.1: Unexplained voice phenomena – 'sit in the chair'

Ask a seasoned researcher in the paranormal field. The best electronic voice phenomena (EVP) you can obtain are the ones that fit the context of what's going on at the time. Here we have a voice saying, 'sit in the chair.' There's nothing unintelligible about what you just heard. You hear the words 'sit in the chair.' What chair is being referenced here? The passenger chair. If you read my book *The Bothell Hell House,* you know the spirits seem to have a fascination with the chairs I sit in (see Fig 16.4). This form of targeting involves the poltergeist manipulating specific objects I own or frequently use. Study the pictures below.

131

Fig 16.4: A.) Kitchen bar stool found in my office B.) A kitchen chair is pulled out. Water puddle you can't see C.) Same kitchen chair found in my office D.) Missing kitchen chair E.) Kitchen chair pulled out similar to B. F.) Office chair split in half – stem resting on the Bible.

When you think of electronic devices, i.e., the sensor embedded inside the passenger seat, understand it's all digitized. A whole series of **010110010100110s**. Notice how the voice was modulated? Sounded computerized. 'Sit in the chair.' Parapsychologists Steve Mera has spoken publicly about an event he and Don witnessed in the Bothell house in January 2016 involving the alteration of the ADT security voice status system. Everybody who've been inside my house knows (Ghost Adventures included because they asked that it be deactivated during their visit) about my ADT security system I had installed. Everyone knows the ADT wall panel blurts out alarm statuses whenever a window or door is opened. The second you open the front door a synthesized voice says, 'FRONT DOOR OPEN!' Open the door leading to the garage a synthesized voice says, 'GARAGE DOOR OPEN.' Same thing for all the other doors and windows in the house. A few days after Steve and Don arrived the first time, both men began noticing a change in how the ADT security responded whenever a person entered or left the house. The synthesized voice started saying, 'DOOR OPEN.' Regardless of whatever door had been opened/closed.

It took a while to notice this change, but The Scientific Establishment of Parapsychology led by Steve Mera confirmed just that. A change had occurred to the existing message. I must bring to the reader's attention that the ADT security system default message 'FRONT DOOR OPEN,' etc. are hard coded into the device. It's coded to a level that a home occupant (like me) could never reach. The same thing for my Sonata's computer system.

[*According to the American Resources Policy Network, the typical U.S.-built car contains more than 50 pounds of copper: approximately 40 pounds for electrical components and 10 pounds for nonelectrical components. Today's luxury cars contain some 1,500 copper wires—totaling about 1 mile in length.*] That's a lot of wires, ladies and gentlemen.

Your average car is a lot more code-driven than you think

https://www.usatoday.com/story/tech/columnist/2016/06/28/your-average-car-lot-more-code-driven-than-you-think/86437052/

"Mainstream cars may have up to 10 million lines of code, and high-end luxury sedans can have nearly 100 million—that's about 14 times more than even a Boeing 787 Dreamliner jet."

How cars have become rolling computers

https://www.theglobeandmail.com/globe-drive/how-cars-have-become-rolling-computers/article29008154/

Tina and I had a lot of electronics commandeered while living in the Bothell house. Televisions would turn on or turn off by itself. Lights, the kitchen microwave, my office stereo, all these things would turn on or off by itself. My passenger seatbelt doing what it is doing now surpasses all those things I've just listed. I asked a question, and the response I got was 'sit in the chair.' I wonder what would have happened to me if I had sat in the chair?

CHAPTER 17

New Bible

If you asked me which items I would like to have back; it would be the two Bibles that went missing late 2014 and the watch Tina gave me marking our fourth-year anniversary as a couple. Researchers told Tina and me that items that get taken do return eventually. Our items didn't. It's like they all fell into a black hole – that's how I would sum up how they went missing. If I had to guess how many items are still unaccounted for, I would have to say about a hundred. That's a lot of missing items. May 1st, 2012 my extra set of car keys went missing. Summer 2012 – Tina's jewelry went missing. Necklaces, Bibles, earrings, rings, candles, holy water, coins, cash, music CDs, iPad, a watch (four year anniversary gift from Tina), cameras, Sony Handicam, motion sensors, crosses, voice recorder, Citrix motion camera, Foscam motion cameras, driver's license, passport, wallet, credit cards, birth certificates, kitchen utensils, Seattle Seahawks shirt, toothbrush, toothpaste, pick up receipt from the cleaners. Those are just a few of the items I know that went missing. Researchers have a name for what I just described. They call it Apport – Asport.

Apport - the appearance of an object from an unknown source, often associated with poltergeist activity and séances - **Urban Dictionary/ Wiki**

Asport - the phenomena of the vanishing or removal of objects (by a spirit) and the subsequent reappearance in another location.

Fig 17.1: Three Bibles that caught fire in the Linder home/Bothell WA. Two out of three had a disappearing act prior to catching fire.

Bibles - Bothell House 2012 – 2016	Activity
Bible #1	Went missing in 2012. Returned 1:34 AM Spring 2014. Was on fire in the upstairs hallway
Bible #2	https://youtu.be/uVZVtcjZzg o - April 2016
Bible #3	https://youtu.be/CjkYw2kleB U May 2016
Bible #4	Summer 2016 - Tina's Bible shredded to confetti.
Bible #5	Manipulation • A bowl of saltwater poured was over it • Thrown off bookshelf • Thrown at me while I was taking a shower • *WENT MISSING.*
Bible #6	Manipulation • Thrown off bookshelf • *WENT MISSING*

Table 17.1: Manipulation and disappearing acts

I've been living in my apartment going five months now. I still hear heartbeats within my mattress. I'm still being poked and prodded. The dishwasher is still acting up. The passenger seat belt light still flashes on and off. Rich Schleifer (the guy who lives a few houses down from the house Tina and I once lived in) emailed me on Facebook today. The husband and wife who moved into the Bothell house (two months after I moved out) have replaced the front door with a dark blue door. *A blue door?* I thought to myself. No one puts a blue on the front of their house unless they're trying to send a message. What message are the current home occupants trying to send?

Google knows best:

- http://www.homecurbappeal.com/what-does-a-blue-front- door-mean-feng-shui-for-your-homes-curb-appeal/ "said to bring lots of positive energy into space."
- https://xenophobia22.wordpress.com/2013/02/12/what -a-blue-door-means/ 'For many Native American people, the blue door prevents any evil presence from entering your home.

When Rich told me that the new tenants had replaced the white door with a blue door, I have to admit it put a smile on my face. The husband and wife that live there are taking no chances. They're heeding the advice given to them. That's good. One of the questions I get from people after moving out of the Bothell house is have, I spoken the new house occupants? Did I warn them? The answer is no. The Scientific Establishment of Parapsychology gave me a report of what they found in the house. They listed the house as an LIH – localized, intelligent haunting. What does that mean? It means the house is exemplifying a lot of paranormal phenomena commonly associated with intelligent hauntings. No one knows what the root cause is. Not yet, anyway. Steve Mera said, and I tend to agree with him that the phenomena Tina and I witnessed in the four years we lived in the house could be the result multiple causalities.

Do the current occupants know the house is haunted? Yes, they know. It's impossible not to know. But don't think of it as me warning them. Telling someone that the house they're about to move into is the house from hell doesn't make their living conditions better. It makes it worse. I go into great detail about why I believe that later in the book. Right now, I want to talk about the Bibles I used to own, and the phenomena known as apporting.

One of the things I like about the company I work for is the promotion of a work-life balance. Individuals are encouraged to have an equilibrium between work and their lifestyle. One of those equilibriums involves taking a break in the middle of one's shift. I'm not talking about a fifteen-minute break. I'm talking about a leisurely break that reboots the mind. Go to the gym. Go for a run. Read the book you bought to work in one of the many break rooms. Take a nap. Or go for a walk. That's what I do when I want to break from whatever it is; I'm doing. I take a walk. This is going to sound weird, but it's true – when I walk, I meditate. I clear my brain by taking in everything that's around me. Thank God, the weather was obliging me today. Rain and more rain. That's what Seattle tends to be sometimes. Not today, though. It was sunny outside today. That was my motivation for going for a walk. A long walk. I was ten minutes into my walk when suddenly I noticed something. There was a book lying in the middle of the sidewalk – ten yards in front of me. A Bible! *Why is a Bible laying in the middle of the sidewalk? It was as if it was put here on purpose.* It was right here in front of me (or about to be) as I draw closer. There were people in front of me, and there were people behind me. It was lunchtime. People were walking about in every direction. I didn't know the book I was looking at was a Bible until I got up close to it. I thought *this is a Bible. What's a Bible doing lying in the middle of a sidewalk?* A well-traversed sidewalk I might add. *Am I the only one seeing this?* I was looking in every direction. What was I looking for? I don't know. I was hoping someone would walk up to me and say, 'pardon me; I accidentally dropped this.' That never happened. If you read *The Bothell Hell House*, you know my history with Bibles. I'm having a hard time believing someone dropped this Bible. I mean, had it been open or facing down that would be different. It doesn't look like it fell out of someone's backpack. No, it's lying perfectly flat. It's perfectly squared up with me. The first thing I thought was *these spirits (in their demented way) are fucking with me? Or maybe this is their peace offering? This is the closest they can come to in giving me back my Bibles. Sigh!* I've never seen this Bible before. It's not a Bible I've previously owned. I can do two things right now. I can put the Bible back down on the sidewalk and keep walking. *Just keep walking, Keith Linder!* That's what I should do. I don't. I can't. Where I come from, people don't leave Bible's on the ground. It's disrespectful.

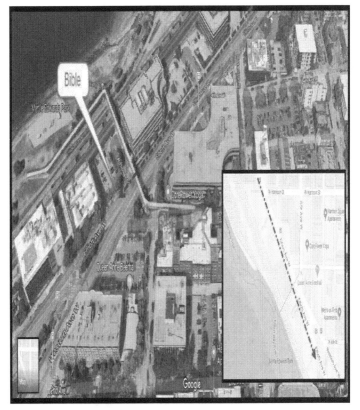

Fig 17.2: Walk path – Bird's eye view

138

Fig 17.3: Walk path – Bird's eye view (1) where I saw the Bible.

Fig 17.4: Close up walk path – fall 2016

Fig 17.5: Bible found in the middle of drive-through – fall 2016

There's no way someone would leave a Bible lying in the middle of a sidewalk. A driveway at that. That's just weird. We've all at different times in our lives have found religious paraphernalia in public places, e.g., laundry mats, our mailbox, our doorstep, bus stops, and on occasion, the public library. Specifically, religious pamphlets. This isn't a pamphlet. This is the Bible. Had this been a Quran or Tora, my reaction would still be the same.

Apport – "the appearance of an object from an unknown source, often associated with poltergeist activity and séances." Is this what this is? Remember – Tina, and I would often find things in our home that neither of us owned. That's what apporting is – items appearing that have no known source. The Bible had to have come from somewhere. We know it didn't fall out of the sky. *Well actually maybe it did*. It's very important you understand how serious I am about the claims I'm making. Objects are appearing out of thin air, and by thin air, I mean between human eye blinks. The only way to describe this split-second movement is to tell you a story of what Tina and I experienced. Imagine you and your spouse are watching TV. There's a giant throw rug between you and the entertainment center.

You and your spouse in amazement leap off the couch together. The rug that lies between you and the entertainment center is now rolled up. You and your spouse have no memory whatsoever of the rug being rolled up. That period never happened. Wasn't your rug rolled up a second ago? No. There's a moment in time that appears to be missing. That moment in time when the rug rolled up completely or halfway. That happened more than once. Second example – imagine you're going to your kitchen drawer to retrieve an item. You retrieve that item, e.g., knife, fork, scotch tape, postal stamp, etc. You've turned your back to the drawer you've just opened and proceed to leave. *Dammit, I forgot something. I need a steak knife versus a butter knife. I open the drawer again.* The same drawer you were just in. As soon as you open the drawer – all these unopened envelopes start pouring out. We're talking twenty to forty envelopes. They all have postage stamps dating back to two- thousand five, two-thousand-eight. Some are dated two-thousand eleven. The only thing these envelopes have in common is their destination address. It's the house I'm currently living in. There's a theory within the paranormal community about objects appearing that perhaps belonged to previous poltergeist sufferers, i.e., previous tenants. That's not a theory anymore. That's a fact. Some of these letters are addressed to Rhonda. The previous tenant who told me her family witnessed strange phenomena also. Some belong to tenants after her. Some of the envelopes appear to be bill payments. Some of them contain tax information. I'm pretty sure these letters were very important to the people who lived here. The fact that they're not opened means the people who lived here never really got a chance to look at them. Everyone who lived in the house before Tina and me, including those who didn't experience anything (that they know of) are poltergeist survivors. It is hard to notice items missing – especially small items. Items appearing? Now that's a different story. When something that's not yours appears in your environment, you notice it immediately. That goes for items inside the house and items outside the house. This Bible shouldn't be here.

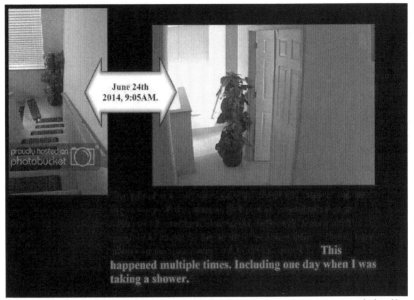

Fig 17.6: June 24th, 2014, 9:05 AM. The plant you see was originally down the stairs. An email alert came that read 'motion detected'. The plant picture on the right was taken by a hallway motion detect camera. The picture to the left (from my cell phone).

Haunted House- Teleport Possibly Summer 2014	https://www.youtube.com/watch?v=gbWXXnjfB9E

Table 17.2: Hallway - Summer 2014

Where do I think the Bible came from (that I found while taking a walk at my job?)

- Bible I found was taken from a previous tenant that lived in the Bothell home.
- Bible I found was taken from the people who recently moved in.
- Bible I found was taken from another home. Any home the world over.
- Bible I found was a good spirits gesture (an angel) letting bygones be bygones.
- Bible I found was left by a good spirit (an angel) as a means of protection.

This Bible was put in my path at the precise time at the precise moment to avoid being picked up by someone else. The idea to go for a walk originated at my workstation. The same workstation where I was attacked (see *The Bothell Hell House* Chapter 31). If the minions were with me, then it's not paranoia to believe that they're with me now. Especially with everything I've experienced since moving out of the Bothell house. Is this some peace offering? Perhaps. It wouldn't be right of me to state that every spirit in the Bothell was evil. There were some protectors there.

I decided to share this particular story of me finding a Bible in broad daylight on a public sidewalk with you because I wanted you to understand the phenomena known as apporting and asporting. These two words can become very confusing because of their definitions being so similar. This Bible and the objects Tina and I found in our Bothell house could be labeled an asport or apport type event. I'm going to go out on a limb and say those un-opened letters that appeared in our kitchen drawer in 2014 had to have gone missing within minutes of those letters entering the house. The question we should be asking ourselves right now is where were these letters before appearing in our kitchen drawers?

Where was this Bible before appearing on the sidewalk? There are multiple theories about where these items go. Some researchers believe they (the items that went missing) are located in areas of the house that the house occupants can't access. I haven't come across one poltergeist case where the researcher or house occupants found the missing items or items no one knew about in areas of the house no one could reach, e.g., behind the walls, in the pipes, underneath the floor, the roof or bathroom tile. That would be an awesome discovery. Tina and I have over a hundred items missing. Could those items be appearing in other people's homes? I'm talking about homes where poltergeist activity is being reported. Think about it for a second. That rug Tina and I found folded up in front of us, happened at such an immense speed that we didn't even notice it. One second the rug was spread out (covering the entire den floor) the next second it was rolled up as if we had just bought it home from the store.

There are only two explanations as to how that could have happened. Explanation number one: the rug was taken as it was. Rolled up and returned to us. All within the blink of an eye. Second explanation: the rug was rolled up in front of us and done so in less than 300 to 400 milliseconds or 3/10ths or 4/10ths of a second. How is that possible? Two words: time dilation. "One of the most revolutionary concepts we learned in the 20th century is that time is not a universal measurement. It doesn't matter how much our lives are governed by the same seconds, minutes, hours, days, and weeks, regardless of where we live on the globe, time will never be absolute. The rate at which it passes depends entirely on your speed and acceleration at any given moment." Have you been on an airplane and looked out your window and saw another plane passing by in the distance? Its looks like it's flying in slow motion. It's not. In Einstein's theory of relativity, "time dilation describes a difference of elapsed time between two events, as measured by observers that are either moving relative to each other or differently, depending on their proximity to a gravitational mass." It states that "the faster we go, the more the time is affected." I can't tell you how many paranormal events that I experienced that felt like it happened within an instance. I'm talking within a blink of an eye. I believe these spirits can move at immense speeds relative to the house occupants. Relative to Tina and me. I'm certain of it. It's the only way they could have pulled off some of their machinations while Tina and I were present. Time dilation and the **observer effect** are scientific theories that I believe poltergeists are in some way, shape, or form exploiting.

THE
EXPERIMENTS

CHAPTER 18

Who's Watching Me?

I've talked to a lot of paranormal researchers over the last couple of years. All of them in some shape or form said: "they wish their field could be taking more seriously." Every last one of them to an extent has craved for the acceptance of both the scientific and skeptic communities. Guess what? Until you set up some form of standardization around your work, that's never going to happen. What is standardization? Standardization is *the process of implementing and developing technical standards based on the consensus of different parties that include firms, users, interest groups, standards organizations, and governments.* The consensus from different parties is one of the values of standardization. In the information technology field, we have multiple standardization models we have to adhere to. We couldn't exist without them. Think about it. Our customers would not be our customers if they knew we made things up as we go. We adhere to multiple forms of standardization. Some imposed on us by law. Some we pose on ourselves. Who governs the paranormal field? No one. Who reviews all findings? Who initiates standards for all to follow? Who certifies the tools, e.g., voice box being used? If I wanted to create a paranormal investigation website right now, I could. Throw up a few pictures of some abandon buildings, abandoned homes, a few dust particles and I guarantee you someone's going to call me screaming and panting about their house being haunted. They're going to invite me over. They want answers. And you know what? I'm going to go. Not because I want to. I'm going because no one's stopping me. No one. That should scare you. Who oversees me entering your house and assisting? No one! Standardization is

146

a set of processes that have been proven to be effective. Everyone (to the best of their ability) follows the same model. When done well, standardization reduces ambiguity and guesswork. The paranormal field is filled with guesswork. Their cup runneth over. Standardization would minimize that. It would limit the amount of ambiguity around certain types of evidence, e.g., orbs. Half the paranormal field believes orbs are real. The other half believes it's not. A governing body overseeing all orb data being captured could help end that debate. Ending that debate would help the paranormal field focus on bigger and better things. I said in my introduction that the possibility of me having attachments was just about guaranteed. You don't do what I do over four years and walk away scot-free. What exactly did I do? I stared into the abyss. I set up motion detection devices throughout my home and in doing so opened myself up to being contacted. I told the spirits to give me everything they got. I dared them. I let them run through me (literally) one morning. I couldn't help it. I was experiencing extreme sleep deprivation that day, which tells you I wasn't thinking right. Tina had not too long got up from the bed when all of a sudden, I started feeling paw prints on the sheets and mattress. These paw print, aka bed indentations, were heading towards me. I was mentally weak that morning. Seriously! I was having thoughts about giving up. *Go ahead and kiss me, bite me, molest me, scratch me, stick your tongue in my ear, do whatever it is you're going to do, get it over with. Do whatever it is you're going to do and call it a day.* All of a sudden, I felt a swoosh feeling. Something ran through me. Or better yet inside me! Weird energy. I started quivering immediately. Extreme goosebumps. It was like a hallucinogenic drug had just invaded my body. Talk about an extreme sense of euphoria. That's what it felt like. All of this happened within seconds. That's just one aspect of how an attachment occurs. The other aspects (for me) involve what I've already mentioned. A malevolent spirit will attach itself to you if you challenge it. Imperfections — a spirit will attach itself to you if it senses your imperfections. The word imperfections shouldn't be confused with the word curse. We all have imperfections. That's what makes us human.

Malevolent spirits can identify those imperfections onsite. That's right. On site. The minute Tina and I walked into the Bothell house we were found wanting. Tina never saw an apparition in the house. She never saw the Gray or White Lady. I did. Why is that? My only guess is the spirits knew I couldn't leave it well enough alone. The spirits knew that. Of course, I would have loved to have been proven wrong. I would have loved not to have seen water dripping from my apartment ceiling. Why couldn't the maintenance guy find a logical explanation as to why that occurred? *Embrace the suck.* When life serves, you lemons what do you do? You turn around and make lemonade. That's all you can do. Problems seem simpler when you do that. In my field, we don't fold into the fetal position whenever a problem develops. No, we have processes built into everything we do that help us out. That's what standardization does. It bails you out. We try to get the job done regardless of the problem at hand. Is it perfect? Of course not. Nothing's ever perfect. But there's a process built into the standardization that takes care of that. It's called lessons learned. I think that's one of the things Zak Bagans couldn't understand about me. Zak made the same mistake other paranormal teams made when they arrived at our house. He thought Tina and I were looking for a savior. Tina and I weren't looking for a savior. We were looking for an institution. Religious institution or non-religious institution. We didn't care. We thought there was an organization out there in the world that deals with stuff like this. An organization with standardization at its core. We were wrong.

How should I deal with my attachment problem? Succumb to my inner demons? Become an alcoholic? The minions would love that. Heck! That's why they're here. My grandfather would always say "demons have their general orders, and we have ours." Can you imagine the amount of mental pain you have to be in to commit suicide? I can't even imagine the thought process that comes seconds before succeeding. Death by a gun! You never hear it. Death by sleeping pill! You never feel it. Death by slicing your wrist! The act is painful – but you go peacefully. Death by hanging! Similar to bleeding out. Death by train?

Imagine how dark your world has to become even to contemplate something like that. Rhonda (previous tenant of the Bothell house) left three beautiful children on this planet. One beautiful little girl and two handsome young men. A mother who kills herself must think her children are better off without her. Who told her that? Someone had to. Remember, (FYI to those who haven't read my previous book) Rhonda tried to commit suicide several times when she was living in the Bothell house. Rhonda told me something was relaying that message to her internally. The desire to end her life after moving out of the house didn't subside. The best thing I can do now besides living my life is document what happens next. What I'm about to do will hopefully make sense to somebody. What am I going to do? I'm going to document all still happening around me. I'm going to keep a video diary of what happens in this apartment. Of what happens in my bed. In my sleep. In my dreams. Who's here? Who's moved in with me? Is Ray here? Are the shadows here that Steve and Don picked up when they were in the Bothell house in April? I believe those minions are the ones that followed me. They're not the only ones. I'd say that there were probably five minions in the apartment with me. How do I prove to you that I'm not alone? I do that by conducting experiments, i.e., by conducting my own investigation. Time to incorporate the six steps to troubleshooting.

Steps of Troubleshooting: (*what I will attempt to do*) *
- Identify the problem (*should be self-evident by now*)
- Establish a theory of probable cause (*to-be-determined*)
- Test probable cause theory to determine the actual cause
- Establish an action plan and execute the plan (*affirmative*)
- Verify full system functionality and if applicable implement preventative measures. (*I'll try*)
- Document findings, actions, and outcomes. (*affirmative*)

It's not my intention to confuse you with the order of events but try to understand, everything I talk about in this book overlaps. Poltergeist for lack of a better word are multifaceted. The things they do interchange and overlap one another.

It made sense that the first experiment I would conduct would center on capturing some EVPs. The most compelling evidence surrounding this case has been the unexplained voices. The one's Karissa Fleck caught when she lived in the Bothell house and the ones Steve and Don caught when they lived there are some of the most profound voices ever caught. If these minions are here, and I believe they are, then they're going to have to talk.

Imagine being poked to the point of only getting four hours of sleep. That's what June 17th, 2016 was like. I woke up feeling more tired than when I went to sleep. Two years ago, I would've gotten up and started screaming. Two years ago, I would've gotten up and started smudging the entire house. I would have been cursing and writing nasty notes on printer paper and leaving them in various parts of the house, hoping the spirits read them. That's one mistake out of many I made while living in the Bothell home. Not anymore. I leaped up thinking to myself *embrace the suck, Keith, embrace the suck*. I reached for the voice recorder I put by my bed the night before and hit record. I want to know who's watching me. The links below are from that morning.

Demons in Seattle – Attachments
Long version - **https://youtu.be/XyiS22Wn1cw**
'See how he stood up' at 23:10

Demons in Seattle – Attachments
Short Version - **https://youtu.be/HYwjMPD2nfU**
Time stamp - **'See how he stood up'** 00:09; 00:21; 00:24; 00:28; 00:34; 00:37

CHAPTER 19

Strange Bedfellows

I must have played the 'see how he stood up' MP3 file, thirty-times before sending it to Patty. I need to make sure I do not wishfully hear things. Let me send it to Rich Schleifer. Let me send to Nikki Novelle. Let's see if they hear it. The response from them and others (including Steve Mera) can be summed up in one word: "interesting." Nikki's and Patty's response was something to the effect of "oh my god!" There's no better EVP in my arsenal that best describes the phenomena known as attachments than the EVP I just captured. One spirit is whispering to another (**which you should have realized has happened several times already**), 'see how he stood up.' It happened right as I was climbing out of bed. Another example of a contextual EVP - the voices you heard match what just happened. The reason I got my voice recorder out in the first place was because of the rough nights I'd been having. Multiple pulsating coming from within the mattress. Non-stop heartbeats, constant poking, and prodding. It's hard to sleep through that. I so want to set fire to my mattress right now. Seriously! That's what I want to do. The minions would love that. It would please these guys tremendously if I in some way, shape or form started going crazy. If you think that unexplained voice 'see how he stood up' is weird, listen to this story. I'm the type of person that rarely gets sick, which means when I do get sick, I'm pretty much bedridden. Uh oh? You're damn right, uh oh. I've always been curious about the level of bombardment I would have should I ever become sick. Would the poking and prodding increase? Would the pulsating mattress sensations intensify? My inner preconceived notion thought, *Keith, they're going to bombard you like crazy. It's going to be open season.* I was not looking forward to the day I would be bedridden sick. Well, that day finally came.

I came down with a severe cold and let me tell you, I was in bed (in my new apartment) for about a week. Coughing, sneezing, and wheezing — that was me. I remember this particular morning as if it happened yesterday. There I was lying on my back (not doing good). It was a little bit after 5 AM. I'd been tossing and turning all night as a result of being sick. I remember switching sides when all of a sudden, I heard the words 'leave him alone.' I heard it as clear as day. It was right over me. My eyes started circling the room. I'm thinking *is someone in the room with me*. Of course, not I live alone. A male voice. A powerful male voice. Who was it? I don't know. All I know is the poking and prodding I've been experiencing for quite some time now never seems to happen when I'm ill. But that doesn't make any sense. Why leave me alone when I'm sick? I understand there is a percentage of individuals reading this book who frown whenever the word demon is used. You don't believe in them. I get that. I don't want to get all bogged down in what a demon is or what a demon isn't. I've learned over the years that debating over what we think something is or isn't doesn't get us anywhere. Let's see what we end up with by reviewing things objectively. The spirits in the Bothell house have never demonstrated their level of friendliness. Tina and I never came home and found flowers drawn on my wall. Oh no. We've come home and found upside-down crosses. No 'welcome home, Keith, we did the house chores for you.' That never happened.

I've come home and found the worlds 'Die KL' written on my wall multiple times. I've come home and found my face burned out of all my pictures. Tina had a light fixture explode in her face. That could have blinded her. Three Bibles had caught fire. Paw-prints — I almost forgot the paw prints. Not on the floor. On the ceiling. I would have no problem naming my first book *The Bothell Heaven House*, had the events that Tina and I experienced been heavenly. The harsh among you will say 'well you were provoking them somehow, you put your religious belief on display. You smudged the house.' I will admit that some of the things Tina and I did elevate the situation. There were some things I wish we had never done like smudging right before bed. Bad move. There are some things I wish we had done more of. Like, hold paranormal teams more accountable. So yes, mistakes were made. But let's keep it real.

The mistakes Tina and I made pale in comparison to the attacks we received. Let's not forget the first thing to go flying in our house was a pottery plant. That happened during a housewarming party. Let's not forget that Steve and Don got the spirits to admit they pushed me down the stairs. There was no activity whatsoever in 2013 — total peace. Then came my mysterious fall— January 2nd, 2014, which we now have audio of them admitting they caused. It was a few weeks after that the activity returned. In a major way, I might add. If what I just described doesn't fit the definition of a demon, then nothing does. I think we all can agree these spirits are mean. They're conniving. They're opportunists, and they're extremely patient. That's not me talking. That's the evidence talking. I remember I had to buy a brand-new bed when Tina moved out of the house – a huge California King mattress. Have you ever carried California King mattress up two flights of stairs? It's a bitch to achieve. The spirits could have easily helped me move that giant mattress upstairs I promise you I wouldn't have objected. They could have done it while my back was turned. I repeat! I wouldn't have objected. 'But Keith, spirits are nice.' 'Spirits are friendly.' They hell they are — not the ones I've encountered. If your world view is demons don't exist, then I don't know what to tell you. Once again, I'm not here to support world views. I'm here, to tell the truth. My world view was altered significantly the day I saw a plant fly across the room. They say, "seeing is believing." It is.

The experiments I'm about to conduct now are a continuation if you will of what Steve and Don did when they were here. I told Steve and Don about the banging noises coming from the hallway before both men arrived. I told them that the poking and prodding were intensifying. That and the new wall markings are what brought them back, remember? April 14, 2016, Steve Mera's notes: *Whilst in the upstairs hallway, myself (Steve Mera) and Don Philips heard a woman scream. The sound lasted only for a second. Though the sound seemed close in the vicinity, it was not loud. Inspection outside revealed no people around. Though the sound did seem to emanate from one of the upstairs bedrooms. No explanation was found.*

April 16, 2016 – Steve Mera's notes *A). Saw a shadow move B.) Multiple vocal responses captured (actual voice phenomena) C.) Picture falling off the wall. Unexplained as to why it fell.*

NOTE: Fell right after the bedroom tripwires went off (which was an unexplained event). Those are just a few of the things they got. You already saw the shadow pictures above (Chapter 11).

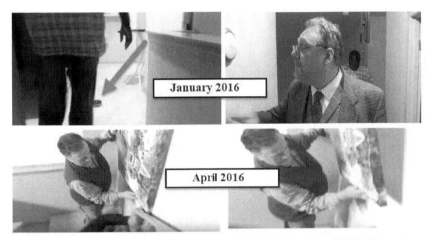

Fig 19.1: Steve Mera, Don Philips, and Nick Kyle (April 2016) had to deal with objects violently falling in the hallway area.

April 14th, 2016 – One of the areas Steve and Don wanted to focus on when they came the second time was my bed. They asked if they could take it apart. I have to admit; I was stumped. What can you find by taking a bed apart? Most researchers will tell you (those with experience) you're not looking for ghosts. You're not looking for the poltergeist. You're looking for anomalies. You're looking anything that deviates from the standard. Something that's not easily classified.

One of the devices Steve pulled out of his tool kit after the bed was disassembled was a hand-held compass. It started behaving weirdly within seconds of it being placed near the bed. The compass "skewing a full 180-degrees" in the opposite direction of what it's supposed to. What would cause a compass to go from the north to the south position in a matter of second? I'm talking over and over. Per Steve Mera, it would appear that the bolts that hold the middle frame together had become magnetized. How does an item become magnetized? Science tells us that items become magnetized due to currents traveling through them. More specifically, electrons. These electrons are what cause a material to be magnetic. Electrons are extremely small particles. They spend their time spinning around the nucleus of an atom. An object can't become magnetized unless the electrons inside it align in the north or south position. It's either one or the other. It would appear based on Steve's test that the metal bolt underneath my mattress was composed of electrons (all pointing in the south position). Contrary to the compass itself, which as you know, always points north. Why would a bolt be magnetized? Steve wasn't sure. This, in Steve words, was an anomaly. Think about it. I want you, the reader, to think about it seriously. I told Steve and Don before them coming a second time that the poking and prodding had increased to the point of driving me out of my room. I'm talking about serious sleep deprivation. When Steve first shared his finding with me, I have to admit I was confused. I'm not a scientist. I asked Steve point-blank, what is the significance of this finding? Steve's written response to me was "paranormally induced ELF (electromagnetic field) can radiate metal nearby and deflect a compass. Taking measurements of this periodically can demonstrate the defusing process of end saturation in the environment until it has diminished." Something with a sufficiently strong magnetic field - magnetized the belt bolts right underneath my headboard and pillow. Causing the compass in Steve Mera's hand to do cartwheels. Please think long and hard about that.

This would be the second time today (April 14th) where an anomaly appeared inexplicably and "defused" inexplicably. Both instances involved my bed (review Chapter 8). Steve's findings were the most important finding of all to me. Steve knows what I've been saying about the bed is true. Anyone who's ever been attacked by a spirit while trying to sleep will tell you it's one of the most uncomfortable events you'll ever experience. I get so many emails from people saying, "I wish that happened to me." Trust me; you wouldn't want this if you knew what was truly happening. Hollywood makes it look exciting. It's not exciting. It's deadly. I've been living in my new apartment for several months now. The only thing detrimental to me (that I know of) is the things I experience while lying in bed. That's where I'll conduct a majority of my experiments. The apartment I live in is not haunted. Neither is my car. I'm the one who is haunted. I'm the one with attachments. I don't say that with pride. Heck no! People look at you differently the second they find out you have spiritual attachments. They stigmatize you. 'Better you than me, dead man walking, sucks to be you' those are just some of the things people say when they learn you have attachments. Some of my friends think that way. Even some family members. I've noticed I'm not invited to major get togethers at friends' houses anymore. I can't get upset. These are my friends.

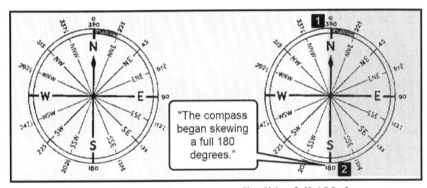

Fig 19.2: Illustration – **1.)** Compass needle did a full 180-degree turn **2.)** When placed near portions of the bed where I've claimed of being poked and prodded

CHAPTER 20

Teddy Bear Experiment

Seotember 2016 – If you asked me four years ago what beliefs I held about the paranormal, I couldn't give you an answer. My interests for as long as I can remember have been informational technology. That's the path I chose and held since I left high school. How people interact with computers is where my fascination lies. Second to that would be science fiction and action movies. After that, it's *Star Wars,* politics, astrophysics, theology, and sports fishing. The paranormal? Never heard of it. Not until May 1st, 2012. There's a gross misconception about the paranormal as it relates to African Americans. I've had a lot of stupid questions, i.e., statements thrown my way as a result of me and Tina's ordeal. The statement that irks me the most has to do with comedian Eddie Murphy's standup routine in the motion picture *Raw.* I can't tell you how many times people have said to me, "There's no way your Bothell house could be as haunted as you say it is. Eddie Murphy said black people don't live in haunted houses. They get the fuck out immediately." These people have no idea how close they've come to being punched in the face. That kind of ignorance permeants throughout both believing and non-believing communities. Am I an African American? Of course, I am. I'm not a Borg? I'm not a member of some collective that says when plants start flying run! I'm my own person. I have my own fascinations about life. My own questions. Don't we all? One thing I learned about poltergeist, about minions, in general, is they don't suffer fools. It's not their job to help you figure things out. Their job is to raise hell! If you can't get the help, you need to combat them. Oh well, that's too bad. 'Poor little you.' That's the mentality they have.

If you read my book, *The Bothell Hell House,* you know there's one truth that's not yet wavered. These spirits love manipulating electronic devices. Let's not forget about the cameras that went missing. Let's not forget about the television going off and on by itself – numerous times. Let's not forget about the electrician visiting the house multiple times. Let's not forget about Comcast, ADT security, and Public Utility District multiple visits to the house. None of them were able to ascertain the problem Tina, and I were having with our electronic devices. If we set all of that aside, what do we have left? We have the US and UK teams' investigative findings. That's what we have. One of the experiments Nikki Novelle conducted when she was here (back in February) involved a shadow detection doll. The EVPs from that experiment (Chapter 52 *The Bothell Hell House*) and the EVPs captured during Steve and Don's first and second visit confirms these spirits love for electronic devices. Seriously, you should listen to those EVPs. The conversations taking place between entities reminds me of the conversation my brother, and I would have while we watched our mom and dad put our Christmas gifts together. Our parents didn't even know we were observing them. There we were huddled together near the hallway entrance. Kevin, Michael, and I — we were guessing which gift belongs to whom. We're whispering mind you. These minions are doing the same thing. The only difference is they're not trying to figure out which gift belongs to who. No! They're trying to guess what type of camera Steve and Don are putting in the hallway. They're using words like 'image detector, nite cam, and cable.' Like I said, the spirits have an extreme curiosity with tools and gadgets. That, ladies and gentlemen, will be the basis for my experiment. What type of investigative devices are at my disposal right now? Zero.

I told Nikki about what I was doing. It had to have been fate because Nikki had just come across something; she felt I might be interested in. One of her friends in the paranormal field had told her about a new gadget they had started using. They call it a trigger alarm teddy bear. I have to admit I was not excited about the name - here's why. Nikki, Karissa, Rich, Steve, Don, and I all have videos on our respective YouTube Channel showing the interaction these entities are having with motion detect devices.

Tripwires work great in a house environment because a house environment is spread out. I'm in a two-bedroom apartment now. What am I going to do, put a teddy bear on each corner of the bed? I don't think so. Nikki saw my hesitance and said, "the trigger alarm teddy bear it's not a motion sensor per se." I'm like, what do you mean it's not like a motion sensor? From what she understood; the bear doesn't detect motion. It detects touch. It'll only go off if you touch it. I cracked a smile that Nikki couldn't see. *That's exactly what I need.* I went to Amazon.com and ordered two trigger alarm teddy bears.

Doll Experiment February 2016   **Teddy Bear Experiment Fall 2016**

Fig 20.1: Shadow detection doll / Touch-activated teddy bear

The teddy bears arrived a few days later and guess what? It looked exactly like the bear on Amazon's website. Talk about simplicity. All the manufacturer did was cut open the back of the bear and insert a touch-activated door alarm. That's all this bear was. This experiment is going to simpler than I thought. That's a good thing. A lot of these paranormal television shows like you to believe that the best way to get evidence is by using expensive gadgets. Not necessarily. The simpler the gadget, the simpler the experiment. How many steps should the experiment have for it to be carried out? In my opinion, as few as possible. I can already tell from looking at this teddy bear that I'm on the right path. If there's one thing I've learned about these minions is they respond to simple experiments. Please review the illustration on the next page.

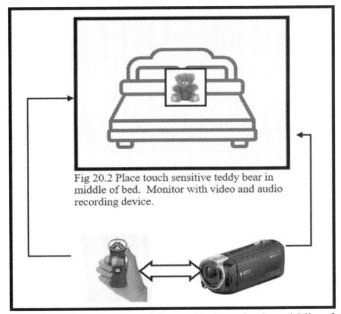

Fig 20.2 Place touch sensitive teddy bear in middle of bed. Monitor with video and audio recording device.

Fig 20.2: Place the touch-sensitive teddy bear in the middle of the bed. Monitor with video and audio recording device.

You can see from (Table 20.1) that the teddy bear experiment was a success. Not only was I able to get twenty plus interactions, i.e., beeps coming from the bear when no one is near it, I also got a few unexplained voices on the video and audio equipment. I am going back to what I said earlier about implementing some form of best practice, i.e., standardization around the experiment I'm conducting. A touch-sensitive device going off by itself is great. Doesn't necessarily mean what just happened is paranormal. That's what a skeptic would say. 'Your teddy bear's malfunctioning; it's giving you a false positive.' Yeah whatever. That's where the voice recorder and video camera come in. A voice uttering the word 'Keith' in and around the time the teddy bear goes off is what paranormal researchers call good evidence. What's my name? My name is Keith. What do you hear when you reach time stamp 3:54:03? You hear a female voice saying 'Keith.' I know that voice. I've heard it in my ear numerous time here and at the Bothell house. Imagine hearing your name whispered in your ear at 3 AM. Talk about becoming aroused. Prepare yourself. I'm going to talk a lot about that in the chapters ahead.

1st Teddy Bear Experiment	Ringing – Time Stamps
	https://www.youtube.com/watch?v=vuOV37PiEk8 **DAY ONE:** 1st Bear alarm goes off at **00:58** goes off again at **1:03** Bear alarm goes off a 3rd time at **3:34** 4th time at **4:48**. 5th time at **5:40** 6th time at **5:54** Alarm goes off a 7th time at **6:13** 8th time at **6:55** Bear alarm goes for a 9th and 10th time at **7:37** and continuous touch at **7:37**. 11th time at **14:14**. Then again at **14:22** 12 times now. 13th time at **15:20**. 14th time at **21:58**. Mic tap at **31:30** EVP at **34:07** dragged out 'Keith.' Re-establishing baseline at **36:53**. **DAY THREE:** TEST 3. Bears go off 1st time at **1:08:13** 2nd time at **1:09:00** 3rd time at **1:12:04**. Mic tap **1:24:31**. Bears go of a 4th time at **1:37:08**. **DAY FOUR:** TEST 4. Bear Rings at **2:58:30**. **DAY FOUR:** TEST 5. I'm ironing clothes, getting ready to meet friends for dinner. This **Day FOUR** Test 5. 1st right at **3:43:42**. 'KEITH' EVP at **3:54:03**.

Table 20.1: Teddy Bear Experiment – Phase 1

The teddy bear ringing in the video is not the huge takeaway here. The teddy bear didn't beep once. The teddy bear, i.e., brand new teddy bear didn't beep twice. It beeped twenty-five times. It shouldn't have beeped at all.

I want to talk about what it is I was doing at 36:53 (Table 20.1). Please review that. You see me throwing something at the teddy bear. It's an EMF reader. Might as well have been a shoe or something. The teddy bear didn't beep. Did you see me tossing the bear up in the air? The teddy bear still didn't beep. It didn't do anything. That's what it supposed to do. That's why Nikki recommended it. It's a touch-activated bear.

I don't mean anywhere either. No! You have to touch the bear on the round sensor. That's the only way it will beep. Where is that sensor located? Inside the belly of the teddy bear.

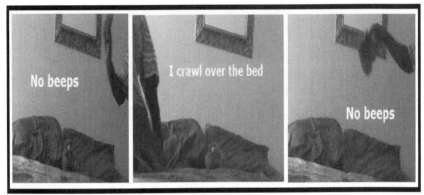

Fig 20.3: I'm unable to debunk my experiment. The touch-sensitive bear is doing what it's built to do. Beep when a certain spot has been touched.

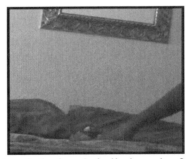

Fig 20.4: have to touch the bear's belly in order for it to beep.

People have asked me, "could you have made the video shorter? My response? Yeah, I could have made the video shorter. But I won't. This video (Table 20.1) is way longer than four hours. The experiment you just watched went off and on for five days. Contrary to what some of you have seen on television, there's no such thing as instant gratification. Investigations take time. That one experiment was five days longer than Ghost Adventures' entire investigation. Can you imagine watching five hours of video? It's not exciting. Not until something happens – in this case, it was the teddy bear finally going off.

2nd Teddy Bear Experiment – Guest Bedroom	Ringing – Time Stamps
	https://www.youtube.com/watch?v=_XQOABz5t-4 Bear alarm at **1:07**; Bear alarm at **2:40** 'No'; Bear alarm at **3:14**; Whisper at **9:24** the word 'Go' is heard; **9:43** something says 'Right'; **10:12**; **10:21**;

Table 20.2: Teddy Bear Experiment – October 2016

9:24 The word 'Go' is heard

9:43 Something says 'Right.'

When I walk out of this room, can you touch the teddy bear? I walk out. Teddy bear starts beeping at **13:12** thru **13:21***

13:55* I'm going to walk back into the room (bedroom) in five seconds. Can you activate the bear (when I enter the room)?

14:05* As soon as I walk in the bear beeps.

The interesting thing about the second teddy bear experiment is it wasn't an experiment. Not an official one. I was experiencing tremendous activity the night before. Tremendous nightmares. Tremendous night terrors. I had forgotten that the teddy bear was in the guest bedroom. That teddy bear beeped that entire Sunday afternoon.

2nd Teddy Bear Experiment –	Ringing – Time Stamps
	https://www.youtube.com/watch?v=qU8X3nT5feI Bear rings at **00:30**; Teddy bear is facing down. The sensor has been placed on its belly - facing mattress. Bear rings at **2:21**; Different camera. Bear rings at 4:03 Bear rings at **5:12**; Bear rings at **6:44**; Bear rings at **6:55**; I'm asleep. Bear rings at **8:20**; Bear rings at **8:28**; Bear rings at **9:57**; Bear rings at **11:28**; Bear rings at **12:52** Diff camera view. Bear rings at **13:12**

Table 20.3: Teddy Bear Experiment – October 2016

CHAPTER 21

Death by Moving Train

Parapsychologists will tell you that poltergeist will do everything within their power to torment you except commit murder. I disagree. Poltergeists have been killing people throughout millennia. They're bullies. That's one way of describing them. Webster definition for bullying is — *use superior strength or influence to intimidate (someone), typically to force him or her to do what one wants.* Doesn't that describe the actions of a poltergeist? If you truly want to understand the actions of a poltergeist, you need to look no further than Maria Jose Ferreira. Maria Jose Ferreira's poltergeist ordeal is one of the harshest "Geist" encounters I've come across. Maria saw death by poison as a means to an end. Not only was she being afflicted by the poltergeist, but she was also being afflicted by the people and organizations that said they were there to help. Sound familiar?

Bullying – "bully-related suicide can be connected to any type of bullying, including physical bullying, emotional bullying.
Some of the warning signs of suicide (as a result of being bullied) include:

- Showing signs of <u>depression,</u> like <u>ongoing sadness,</u> withdrawal from others, <u>losing interest in favorite activities,</u> or trouble sleeping or <u>eating.</u>
- <u>Talking about or showing an interest in death or dying.</u>
- <u>Engaging in dangerous or harmful activities, including reckless behavior, substance abuse, or self-injury.</u>
- Giving away favorite possessions and saying goodbye to people.

- <u>Saying or expressing that they can't handle things anymore.</u> <u>Making comments that things would be better without them.</u>

NOTE: What I underlined in the bullet points above and below are acts and emotions Rhonda had while living in the Bothell house.

<u>What We Know About Suicide</u>

- Suicide-related behavior is complicated and <u>rarely the result</u> of a <u>single</u> source of trauma or stress.
- People who engage in suicide-related behavior often experience overwhelming feelings of <u>helplessness</u> and <u>hopelessness</u>.
- ANY involvement with bullying behavior is one stressor which may significantly contribute to feelings of helplessness and hopelessness that raise the risk of suicide.

<u>https://www.cdc.gov/violenceprevention/pdf/bullying-suicide-translation-final-a.pdf</u>

Another imagination requests from me to you. Imagine you're isolated. It's you and not Maria Jose Ferreira that's being attacked. It's your clothes catching fire and not hers. I'm talking about the clothes you currently have on. Your world and those around you have been turned upside-down. Friends and family have no clue what to do with you. Here comes a paranormal organization with his or her world view. They've concluded that you (not a malevolent spirit) are what's behind this. The word they use is "agent." It's RSPK - Recurrent Spontaneous Psychokinesis. They try to tell you that your problem is not spiritual. It's mental. *Ghost Adventures* told the entire world first (not Tina directly, their client) that she might be the one causing all the activity in the Bothell house. Excuse me, but are they doctors? I didn't know Zack Bagan, and Dave Schrader had a degree in psychology. That innuendo, i.e., conjecture was uttered at the tail end of the "Demons in Seattle" episode. Can you imagine Tina's reaction? Can you imagine her family's reaction? Tina and her family were livid and rightfully so.

Maria Jose Ferreira took her own life because she was feeling hopeless. If fifty needles were inexplicably appearing inside the heel of your foot (while your shoes were on), you'd feel hopeless too. You would think there was no end to your torment. *Screw this! I'm killing myself.*

Rhonda Lee Jimenez and her family lived in the Bothell house four years before Tina, and I arrived. That alone debunks *Ghost Adventures'* ridiculous conjecture about Tina being an agent. And just for the record, *Ghost Adventures* knew a previous tenant had reported similar activity. Rhonda told me a year before she died that "I hope you and Tina succeed. I hope you two can maintain your faith, maintain your belief system. I hope you two win." Rhonda wanted us to beat whatever was living here. In Rhonda's own words the Bothell house was a "living hell." She said it was "the beginning of the end." She said the house destroyed her and her husband's marriage. She told me in not so many words that the house was the reason for her depression. That depression is what led her to drug and alcohol addiction. Did Rhonda have spiritual attachments she didn't know about? Did her family? I'm almost certain that they did. By the time I caught up with Rhonda, she was living in Yakima, Washington. It was weird – she told me she and her husband "had just gotten back together." She told me her youngest son (the one who developed meningitis inside the Bothell home) "still sees shadow figures." He still sees them!

August 15th, 2016. Rhonda Lee Jimenez committed suicide. The death occurred in Bonna, Montana. Multiple news outlets saw fit to cover the story.

MISSOULA -

https://missoulian.com/news/local/name-of-woman-hit-and-killed-by-train-in-bonner/article_d4384644-39d9-5001-8009-86b272b46abf.html

https://newstalkkgvo.com/train-strikes-kills-unidentified-woman-near-bonner/

Missoula County Sheriff and Coroner T.J. McDermott identified the woman who was killed after being struck by a train on Monday evening as 48-year-old Rhonda Jimenez of Yakima, Washington. The cause of death has been determined to be suicide, and the manner of death was blunt force trauma. The investigation into her death has been officially closed. An unidentified woman was struck and killed by a train near Bonner late on Monday afternoon. Jeremiah Peterson with the Missoula Sheriff's Office said the initial call came into 9-1-1 at about 6:15 p.m. "Deputies and emergency personnel responded to the area near the old Milltown Dam where an eastbound train struck a female pedestrian on the railroad tracks," Peterson said. "She was subsequently killed. The county coroner responded, and the sheriff's office is currently investigating," Peterson said personnel from Montana Rail Link responded to the scene.

Fig 21.1: Coroner T.J. McDermott identified the woman forty-eight- year-old Rhonda Jimenez of Yakima, Washington.

Rhonda's death didn't surprise me. People who repeatedly try to kill themselves end up succeeding eventually. Especially if they have a demon urging them on. By urging, I mean addicted to alcohol, suffering from depression, abuse, and rape. Hopelessness! It's impossible not to feel that when being bombarded twenty-four-seven by phenomena, you have no understanding of. In Rhonda's case, that would be her drug(s) and alcohol addictions and hard to treat mood disorder. Rhonda's son said it best when he said: "my mom's demons had finally caught up with her." What Rhonda's son said gave me chills. The spirits inside the Bothell house have successfully taken a life. Who's next? I'm telling you the honest to God's truth. Have I ever thought about killing myself? Yes, I've thought about it. If you were constantly harassed and followed by a force, you couldn't see you'd think about killing yourself too. A feeling of hopelessness is one of the main ingredients for committing suicide. It's one of the main emotions you feel when being bullied. Here are a few myths I found online about suicide.

Myth#1 - you have to be mentally ill to think about suicide. That's false. Most people have thought of suicide from time to time, and not all people who die by suicide have mental health problems at the time of death.

Myth#2 - people with suicidal thoughts want to die. False - the majority of people who feel suicidal do not want to die; they do not want to live the life they have. The distinction may seem small but is in fact very important and is why talking through other options at the right time is so vital.

I'm pretty sure <u>Maria Jose Ferreira </u>didn't want to end her life. But she did by drinking a bottle of liquid poison. There are other documented cases of people committing suicide as a result of "Geist" attacks. The idea that a poltergeist can do just about anything it wants except kill you is in my opinion grossly inaccurate.

<u>49-States-Now-Have-Anti-Bullying-Laws</u>

<u>Get Help - Stop Bullying</u>

CHAPTER 22

The Heartbeat Experiment

I can't tell you exactly when the heartbeats started appearing. It probably started without me even noticing it. When I speak of heartbeats, I'm not referring to the pulsating mattress phenomena. The pulsating, i.e., throbbing mattress and the phenomena I refer to as poking and prodding are two sides of the same coin. How long has all this combined been going on? My best estimate would say about five years (before this book was written). It's weird even by "Geist" standards. Every night after 3 AM, the heartbeats begin to happen. Where do they happen? Under my pillow. Always under my pillow. Doesn't matter what bedroom I'm sleeping in; I still hear it. In hotels during a business trip? I hear it then also. Sleeping at a friend's house? I still hear it. Doesn't matter whose house I'm sleeping in. If I'm there more than two nights, I hear heartbeats.

You've heard of having a bad day? Imagine having a bad night. My worst nights include heartbeats, night terrors, and non-stop poking. Occasionally they'll yank the sheets off the bed. No way you're sleeping through that. Guess what? The spirits are not always that blatant. There is a sensual side to this affliction I've yet to share. Now and then in the middle of my sleeping, I'm awakened by a female voice. The most soothing and angelic voice you can imagine. Talk about a sudden release of endorphins. The voice might as well be a siren's call. That's about the best way I can describe it. Hmm, I can describe it way better than that. I will, in the coming chapters, describe exactly what I'm hearing and feeling. There's a lot of explicit detail coming your way. Please prepare yourself.

I've been living in my apartment a little over three months. The poking, the pulsations coming from within the mattress, and the heartbeats from inside my pillows are all connected. The shadows parapsychologists Steve Mera picked up when he was here back in April 2016 sort of helped me put this puzzle together.

Fig 22.1: 1.) I've just laid down in bed 2.) Watching TV or texting. Poking and what feels like pulsating softballs within the mattress starts soon after.

Fig 22.2: 3.) Heartbeats start at 3 AM 4.) They keep going till time to wake up.

Fig 22.1 and Fig 22.2 describe it perfectly. Can you understand why someone over a period of time (in my case five years) would want to kill themselves? Has it ever happened to me when a woman was in bed with me? The answer is yes - the poking has. Do the women ever notice? Tina didn't. Other girls, I've dated after Tina haven't noticed. The pulse underneath my mattress, underneath my pillow is happening more and more to the point where I can now hear heartbeats. I can hear scratching noises now. The scratching sounds are weird. The next time you're in Home Depot, walk over to the plywood section. Find a good piece of four-by-four. Drag your fingernails across that piece of plywood. That's what my ears are picking up at 3 AM. Doesn't matter if it's the weekday or the weekend. The same thing happens. Every morning I ask myself the same question, when does it end? I can understand if I was still living in the Bothell house. I've moved out. I've been out for quite some time. Why am I still experiencing some of this? I thought I was free. I'm not sure now. My friends, they don't get this. They don't understand that it's not over. If you should by any chance ever make your way unto my YouTube Channel. Or make your way to my WordPress or Facebook page – there awaits a lot of what I've already talked about. That's what the internet is – our planet's biggest library. Someone's going to read this stuff (all of it) and in doing so come up with an explanation as to why this is happening. I don't mean they're going to debunk it. No. They're going to prove beyond a reasonable doubt that poltergeist exist. I'm trying to help that person out. That's why I wrote this book and *The Bothell Hell House*. When you break it all down to its finest compound, all you have in regard to evidence is information. In the IT world, we call it data. As you're about to see I've run into a slight problem. I've reached a dead end. Nikki said it best when she said, and *I'm paraphrasing*, she has no way of capturing the heartbeat she <u>felt</u> when she took it upon herself to put her hand on my mattress. She was perplexed. We all were. How do you research that? How do you quantify it? That's where I'm at right now. How can I share that part of what's happening to me? I can be descriptive as all get out. Something tells me that's not going to be acceptable to someone like yourself.

And that's understandable. People buy books for different reasons. Especially a book like this. People have questions. Questions about life after death. About ghosts. About demons. About angels. About elementals. About poltergeists. One person's prism is another person's life experience. Maybe you're a skeptic or worse a cynic. Skeptic or believer, my reason for writing this book is still the same - to tell my story to the best of my ability. One of those stories involves the heartbeats I'm hearing when I'm trying to sleep. How do I make you understand what that is? What that feels like? There has to be a tool out there that can capture what it is I'm talking about. *I'll be dammed there is.* A digital stethoscope! That's what I need.

I pondered about buying a digital stethoscope for over six months before finally saying to myself I got to buy myself one of these. I've lived in my apartment for a year now. Nothing I've told you thus far has subsided. The fact that I'm still being bombarded with everything I've just told you about is what motivated me to go out and buy a digital stethoscope. The thing I had to come to terms with before actually buying a digital stethoscope can be summed up with one word: Practical. Should I be buying something that expensive? Something the spirits can take within a bat of an eye. Nothing went missing in my apartment. *Not that I know of.* The possibility still does exist – this is a new piece of electronic equipment. Digital stethoscopes are not your average ghost gear. We're talking about a medical device — one of the most important medical devices that ever was created.

My deliberation would not have taken this long had the idea been to buy a regular stethoscope. Regular stethoscopes are a dime a dozen. I don't need a dime a dozen stethoscope. I'm not doing this for me. I can hear the heartbeats just fine. I'm doing this for you. Digital stethoscopes have a capability that a regular stethoscope doesn't. Digital stethoscopes can record what it is they hear. That's ones of the reason why they're so expensive. My biggest fear is I buy something like this, and within seconds of me bringing it home, it's gone. Or the circuit board gets fried – for reasons I can't explain.

That happened multiple times with other pieces of equipment. What the spirit wants, it takes. No questions asked. If you understand the EVPs, I've shared in this book and most importantly the EVPs I've shared in the book, *The Bothell Hell House* you'll know the minions have on more than occasion admitted to manipulating electronic devices.

The ultimate manipulation is the outright theft of an electronic device. Remember the unexplained voice saying, 'go and lift one of these.' The stethoscopes I want to buy cost five – hundred dollars. Suffice to say I thought long and hard about the consequences of buying digital stethoscopes. I did a lot of research. The reviews about the stethoscopes I was planning to buy were pretty good. I'm keeping with the theme I thought of earlier. Simplicity. Keep the experiments simple. The digital stethoscopes I was thinking about buying were just that. Simple. No learning curve whatsoever. I'm not trying to determine which spirit has atrial fibrillation. I'm not looking for a bad heart valve. I'm trying to record heartbeats. Like Steve's chief researcher said, "If you ask a direct question while holding up a voice recorder, and the response you get is a direct answer to the question you asked. We're not talking about ambient sounds, or grunts and groans. The response in question is vocal. It's intelligent." That's an EVP. That's an unexplained vocal response. The question we can't answer is where did that voice come from? Why is there a voice in the first place? It shouldn't be there. The same rules apply with the digital stethoscope. If the stethoscope can pick up heartbeats from both my mattress and pillow, the question soon after that discovery is where are those heartbeats coming from? Beds and pillows don't have heartbeats. They're not living things. The world deserves an answer. I know I do. That's it; I'm buying two digital stethoscopes.

The two digital stethoscopes I bought are:

- EKO CORE Digital and the
- ThinkLABS One digital stethoscopes

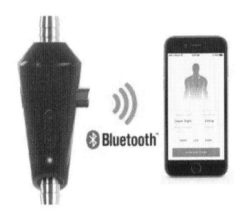

Fig 22.3: EKO CORE Digital stethoscope attachment
https://ekodevices.com/

EKO CORE Digital stethoscope:

- **40x audio amplification**
- 7 volume levels for listening comfort
- Digital (on) and analog (off) modes
- Rechargeable (9 hours of continuous use per charge)
- Bluetooth LE for wireless Mobile App connection
- Free Eko Mobile App – available on iOS and Android

This unique device (see above) easily attaches to your current analog single-tube stethoscope and provides a wireless connection to your mobile device so you can see your patient's readings in a whole new way.

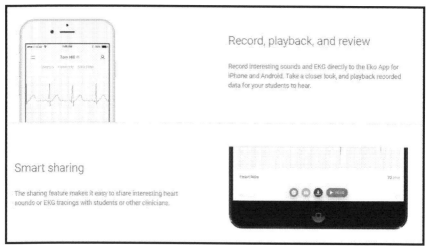

Fig 22.4: Eko smart technology stethoscope

- Live streaming with video/audio conferencing
- Listen to your digital stethoscope from anywhere in real-time. Simply activate live streaming on your phone and share the URL.

Fig 22.5: includes video conferencing capability.

Fig 22.6: ThinkLABS One digital stethoscope

ThinkLABS One digital stethoscope:

- High strength sapphire crystal, robust enough to be used in deep-sea chronometers.
- Precision-machined aluminum, hand-polished by people who work with satellite systems and other advanced applications requiring the perfect finish.
- Specialized electronic components that are custom manufactured for ThinkLABS.
- Gold-plated connectors and jacks to ensure low impedance connections.
- Design refinements that focus on minutiae, which achieve the last details of performance.

ThinkLABS' amplified stethoscope is the loudest stethoscope ever made and has fully adjustable volume (1-10) to fit the audio needs of any individual. Voltage doubling charge pumps provide extra headroom for low distortion reproduction of S1 and S2 heartbeat peaks. The headphone amplifiers have sufficient power to drive low-impedance audio headphones, producing 45.2mWatts Competitive stethoscopes operate on lower voltage, use a single amplifier and high impedance speaker, resulting in clipped heartbeats at significantly lower power output.

IMPORTANT - Audio Filter System - Multiple filters give you control over the sound with far more nuanced than the blunt instrument of a "bell" or "diaphragm." You can also limit bandwidth to exclude ambient noise.

https://www.thinklabs.com/thinklink

Thinklink provides a connection between One and your mobile or laptop devices to capture and send via iPhone, iPad, Android devices, and Mac/PC.

I've had just about every paranormal device you can think of in my house. I can't think of one paranormal device that's been certified by some of group or organization. I've not seen one with built-in Wi-Fi and built-in Bluetooth. Not one paranormal device that's come into my Bothell house was cloud or SaaS-based. These stethoscopes I've obtained are state of the art. There's no getting around that. Both stethoscopes are brand new. No time for half measure. *If the spirits steal them, I guarantee you I'll be downing a bottle of Jack Daniels while crying my ass off.*

I believe these devices will help me explain the phenomena known as attachments. Or better yet help someone else explain it. The Eko and the ThinkOne stethoscope have only one mission: Capture the sounds coming from my pillow and mattress.

https://youtu.be/gKQbHABcA8o

Experiment I

https://youtu.be/RuXBdZoPPZE

Experiment II

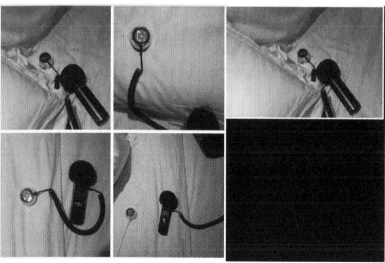

Fig 22.7: Hotel room Spokane WA

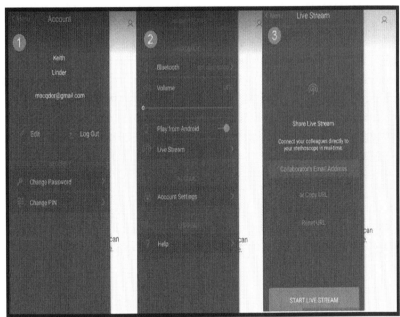

Fig 22.8: Eko Smart Phone App Interface – Droid

1. Login into the phone app.
2. Bluetooth / Volume / Live Stream controls
3. Live Stream Setup

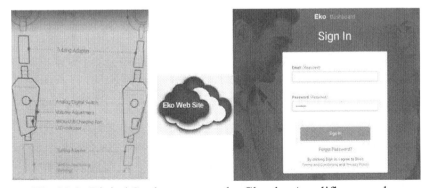

Fig 22.9: Digital Stethoscope on the Cloud – Amplifies sound 40X.

The Eko and ThinkOne stethoscopes would have never survived the Bothell house. They either would have gone missing (odds are that's what would have happened) or they would have malfunctioned. The two videos two pages back show me sleeping in two beds. The master bedroom and guest room. Heartbeats (as I've been stating) coming from two state of the art stethoscopes. The heartbeats I picked up aren't mine. And how do we know that? We know that because science tells us. "A normal resting heart rate for adults (18+ or higher) ranges from 60 to 100 beats per minute. I've given the reader a view of what my heart rate was while living in the Bothell and more importantly, while living in my new place (see Table 22.1). My medical record (available upon request from any skeptic org) bears witness to that.

Date	Blood Pressure	Heartrate / BPM
3/17/2015	122/82	74
6/6/2016	122/90	56
6/28/2016	124/86	57
6/30/2017	138/90	63
9/25/2018	112/72	70
1/26/2019	118/80	72
Average		**65**

Table 22.1: Kaiser Permanente BPM medical records – Keith Linder.

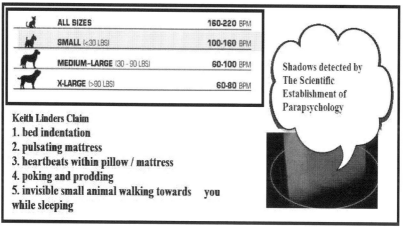

Fig 22.10: Animal BPM chart mixed. My claims and S.E. Ps findings

Once again, the best way to conduct these experiments is to keep them simple. That's easy to do with these devices. The first thing you need to know when adhering to a process is knowing where the trigger is. A better word for that would be an event. An event is what kicks off a process. The event, in my case, is the heartbeats themselves. When I say I wake up hearing heartbeats what does that mean? It shouldn't be complicated to understand, so here goes. If you sleep like me, you're probably sleeping with your ears pressed against the pillow. Now imagine you're hearing 'ba bump,' or 'lub-dub' non-stop. The 'ba bumps' I hear began after 3 AM. It's very irritating, but what can you do? You eventually get used to it. Or least I do. I mean, what choice do I have? I have to maintain some form of normalcy. So, I've learned to sleep through it. Does it go away? Of course not. By the time I wake up (which is a few hours later) the beats have intensified. Sometimes the 'ba bump' is rampant. Sometimes it's not. Most of the time, especially on the weekend when I try to sleep in the heartbeats, are always louder. That's my trigger, ladies and gentlemen. When the beats have reached the point of almost driving me insane as described in Edgar Allen Poe's book *The Tell-tale Heart,* that's when I will conduct my experiments. As to how I was able to capture these unexplained beats. The answer to that question is simple. I wake up from a relentless night of 'lub-dub' beats and poking-prodding.

Step A. march over to my computer desk.
- **Decision** - how in-depth do I want to be with my experiment?
- **Decision** - which stethoscope do I use? The Think One stethoscope is perfect ad-hoc experiments. REMINDER: *I have to avoid putting too much thought into these experiments for fear of jeopardizing what I'm about to do.*

There's a level of spontaneity that needs to be incorporated in carrying an investigation such as this. These spirits (based on the evidence we've captured) seem to have the ability to read minds. I can't risk the heartbeats dissipating before my experiment even starts, which is where the ThinkOne comes in. Three steps are all it takes to get going.

- Step A – turn on both devices
- Step B – connect my ThinkOne to my H1 Zoom device.
- Step C - place the ThinkOne stethoscope on the bed and hit record on the Zoom H1 and I'm done. That's it.

The Eko stethoscope is a little more cumbersome – and not in a bad way. Before I put my Eko, on the bed, there are a few things I have to do first.

- Step A – turn on the phone app.
- Step B – turn on the Eko
- Step C – turn on the blue tooth (synchronization begins)
- Step D – setup LIVE streaming (ability to hear the heartbeats in real-time) on my PC or laptop
- Step E – access my dashboard on Eko website
- Step F – place the Eko on my bed.
- Step G – begin recording.
- Step H – Observe / Listen

There's a lot of thought that goes into setting up the Eko. A lot of dependencies, e.g. Wi-Fi. When using my Eko - there's an enormous amount of opportunity for a spirit to sabotage The possibility of experiencing technical difficulty goes up significantly – which by the time you've corrected everything. The heartbeats you were after are gone. They've dissipated. It doesn't happen all the time. But it does happen. I showed these readings (**heartbeats**) to several of my friends in the medical field, and the response I got was:
https://youtu.be/cZVUmfKOxio

- "crappy recording of a sinus Brady
- "long QT" syndrome

- "almost like the person is atrial paced....see small spikes...hard to tell with one strip. Would need a 12 lead EKG."
- "Are they symptomatic?"
- "looks like a normal sinus rhythm."

My friend, a Certified Transport Registered Nurse (CTRN), finally asks me after looking at all the ECG readings, " who is this?" I tell her these readings came from my bed (all my friends know about my ghost experience). Her response.

- "That's freaky."
- "Dude....the ghost is about to die."
- "If I saw that (ECG readings) on a live human, I would think they were nearing the end."

Try not to lose sight of the fact that these readings were taken from my bed. Fact number one. These are not my heartbeats. I'm rarely in the room when these experiments are conducted. The heartbeats I've provided you in this book come primarily from the master bedroom (the bed I sleep in the most). I've captured similar heartbeats from hotel rooms. The hotels I've stayed in while traveling on business – the ThinkOne is perfect for that. I conduct these experiments to the best of my ability for the hopes that you might have an idea of what it is I'm reporting. I didn't invent the term 'phantom heartbeats.' That term has been around for quite some time and rightfully so. There are tons of documented cases of house occupants hearing heartbeats from inside their bedroom, behind their headboard, behind their bedroom walls, underneath the floor and extreme cases of heartbeats coming from within the mattress and bed sheets themselves. The average beats per minute coming from these experiments I conducted using both Eko and ThinkOne digital stethoscopes has been 114+/- beats per minute. Science says we can guestimate the size of the animal by its heartbeat. If that's true (and I can't see why it wouldn't be), then it reveals something remarkable. It means whatever it is that's been causing the bed indentations, the poking, the prodding, and the pulsating mattress whenever I try to fall asleep is the size of a small dog or small cat.   Whatever this is that's how big it is. The findings from this experiment support what Rhonda's son has been saying about "seeing shadowy figures out the corner of his eye." It says a lot about the shadowy figures the women I've dated have seen – which we'll get to in the coming chapters. Earlier I said what I feel lying across my extremities at night reminds me of a sandbag. I'm talking about weight and size. I mentioned in my previous book (years before this experiment was conducted) the indentations I feel in my bed mattress when I'm sleeping reminds me of the pet cat I had when I was growing up. That pressure in the mattress, i.e., the indentation you feel as your pet approaches. Take the shadow figures Steve Mera captured from his hallway light experiment and add it to everything I just said and what do you have? You have the dimensions and proportions of the minions I keep mentioning. In short, you have proof beyond reasonable doubt about what I and others have been describing. I want the reader to understand that every experiment I conduct always begins and ends with a prayer. Not because I'm super religious. I'm cautious. I'm respectful. At least I'm trying to be.   Every experiment that involves contacting spirits is dangerous. That includes investigations. I cannot afford to open (for lack of a better word) a portal right now. Look at everything I'm dealing with already. The last thing I hear before I fall asleep and the first thing I hear when I wake up in the morning are phantom heartbeats.

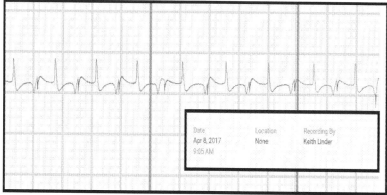

Fig 22.11 April 2017 Eko Digital device - Electrocardiography

https://youtu.be/cZVUmfKOxio

Poltergeist Heartbeats Experiment.

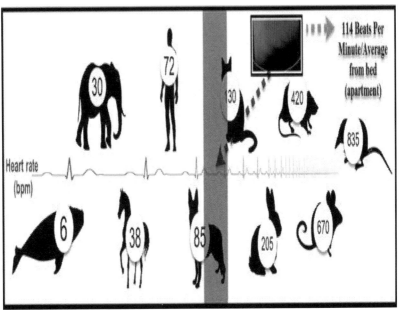

Fig 22.12: 114 BPM was the average BPM I captured. Cats average BPM is 130 +/-

Fig 22.13: ThinkOne Digital Stethoscope – master bedroom

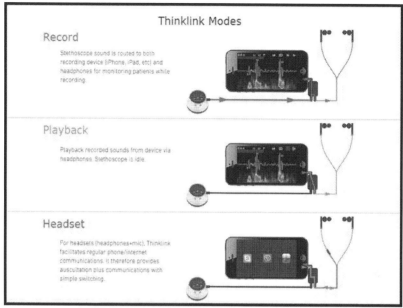

Fig 22.14: Modes – Smart Technology

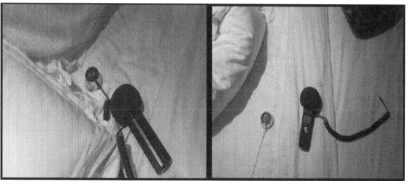

Fig 22.15: ZOOM H1 portable handheld digital voice recorder hooked to the ThinkOne Labs digital stethoscope. Location - Davenport Hotel bedroom.

https://youtu.be/s-ge3L0A6nk
Poltergeist - Heartbeats [headsets required]

CHAPTER 23

Night Terrors

Stop pressuring me. Make me wanna scream
~ **Michael Jackson**

You would think with all the activity Tina, and I were experiencing while living in the Bothell house that one the questions we would have been asked would have been: are we experiencing any nightmares. We were never asked that question. Come to think about it, there were a lot of questions that never got asked. One question in particular was: how are you and Tina able to sleep? Crying, screaming, kicking, and waking up in a cold sweat multiple times in summer of 2013 – that was Tina. In the two years I've known Tina she's never woken up kicking and screaming. Not till after we moved into the Bothell house. The only thing I could do at the time was to put my arms around her. When I asked her what the dreams were about, she wouldn't tell me. The dreams I'm having right now in my new apartment I learned are called lucid nightmares. According to Patrick McNamara Ph.D., a lucid nightmare is when "the dreamer is aware he is dreaming and that the dream is a nightmare. The nightmare themes often involve demonic figures out to inflict terrible harm on the dreamer who struggles to wake up but can't." I didn't know what a lucid nightmare was until after I moved out of the Bothell house. I had already started having nightmares weeks before moving out of the house. Imagine having both — lucid nightmares and night terrors. I mean, interchangeably. If you ask me which is worse, the nightmares or the night terrors, honestly, I couldn't tell you.

The answer I want to know is why are my dreams are intensifying? The dreams I'm having now are worse than the dreams I had while living in the Bothell house. I would hope that they would be lessening. What are they like? Imagine Quintin Tarantino, Robert Rodriguez, James Cameron, Stephen Spielberg, and Eli Roth all working on a project together. The script they're working off of was written and prepared by *Death Note* creator Tsugumi Ohba. Try to imagine what that movie would look like? Got an idea? Now throw some gasoline and a match behind it. That's what my dreams look like now. These night terrors I'm about to discuss with you are unlike any other bad dream I've ever experienced. Every last one of them is demented and twisted. The dreams I've had before moving to the Bothell house I tend to forget about them within seconds of waking up. Not these dreams. These dreams I'm having now pause themselves the minute I wake up. There have been times where I've woken up kicking and screaming. I'm drying my eyes with whatever tissue I can find while fumbling my way to the kitchen for some cold water. I come back to the bedroom and lay back down. Knowing that it's going to take me thirty minutes or so to fall back asleep. There's that bad dream again. The terror that caused me to wake up in the first place is still here. Remember those movies were the bad guy hacks into the government computer mainframe and starts downloading files? That's what this feels like. Someone has found the password to all my memory files. The folder where all my life experiences are stored. My triumphs. My failures. My regrets. My loss. My fears. All that stuff I just mentioned is what makes me who I am. It's what makes you who you are. NOTE: I believe the spirits got to Rhonda this way.

What makes this an uncomfortable moment is the level of sloppiness that's taking place. Pulling one folder titled *Major argument with Dad* and inserting it into another folder titled *the day Dad died*. Doesn't cause you to wake up feeling warm and fuzzy. Quite the opposite. These pages and files are my memories, ladies and gentlemen. Thing's I forgot. Patrick McNamara Ph.D. says the dreamer "can discriminate the real from the unreal, so he is not insane.

The ability to reason and to engage in logical thought is intact. Access to the dreamer's autobiographical memories is intact. The ability to take on a third person perspective is intact, so the dreamer can consider, entertain, and imagine what another character in the dream is thinking or feeling as well. Indeed, whole interactions, dialogues between the dreamer and dream characters can take place just as in waking life." That last part, ladies and gentlemen, is where the tears begin to fall. Loved ones who died are back saying unforgivable things. Some of the words I heard as a kid growing up have now changed. Some have not. This act of stacking bad memories on top of bad memories while I'm trying to sleep is heartbreaking. These spirits know exactly what they're doing. Metaphorically they're raising the Titanic from the bottom of the ocean floor with the desired purpose of sinking it again. They're looking for a weakness. Chinks in the armor. Some of you might be wondering why I feel these dreams are demonic. I'll tell you – please study the picture below.

Question: What two parts of my bed (in the master bedroom) did Steve Mera pick up anomalies?
Answer: Foot of the bed and headboard area.

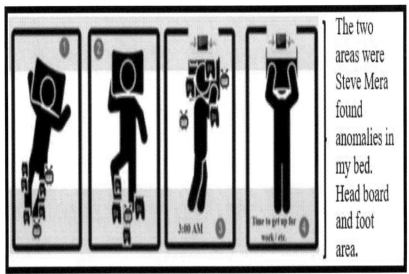

Fig 23.1: Poking and prodding – Night terror/nightmare sequence

1. I feel pulsating, breathing mattress lower leg area within seconds of lying down.
2. Usually doesn't let up or subside
3. I fall asleep. In my midst of toss/turning, I feel pulsation and heartbeats have migrated north.
4. I wake up (weekday/weekend) and find both heartbeats, and the pulsating mattress has intensified. My head feels heavy. Dizzy. Disoriented.

The poking and prodding didn't stop the day I moved out of the Bothell house. I was hoping it would, but it didn't. As the previous chapter demonstrated neither did the pulsating from inside the mattress. I explain in my book *The Bothell Hell House* that the poking and prodding is one of the extreme forms of being tormented. You thought death and taxes were unshakable. Pray you never have attachments. This is what keeps me up at night. Correction! It used to keep me up at night. I'm embarrassed to admit this, but I've learned to sleep through it. Or I try to at least.

Understand when it comes to malevolent activity regardless of how you deal with stuff everything tends to escalate. It's the ultimate dammed if you do, dammed if you don't type scenario that you can ever find yourself in. I started to notice within days of moving into my new apartment that the poking I feel in my rib cage and kidney area would begin sooner than usual. What used to start minutes after I've laid down in my bed has now turned into seconds. Doesn't matter which bedroom I'm sleeping in 👉 👉 👉 👉 👉 *non-stop*. What makes this a helpless situation is a realization that you have to fall asleep eventually. There's no getting around that. My alarm clock is going to wake me up at 5 AM regardless if I fall asleep or not. The question becomes how productive do I want to be at work tomorrow? Can you imagine an animal falling asleep while its predator hovers above him? That's exactly what this is. 3 AM is when the night terrors start. I'm telling you it's extremely weird. All that pulsating and throbbing I was feeling from underneath the mattress in and around my feet (before I fell asleep) has shifted to my pillow and headboard area. The same area where Steve Mera's compass was doing cartwheels. Let me share with you one of the darkest moments of my life.

Most of us who've attended funerals (our first funeral) attended due to a death occurring in the family. Not me. The first funeral that I attended was my best friend, Timothy Johnson's sibling's funeral. Law enforcement called it one of the most horrific murders in Austin, TX history. Still is in my opinion. "The Johnson Family Murder" March 4th, 1984 involved the brutal death of three children – ages fifteen, six, and three. Angela Barnado, 14; Timothy Johnson, 13; Yvette Johnson, 15; Tyrone Johnson, 6; and Tony Johnson, 3 were all asleep in their duplex when a murderer by the name of James Carl Lee Davis, age 21, broke in and proceeded to murder everyone. My best friend Timothy and his cousin Angela were the only ones who escaped with their lives. Timothy and I had developed a friendship while attending Pearce Junior High. We had gone into The Debbie's cake selling business together. Back then, the craze in our school was selling candy and Debbie cupcakes. Every morning Timothy and I would meet at the Safeway down the street from Pearce Jr. High. We'd both buy two boxes of the Debbie oatmeal pie box (which at that time cost seventy-nine and eighty- nine cents).

March 3rd, 1984, I decided to go to Mrs. Baird's bakery down the street from my house. That's where I met my best friend Timothy's two little brothers (for the first and last time). Tyrone and his younger brother Tony were at the cash register buying cupcakes. I knew right away; they were Timothy's brothers. They looked just like him. Something's wrong. *Why isn't the line moving?* I suddenly realized after hearing the conversation Tyrone and Tony were having with the bakery clerk that they didn't have enough money to buy the cupcakes they wanted. The cashier was getting irritated; they were tying up the line. He was this close to kicking Tyrone and Tony out of the store when suddenly I did something unexpected. I reached over Tyrone's shoulder and put a dollar bill on the counter. "I'll pay for it," I said. Tony, who is three years old, didn't understand the concept of paying for things. Let alone coming up short. The look he had on his face about possibly leaving that establishment without a cupcake was moving. All he wanted was his cupcake. Who can deny a three-year-old kid a cupcake? I can't.

So, I paid for Tyrone and Tony's cupcakes and let me tell you the look on Tony's face was priceless. Neither one of them said thank you to me, and you know what? They didn't have to. Timothy (their older brother) was my best friend. I'll never forget the look on Tony's face when he saw me reach over him and his brother. His face lit up like a Christmas tree. Might as well had been Bambi standing there. That's how handsome and delighted he looked. I walked out of the store twenty seconds later, and there was Tyrone and Tony, walking up the street while holding each other's hand. I don't know what compelled me to watch them as they walked up to the hill. But I did. They were about fifty yards from me now. Finally, Tony turned around and looked at me. I guess he felt me looking at him. He waved at me. I knew right then; he was saying thank you. *I thought to myself; I can't wait to see Timothy at school on Monday. I can't wait to tell him that I bought his two brothers some cupcakes. That's going to solidify us being business partners. I'll tell him about how it all went down and watch us both bust out laughing. I went home with four Debbie cakes oatmeal boxes. It's true they are cheaper in the bakery than they are at Safeway. Timothy's going to love this.*

Sunday, March 4th, 1984 – My mom and dad entered my room around 9 AM that morning. They'd never done that before. My dad was holding the front page of the Austin American Statesmen in his hand. I saw a familiar face on the front page. It was my best friend, Timothy. His mom was sitting next to him. He looked sad and distraught. His mom looked even worse. My brain couldn't compute. *What's going on? Why is Timothy on the front page of the Austin American Statesmen?* My dad looked at my mom to signal she should do most of the talking. "Keith, isn't this your friend Timothy?" I'm like yeah. That's when my mom replied, "Keith, Timothy's family was murdered last night. Someone broke into his mom's house and murdered his older sister and two younger brothers." When you're thirteen years old, you don't understand the word murder. At least I didn't. What do you mean Timothy's brothers and sister were murdered? Murdered how? Dad and Mom sat on the bed together and let me read the horrific story. You may want to take a deep breath right now.

Austin Texas -- A 13-year-old boy who feigned sleep while three members of his family were beaten to death with a lead pipe said the children had warned their mother about the suspect, a next-door neighbor. Police Sunday was holding James Carl Lee Davis, 21, without bond on capital murder charges in what one policeman described as the city's most brutal homicide since the 1966 Tower shootings. Officials said Davis, who was unemployed and had no criminal record, would undergo psychiatric examination. The children's mother, city employee Pauline Johnson, 35, was visiting a friend at the time of the killings. 'This is so unreal, so crazy,' she said. 'This seems like a <u>bad nightmare</u>.' Police Sgt. Lloyd Sigler said officers responded to a call about 1 a.m. Saturday at a northeast Austin duplex and found Yvette Johnson, 15; Tyrone Johnson, 6; and Tony Johnson, 3, dead from blows to the head. Investigators said the suspect entered the house through an unlocked back door and slipped into the bedroom of Angela Barnado, 14, a cousin of the slain children. 'I looked into his eyes, and <u>they had a demon look in them</u>,' Miss Barnado said. 'He didn't say a word. He just started hitting me. I tried to hit him with a glass that was on the nightstand, but he smashed my finger.' The girl said her screaming woke up the other children and their commotion diverted the suspect's attention while she fled. A brother of the victims, Timmy Johnson, 13, told investigators he pretended to be asleep while the suspect beat the other children to death. The Travis County Medical Examiner reported Yvette Johnson was raped before she was killed. Timmy Johnson said the children had been spooked by the suspect since he had moved into the duplex next door to live with his mother.' He'd tell us he'd killed for money,' Timmy Johnson said. 'It sort of messed with your brains the way he'd look at you.' Police arrived at the scene, then went next door and arrested Davis, who led them to a 2- foot length of lead pipe bearing traces of blood and hair, buried in the Johnsons' back yard. 'As far as the fierceness of the attack is concerned, I'd have to say it was the most brutal I've ever worked,' said Sgt. Ron McDavid. 'These children were defenseless. That's what was so brutal about it.' Officers said it was the worst homicide in the state capital since Aug. 1, 1966 - Austin American Statesmen – **More info at end of this book**

Timothy had been telling us at school for weeks how terrified he and his siblings were of their new neighbor. He said they always saw James Carl Lee Davis outside on his lawn practicing Judo. He'd be practicing with a lead pipe, Timothy said. The same pipe he used to murder Timothy's brothers and sister. What scared Timothy the most was James Carl Lee Davis' eyes. That and a statement James Carl Lee Davis made one day about killing all of them in their sleep. When Timothy told us this in art class, we didn't give it much thought. We were just kids at the time. Your next-door neighbor tells you he's going to kill you and your siblings in your sleep one night when you least expect it. You don't seriously think that's going to happen. Not when you're thirteen years old, you don't.

March 4th, 1984 was a rough Sunday for me. I realize (maybe a little bit too early in life) the horrors that men are capable of doing to another human being. To children. I had bought three-year-old Tony and six-year-old brother Tyrone cupcakes a few hours before their death. Their sister who I never met was raped, sodomized, and brutally beaten. Timothy survived by pretending to be dead. The official report said that James Carl Lee Davis walked into each room and began swinging. Tony and Tyrone had fallen asleep in their sister's room that night which was unfortunate. The killer then went into Timothy's room (after doing what I just described above) — tapped Timothy on his foot with the bloodied pipe. Timothy didn't move. The killer returned to the previous room and began killing again. Can you imagine what that looked like for all those individuals?

Five days later. I remember looking at my mom in the middle of the funeral ceremony and asking why there were pictures of Yvette, Tyrone, and Tony of top of each casket? Shouldn't the caskets be open? She wouldn't tell me till after we left the church. Her answer was short. "Closed caskets are done out of respect for the family.

Respect for the condition of the bodies." Why did I go to the funeral? Not necessarily knowing what I was getting myself into. I wanted to go. Timothy was my best friend. I knew I wasn't going to be able to talk to him. That's not why I went. I needed to see him. More importantly, I needed him to see me. I wanted him to know just by looking at me that I was here for him. We were business partners. The rumor going around at school was he and his mom we're moving back to California. I will continue selling Debbie cupcakes in your name! You're my best friend! Curse these demons for making me relive that horror. For making me relive that day. I'm seeing things (present-day) I've never seen before about that entire incident. The minions have figured out a way of taking me back to the night of the murder. To March 4th, 1984. That's the night terror. They say you never forget your first love. Your first kiss. I'll never forget my first best friend. I'll never forget the hand wave Tony gave me the minute he got up the hill near his house. He and his older brother Tyrone didn't know me from an atom. They didn't have to. I knew who I was. *I'm your brother from another mother! Now grab your cupcakes and hurry home. I'm sure we're be introduced sooner or later.* When Tyrone waved at me, that's what was in my head. That would be the first and last time I saw them.

I don't know who arranged it, but Timothy and I did finally meet after the funeral. He stepped forward from a horde of male family members and walked over to a bunch of us classmates. We hugged and shook hands. We all got around to exchanging a few words, and that was it. The deacons of the church came back ten minutes later and hurried him away. That was the last time I saw Timothy.

Fig 23.2: Memorial for Tyrone, Tony, and Yvette Johnson at Pecan Springs Elementary School – Austin TX. Erected 1984.

Fig 23.3: "The Johnson Family Murders" picture was taken in October 2018.

You might be asking yourselves, what's the relationship between this story and the phenomena known as attachments? Everything. Ask anyone who's had attachment, and they'll tell you their past experiences in life play more of a role in why they have attachments than whatever it is they're going through now. The things we've lived through. The things we've seen as children impacts us greatly. It leaves a lasting impression. The spirits accessed a period of my life I had forgotten. These past experiences are adhesives. The spirits have raised these past experiences to the surface sort of speak. Why did they do that? Short answer, they're looking for vulnerability, i.e., chinks in my armor if you will. They've uncovered acts of <u>rape</u>, <u>death,</u> and violence that are almost identical to the some of the horrors they've created. They now know the regret I have about that incident. My regret, if you can call it that, is me not being there. Timothy asked me that Friday before school let out if I'd be interested in spending the night with him. I told him I would need to ask my parents. And I did. I asked my mom when I got home. The first thing my mom said was, "ask your dad." I knew that was automatic no. My dad was never a big fan of his children having sleepovers with friends. But I asked him, anyway, hoping that he'd reconsider. He didn't. The answer was a flat-out no. That's why both my parents came into my bedroom that Sunday morning. I would have been in that house when the killer came in. I like to think Timothy, and I could have fought him off, but that's bravado talking.

James Carl Lee Davis had the element of surprise when he broke into that house. When you hit somebody with a lead pipe repeatedly, you've greatly hindered their ability to defend themselves. At the very least, you've knocked them out. The killer didn't even know if he'd killed Timothy already. That's how berserk he was. Had I been there lying next to Timothy I'm pretty sure he would have realized he hadn't. The cousin who got away said he had "demon eyes." That's what Timothy told us in class – weeks before his siblings died.

This murder happened over thirty-four years ago (at the time of this writing). It's inconceivable that I should be having these night terrors now. People who have dark attachments will tell you the experience is morbid. It's way more personal. More intimate than you can imagine. That's what this book is about. The demons attached to me have thrown me in a chair. Their talons are deep in me. 'Watch this! This is who we are. This is what we do. Watch the killer murder Tyrone and Tony. Watch the killer sexually assault the sister. Watch, watch, watch, and watch some more' I'm crying.

They're laughing. My only out is to wake up. Guess who's waiting for me when I wake up? You guessed it. The minions responsible for the pulsating mattress and phantom heartbeats. It feels like someone buried me under numerous pulsating sandbags while I was sleeping. Who out there wish this was happening to them? If you said 'me,' I think I know why. Investigators on television have done a poor job at explaining what this experience is really like. It's not glamorous at all. The spirits (at least the ones in my house) know who and what you are the minute you walk through the door. By the time you've pulled out your K2 meter, they've already decided if they want to interact with you or not. The morbid ones have already arrived at your home (while you're still at the client's house). Each spirit knows your life's history. They know it better than you do. Telling me that you "wish this was happening to you" doesn't prove to me that you're brave. It proves to me that you're ignorant. It proves to me that you don't have a grasp of what this stuff is. I keep a diary of every nightmare I have. There's no comparison to the dreams I'm having now and the dreams I had while living in the Bothell house. Naps? Oh, naps are worse. They're the worst of the worst. Why are the spirits doing this? Short answer: malevolent spirits are assholes. Long answer: they're looking for unresolved issues, i.e., skeletons in your closet. Malevolent spirits are good at exploiting weaknesses. Character flaws – regardless of age, is fair game. Things you might have regretted but may have forgotten. The spirits are pulling out all the bad experiences I ever had. They're combining this experience with other past experiences. Think of it as a spiritual mind-meld.

I don't want to keep reliving my father's death. My grandmother's death. I'm tired of seeing the biggest disagreement I ever had with my mom. The time she was most disappointed in me. I was seventeen years old then. My dad and I had a lot of falling outs up until the time of his death. I attribute that to us too much alike. My dad viewed our family as being a collective. Every decision is based on a unanimous vote – mainly his. I stopped believing in that once I turned twenty-one years old. Not all my siblings did. I'm tired of dreaming about those disagreements; I had with him and my twin brother. It riddles me why they've resurfaced all of a sudden. I remember the negative reaction I got from my siblings about me moving to Seattle.

None of my brothers agreed with the idea – going back to that collective mindset of if one person disagrees, we all disagree. I couldn't conform to that mindset. Therefore, I was out of there. I've moved past all of that stuff.

Who wants to relive that? I don't. I don't want to relive my first crush cheating on me. But I am. Those are the type of dreams I'm having right now. I wasn't having them while I lived in the Bothell house. I wasn't having them before I moved into the Bothell house. When the minions put me back in those situations, understand they're not putting me back in those situations as an adult. Oh no, that would be doing me a favor. The minions are taking me back to the mentality I had when these events were occurring. When my girlfriend (first crush) told me, she cheated on me; I was devastated. I decided to become promiscuous. Break as many hearts as I can. Better them than me. I held that belief for quite some time. It would be easy if I adopted that mindset while living in Seattle. I'd be the town _player_ if I did that. That's what the spirits are hoping for. They know before any life can be taken or misled; you must first succumb to your inner demons. You must be broken first.

These nightmares I've described. They're like a kaleidoscope of past and present experiences. Not all these experiences belong to me. That's right. Some of these dreams I'm having are of other people. I'm sometimes the fly on the wall. "The Johnson Family Murders" was one example of that. Then there are nightmares of people I don't even know. Talk about weird on top of weird. The people are so real as are the environments. If I didn't know any better, I would say those specific nightmares are from individuals these spirits have already encountered. Or encountering right now. Very similar to what I was talking about earlier about objects appearing in the Bothell house that Tina and I didn't own. Who's to say consciousness, i.e. dreams, etc. can't be teleported. Based on what I'm seeing when my eyes are closed, I'm telling you that might be possible. One spirit I encountered (in the coming chapter) admitted as such. Astrophysics having never been inside a black hole often theorize what the experience would be like. If I'm to understand the description correctly, things go horribly wrong inside a black hole. Up is down. Down is up. Left is right. Right is left. Everything inside "curves infinitely." That's kind of what my dreams are like. I'm both infinitely powerful and infinitely weak. Infinitely sensitive and infinitely insensitive. Success, failures, grief, happiness, death, life, fear, and lust. All of that zooming by my eyes at a speed of a thousand frames per second — in the course of one night.

Fig 23.4: Spring 2015 - Countless psychedelic dreams involving a very muscular shadow demon with claws yanking me through the windshield of my car

CHAPTER 24

Keith

".... a person's name is, to that person, the sweetest and most important sound in any language."
Dale Carnegie, How to Win Friends and Influence People

I can't have you believing everything I've gone through has been all doom and gloom. I'm glad to be out of the Bothell house. Four years is a long time to be walking on eggshells. I can't tell you which is better where I live now or where I lived previous because the experience is different. The horror's Tina and I had in the Bothell house fall under what people call a poltergeist infestation. A vast majority of it all was physical. Yes, there were mental elements. Some that Tina and I will probably never be made aware of. What's happening now is both mental and spiritual. The spirits are coming at me from multiple angles for the sole purpose of wearing me down. Attachment aside, I have a pretty good life. A blessed life. I'm still alive. I still have my health. My work-lifestyle balance is the best it's ever been. I've been with the company that I work for going on six years. I've had multiple performance reviews at work. I've passed all of them with flying colors. Have the spirits encroached upon my workplace? Oh yeah! They've shown up at my job a few times. How do my co-workers feel about all of this? Some of them refuse to get on the elevator with me — those that know about the Bothell house. Some have done their research. Most of my friends are not aware of the dreams I'm having. They think the hauntings stopped due to me moving out of the house. I want to tell them so bad that it hasn't. Why don't I tell them?

I guess it has to do with my fear of being given a stigma. One of the reasons why Maria Jose Ferreira decided death was a better alternative to living was because of the reaction from people around her. You have no idea what it's like having an attachment. It's sort of like spiritual solitary confinement. I've had friends sever ties with me as a result of Tina and me living in the Bothell house. These were people that I loved. Can you imagine the friendships I would lose if they learn I had attachments? I can. That scares me. The friends I have now? They see me out and about. They see me advancing career-wise at work. They see me at social events. We're always together, my friends and me. If we're not in a wine bar somewhere, we're in a restaurant. If we're not in Portland, we're in Austin. If we're not in Austin, we're in Vancouver. Every city I visit with my friends or with my co-workers has a hotel room. Every hotel room has a bed in it. When I lie down and go to sleep, guess who's there? The spirits.

These wine tasting events I attend with my friends. They're spectacular. I use these weekend getaways with the guys as a way of relieving stress. Guess what? It works. It does work. But reality does set in eventually. These social events are not infinite. Parties have to end, right? My married friends hug and kiss me and say, "Oh, what a night it's been. Let's do this again soon!" And we do. We always do. But it's time to leave. It's time for everyone to go home. Oh, not quite though. The single men (that includes me now) want to keep the night going. You know I'm not in a hurry to get home. So, we keep the night going for a few more hours. That has to end, too, eventually. Now my single guy friends are ready to go home. Everyone's ready to go home. Look at what time it is. It's 3 AM. Even the adult clubs have closed.

I wonder how many of my friends (both sexes) have seen their passenger seat-belt light go on and off in the middle of the night while they're driving home? How many have walked to where their car was parked and found every car door open? Or found their car lights flashing all at once? Every car light imaginable! I wonder how many have witnessed their garage door open by itself as they pull up to the house. That's what I experience after a night on the town with my friends. I don't necessarily view it as doom and gloom. I could. But I don't.

I'm still alive. I still have my health. I wish it would stop, though. I'm on the highway driving home. The night terrors will be arriving in a few hours. If I had to choose which I would get rid of first the nightmares or the night terrors, I would choose nightmares over night terrors in a heartbeat (pun intended). That doesn't mean the night terrors aren't bad. They're bad! As dreams go, they're about the worst thing you can experience. The emotion you have after waking up resembles the feelings you have after a loved one has died. These night terrors I'm having are horrific. That being said if I you gave me a choice as to which dream category to get rid of, I would choose nightmares first. Weird, I know. It might not be as weird as you think. Try to hear me out. The nightmares I'm having are a threat to my spiritual wellbeing. The spirits in charge of creating the night terrors would love nothing more than to see me go off the deep end as a result of their torment. That's how they define success. 'Keith, you're going to have night terrors for the rest of your life so you might as well jump off a bridge. Why don't you end your life right now?' That's what they suggest. But they have competition, ladies, and gentlemen. It might be a shock to some of you – others it might not be. Demons compete with each other. They share the ultimate goal, which is ruining and ending lives. Each spirit (depending on rank) has a different way of achieving that goal. The goal is the same, but the method is not. Try not to think of their methods as being harsh or less harsh than their counterpart. No, it's much more sinister. The analogy I would use would be the analogy of playing with your food. I could be wrong, but the ones in charge of creating nightmares seem to prefer acquiescence over acts of suicide. If you think about it long enough, it makes sense. Regardless of life's success and failures. We still die. That's one thing we all probably can agree on. In the spirits' mind — taking your soul now versus when you're on your death bed are essentially the same thing. To some, it's just a contest of sooner rather than later. Acquiesce, Keith – give up your soul willingly. That's the feeling I get after I wake up from a night of nightmares. The nightmares are not violent. Most of the nightmares I have bring extreme pleasure. That, ladies and gentlemen, are what scares me the most!

I'm averaging about four nightmares a week: nightmares, not night terrors. Weekends are the worst – probably because that's when I try to sleep in. Both nightmare and night terror tend to overlap during the weekend. They're like two tornadoes forming north and south of a town only to merge at the center of the city. Nightmare and night terror operating as one is nuts. As you can see from looking at Table 24.1, I rarely have a dream-free night. It's either nightmare, night terror or both. Let's talk about the most frequent nightmare of all. The nightmare that begins with the word 'Keith.'

Sunday	Monday	Tuesday	Wednesday	Thursday	Friday	Saturday

Night Terrors
Nightmares
Both
Nothing

Table 24.1: Number of nights when nightmares and night terrors occur. Exact days vary.

5 AM May 9th, 2016 – I was sleeping in my bed when all of a sudden, I heard 'Keith.' It came from out of thin air. As soon as I heard it, my eyes shot open. This sounded real. I immediately rose from my bed and started looking around. I know this voice. This is a female's voice. The voice sounded Irish.

I've heard my name called when I was living in Bothell house numerous times. Tina and I both did. Tina and I thought we were calling one another. We soon learned that it was the spirits themselves that were calling us. This was their definition of a prank. What I just heard was not a prank. This is something more, how can I say it, seductive. How close did it feel? The voice was positioned right above the tragus portion of my ear. That's where I felt a warm breath. Yes, the 'Keith' voice came with a warm breath. Fast forward a few weeks. I was sleeping in the guest bedroom now. Something whispered 'Keith' in my ear again. Exactly like before. My reaction was different this time. I was so sleepy and tired that I decided just to lay there. Color me tired. That's all it was. The spirit seized on my level of fatigue. Talk about the art of disarming someone. Hearing your name called in the dead of night in your ear by a sexy voice, in my opinion, is the perfect aphrodisiac. An ambient, angelic voice followed by a subtle wind, which was undoubtedly a breath of air. Pardon me, but I'm having a hard time deciding which was sexier. The female voice or the warm breath of air that came with it. How close is it? Very close.

Had a real woman climbed into bed and did that exact thing, we'd be making love right now. I'd be open to anything sexually. ANYTHING! That's how seductive the voice was.

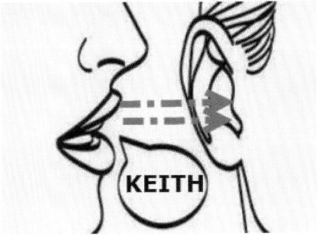

Fig 24.1: 'Keith' whispers in the early morning hours.

My reward for just lying there was something I would never have expected. I felt the mattress dip a little bit. This indentation in the mattress was different than the ones the minions create. This was significantly heavier. It felt like a person was climbing into bed with me. This is a dream. It has to be. Right? Whatever this is, it successfully draped itself over me. There was no paralysis whatsoever. I was not being held down at all. I felt relaxed. *Too relaxed!* The whisper I heard didn't cause me to jump. Why would it? It was my name being uttered. It was uttered sensually. My brain was trying its best to understand it. It was trying to ascertain if it should execute the fight or flight response when suddenly it happened. A kiss. Something just kissed me on the lips.

A warm wet peck. Time to wake up! I have to admit I hadn't been kissed like that in a long time. *A long time!* I know a real kiss when I feel one. This was a real kiss. Based on the woman I've dated; this was a woman with luscious lips. *My favorite.* Before you ridicule me for accepting a beautiful kiss like that, ask yourself the question. How could I have avoided it? I couldn't. I didn't see it coming. I'm not sure what just happened. I've had women whisper in my ear a few times. I know the warm air associated with it. I felt that just now. The kiss too. I felt that as well. But let's put the kiss on the back burner for a while. I want to share with you several EVPs I captured as a result of this incident. That's right, I got some EVPs. EVPs of the female voice. One of the first things I do when an event like this occurs is to reach for one of my voice recorders. The ones I have stationed by the bed. Remember I'm still conducting experiments. The EVPs I captured below took place within six months of me living in my new apartment. One experiment which you already know of involved the touch-activated teddy bear.

Title	YouTube
Washington State Haunting	https://www.youtube.com/watch?v=BmkMoc1plIU *00:12 'Keith' August 2016*
Demons in Seattle - Female, Male EVP.	https://www.youtube.com/watch?v=tD8GVmCi7C_0 *The female voice at 00:04 "Keith" Male voice at 1:31 "Keith" August 2016*
*Haunted House - Keith EVP	https://www.youtube.com/watch?v=Ks4hRTY7kE_E *00:37 'Keith' September 2016*
*Haunted House - Keith EVP	https://soundcloud.com/user-423872078/loud-keith-evp *00:37 'Keith' September 2016*
Demons in Seattle - Keith	https://www.youtube.com/watch?v=KsqlPa2Ytt4 *01:56 'Keith' January 2017*

Table 24.2: * Highest quality 'Keith.'

How many 'Keith' voices have I heard since living in my new apartment? Impossible to count. They happen at different times of the day. That's why I have voice recorders (that run constantly). That should give you an idea as to how often this happens. I'm very picky when it comes to paranormal equipment. I can't just go out and buy any old voice recorder. I have to buy the best. I have to buy the gear that the industry speaks highly of. The industry speaks highly of Zooms. Highly of Tascam's.

ZOOM
https://www.zoom-na.com/

Tascam
https://tascam.com/us/

The point I want you to understand about the 'Keith' voices is they were happening morning, noon, and night. I hear a female voice whispering 'Keith' in the middle of me ironing my clothes. In the middle of me cooking dinner. Seconds before I fall asleep. I hear a female whisper my name while I'm sleeping. I hear a female voice - a sexy angelic voice within seconds of waking up. I even hear it when I'm taking a shower. Even at work.

https://www.youtube.com/watch?v=Ks4hRTY7kEE
00:37 'Keith.'

The 'Keith' voices, unfortunately, are not the most interesting thing going on. Multiple things are going on. The one I want to talk about now that might have been overlooked is the accent. Did you catch it? It's OK if you didn't. I didn't catch it either. Not the first few times I heard it I didn't. I combine these voices with the voices I hear while I'm going about my daily routine and I noticed something. Why are the spirits pronouncing my name wrong? How can you mispronounce the word, Keith? It's only one syllable. Why are they leaving off the **th** sound? My nieces and nephews when they were toddlers used to call me 'Uncle Key'. It took them a while to under the true pronunciation of the word. It's a natural development humans go through when learning the English language. This is where my book *The Bothell Hell House* comes in. Go back to the UK's first investigation!

https://q13fox.com/2016/02/15/bothell-home-haunted-by-poltergeists-parapsychologists-have-proven-it-resident-says/

February 2016 – ".... A team from the Scientific Establishment of Parapsychology just released their report that says the disturbances and noises in Keith Linder's home may be from **Irish settlers.**"

Steve Mera and his chief researcher Don Philips surmised that based on the number of EVPs they found; the majority of the EVPs had Irish accents. As you know from reading this book, we dug deep into the history of Bothell Washington. We dug deep into the neighborhood this house was built on and discovered a percentage of Bothell's residents migrated from Ireland. That revelation has never been more important to me than now. Irish people, ladies and gentlemen, have an almost impossible time pronouncing the **th.**

"There is no **th** sound in Irish (Gaelic), the broad Irish d covers a range of sound from d to dh (soft th = /ð/), and the broad Irish t covers a range of sound from t to th (hard th = /θ/). Before English influenced Irish speakers, Irish-speaking brains were hard-wired to process d and dh as the same sound, and also to process **t** and **th** as the same sound, much as Japanese people process l and r as one sound and cannot differentiate between them without extra training. When Irish speakers first started learning English a few hundred years ago, they approximated the **dh** and **th** sounds to the d and t of their native language and that is how the accent of their dialect arose. That dialect is sometimes called Hiberno-English."

https://www.quora.com/Why-cant-Irish-speakers-many-who-have-been-using-English-all-their-lives-pronounce-the-English-th-sound-correctly.

Th doesn't exist in the Irish language. That's why the EVPs sound like 'Kei' instead of Keith. January 2016, medium Karissa Fleck conducted an EVP session on the back patio of the Bothell house. She asked how many shadow people were out on the patio with her. The response she got was 'three.' To some, it sounded like 'tree.' In my book *The Bothell Hell House*, I made a note that the child sounded like he had a lisp. That lisp altered his enunciation of the word **th**ree. I didn't know then what I know now. It's not a lisp. Irish people have difficulty with the **th**- sound.

Demons in Seattle – 'Three' EVP
https://www.youtube.com/watch?v=IJdqk8xPKVE
1:02 'Three/Tree'

This is why I post evidence online. Viewers on my YouTube channel bought this to my attention while I was writing this book. Had I not shared all this information (including the information obtained by Karissa and others) the dots might have never been connected.

As it exists today

... In the Kennard Corner neighborhood (where Tina and I lived) in Bothell, WA, residents most commonly identify their ethnicity or ancestry as Mexican (17.5%). There are also several people of German ancestry (13.8%), and residents who report Asian roots (13.6%), and some of the residents are also of English ancestry **(7.3%), along with some Irish ancestry residents** *(7.0%), among others. In addition, 28.7% of the residents of this neighborhood were born in another country.*

Bothell Kennard-Corner

Irish in Washington — The Early Years (the 1840s to 1890)

CHAPTER 25

Nightmares

"... In this world, is man ever able to possess anything more solid,
than a dream?"
Berserk Animae

If you think about it, it kind of makes sense why I would be hearing 'Keith' during the deepest hours of my sleep. Science has proven hearing one's name called causes immense activation in certain regions of the brain. "The medial prefrontal cortex is responsible for many of the important processes that make you, you. Many of these processes run in the background or are in a resting or autopilot state. They aren't processes you'd actively control, but your brain reacts to them in predictable patterns that help form your identity and personality. Researchers have discovered that there is unique brain activation when a subject hears their name. This pattern is very similar to patterns that were observed in patients in a persistent vegetative state (PVS)." You heard it correctly. People in a vegetative state have been shown to have immense brain activity after hearing their name. If a PVS person can have brain activity after hearing their name, imagine the activity taking place in a person who is asleep. Imagine their subconscious response. "A PVS is defined as a condition in which awareness of both the self and the environment is absent. Patients in PVS are unable to move, speak, identify others, and in some cases, even open their eyes." But their brain still responds to its name being called. Dale Carnegie "lecturer and developer of famous courses in self- improvement," said it best when he said: "...a person's name is, to that person, the sweetest and most important sound in any language." He's right. Whispering my name in my ear at 3 AM lowers my inhibitions. It removes it. Think about it – a beautiful voice has just whispered 'Keith.' The whisper sounded like artists **Claudia Brücken**. I hate to admit it, but I became instantly aroused. The warmth and coldness of her breath leave you no choice but to be turned on. The air coming from what I hope is her mouth is extremely soothing. We're talking only a few centimeters away. I know what it feels like to have a woman lay on you. I know the feeling quite well. This is not sleep paralysis. I'm not being held down. I don't feel fixated. I feel at ease. I feel bliss. I have to admit the first few times this happened to me I was startled. I'm thinking *where is this going? What's happening?* Then poof! The sensation (the dream) is gone. Whoever this is that's approaching me knows to scatter at the slightest signal of refusal. It's like she has to obey the word 'no' even when I've not mentioned it. She leaves based on my body reacting the wrong way. You would think they would take that as a form of rejection. I'm shaking my head in disbelief. They don't. They come back. The spirits (if I can call them that) know better than me that it's all about breaking me down. It's about lowering my defenses. When she says 'Keith' she's not saying 'Keith,' she's saying 'relax, chill, let me take care of you.' That first kiss scared the crap out of me. Do you know why it scared the crap out of me? I live here by myself. Who in the world is saying 'Keith?' I noticed my body was fighting less and less after each visit. That scares me. If this spirit looks anything like she sounds, I'm in trouble. Deep trouble.

If you want to understand how this disarmament dance works, you need to look no further than man's most hated parasite: the mosquito. That's right, the mosquito. The steps a mosquito takes to abstract blood from its victim is interesting. The first thing a mosquito does when <u>she</u> bites you is release saliva. This saliva is nature's anticoagulant, i.e., blood thinner. It's also an anesthetic. The mosquito numbs that section of the skin it's about to drink from. Think about it. How successful would a mosquito be if all they did was stick us? We'd feel their needle going in and slap ourselves immediately. That doesn't help the mosquito out. The mosquito needs a little bit of a head start. Nature has blessed the mosquito with an anesthetic.

This anesthetic, i.e., saliva makes the host unaware of their blood being drained. On a spiritual level, it lowers their inhibitions. That's what's happening with me. So, this ephemeral spirit enters my bedroom (enters me). It never changes its tactic. I hear a female voice whispering 'Keith' right above my ear. It's happening over and over. Care for a more erotic example? Here it comes. Have you ever watched those old Count Dracula foreign films? Have you ever noticed the woman's reaction? It's interesting how the women slowly but surely begin unclothing themselves as Count Dracula draws near? The Count is not even in its victims' room yet, and their clothes are already off. Neck and breast are slowly exposed. Totally accessible. The women (in their sleep state) are enablers to the wonderful that's about to happen. That's kind of where I'm at right now. I'm not going out of my way to say yes, but I'm not saying no either. I'm asleep. The communication between these spirits and myself is mental. If I had to guess I would say, there's some form of telepathy taking place. I can almost hear several female voices say, 'he's not objecting to us being here.'

Let me tell you the second these spirits realize you're not going to put up a fight. Game on. The dream I'm having suddenly takes on a life of its own. Euphoria on steroids. Imagine having a non-stop orgasm. That's the only way I can describe it. I can feel myself being physically mounted. That voice I heard suddenly takes shape. A beautiful woman has just appeared. She manifests right on top of me. The lower me. The best parts about her are all within inches of my hands and lips. It never occurred to me that a man could be caressed this way. That I could be caressed this way! So gingerly and delicate. Based on how she's kissing and massaging me you would think I was the hardest working man in the world. I embarrass myself by trying to speed things up. I lean in for a kiss. Her eyes tell me no. Don't move. Don't speak. She resumes what she was doing before I rudely interrupted her. Unbelievable kisses and massages. This unbelievable amount of physical attention I'm getting feels like an eternity. And she's just starting. What I call act one – eventually does give way to act two. Act one was all about satisfying me — disarming me. Get me used to the idea of having sexual relationships with them. They've been providing me unbelievable pleasure for weeks now. Unbelievable eye-candy. When I tell you I'm drowning in cleavage, I mean that. I'm drowning in kisses. Drowning in 'Keith' whispers – oh yeah that verbal anesthetic has not been turned off. How did they know what my fetishes were? How did they know I was a breast guy? How did they know that my fantasy (since childhood) is to be in a bed with several women with 36DD breasts? Teardrop-36DD's. Smooth skin. Luscious lips. Emerald eyes. How did they know this would get me? They know because they've (maybe not them specifically but others like them) have been coming through my mind for quite some time. Those mornings where I woke up with an extreme headache after a rough night of being poked and prodded are precursors to what's happening now.

Act Two is the spirits switching positions. By positions, I mean switching focus. Up until now, the focus has been centered on kissing me all over. Nibbling my ear to the point of me screaming *take me, take me, take, take me*. What is all of this? It's a sexcapade that's what it is. When I said, I was being mounted by what I can only describe as being the most beautiful women in the world. I didn't mean in order to have sex. That hasn't happened yet. I have to say, what they're doing now if it was real would put sex out of business. There's so much tantalizing going on right now. So much teasing. I could very easily become the universe's next Big Bang. I could pop any minute now. That's how close to the edge they've gotten me. 'We're not going to let you inside us yet.' That's the message being sent with each hand stroke across my manhood. Then something unexpected happens. This woman that's been loving me and leaving me each morning (on edge) for weeks, succumbs to her tantalization. This woman with the juiciest lips you can imagine leaned in toward me. The breath I smelt as a result of her opening up her mouth reminded me of a field trip I took as a kid to a cotton candy factory. When a woman rests on her tongue on the edge of her lower lip while sitting on top of you, you know she's ready to connect with you. What happens next reminds me of a shotgun kiss. Have you ever gotten a shotgun kiss? I have.

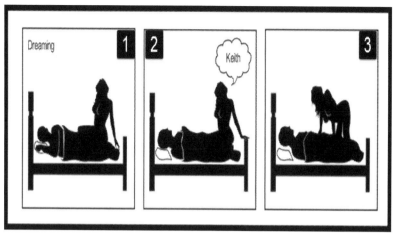

Fig 25.1: 1.) Dreaming 2.) 'Keith' whisper mattress weighs down 3.) Something draws nearer.

My ex-girlfriend (in Texas) gave me one when I was in high school. They're amazing if done right. This is not that though. This a shotgun kiss in reverse. Instead of breathing smoke into me (like my ex did), the spirit began breathing air out of me. She was extracting something from me. It felt amazing. *Take me. Take me now. Take all of me. I'm yours.* RED ALERT. My desire to be their food reached the desk of what I call my spiritual committee. I would describe this as a spiritual defense mechanism. Bells and whistles start going off. ABORT! My spiritual antibodies kicked into high gear and shut down everything. As I'm gasping for air, my eyes popped open. I was awake now — God's truth. I heard the mattress squeak (the sound it makes when someone gets on or off the bed) while my eyes were opening. Something was on the bed with me. Did I just drink a gallon of dark black coffee or something? I'm so out of it right now. So jittery. It's not even funny. *What just happened?* Can someone tranquilize me, so I can back to sleep? I want to pick up where I left off. Notice how quickly my response has changed? I told you they know what they're doing.

Let's RECAP everything you read in this book so far:
- Water puddles morning after I moved in
- Electrical issue with household appliances

- The electrical issue in the car
- Night terrors / nightmares
- Poking and prodding
- Heartbeats
- Mattress indentations
- Shadowy figures here and elsewhere (coming up in the next chapter)

Heraclitus said, "No man ever steps in the same river twice, for it's not the same river, and he's not the same man." The same thing can be said about dreams. The demoness's mission, if one can call it that, is to by-pass my spiritual defenses. Bring me to the point where I'm spiritually vulnerable. Are we talking possession? I don't know. What is possession? I've seen the movie The Exorcists. I've seen Stigmata and the movie Emily Rose. Neither comes close to resembling what I just experienced. Why am I not surprised though?

I've tried everything I can think of to rid myself of this attachment. Lavender, Epson, Kosher, and other types of salt baths. You name it I've tried it. Everything's failed. I've participated in multiple cleansing sessions. Have been laid hands on and prayed over by various clergies. Various shamans. I'm embarrassed to admit that I paid some of them. Which I'm told you should never do. Everyone I've talked to says they can remove these attachments I have. The problem remains.

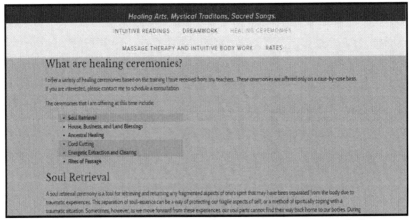

Fig 25.2: Screenshot of cleansing services I attended.

Soul Retrieval

*A soul retrieval ceremony is a tool for retrieving and returning any fragmented aspects of one's spirit that may have been separated from the **body due to traumatic experiences**. This separation of soul-essence can be a way of protecting our fragile aspects of self or a method of spiritually coping with a traumatic situation. Sometimes, however, as we move forward from these experiences, our soul parts cannot find their way back home to our bodies. During a soul retrieval, these parts can be retrieved and returned to the body to be reintegrated, thus restoring well-being and wholeness. The coping mechanism of soul fragmentation could be triggered to occur because of injury, abuse, an accident, addiction, feeling unsafe for prolonged periods of time, the loss of someone close to us, or any situation that results in trauma. Symptoms of Soul Fragmentation could include - feelings of anxiety, apathy, obsession, depression, fear, paranoia. Suicidal thoughts and/or actions. Uncontrollable emotions, or emotions that do not dissipate. Disconnection from our ability to feel and/or express our emotions. Panic attacks. Addiction. Blocks in creativity. Being afraid to socialize and/or go out into the world. An inability to **"get over" a relationship** or put **an event behind us**. The pervasive sense that we are missing something, or that we are not living the life we are meant to live. The ceremony lasts 3-4 hours.*

Cord Cutting

A ceremony to help clear any energetic connections or "cords" between you and another person, place, or experience.
The ceremony can be combined with other ceremonies or scheduled on its own for 60 minutes.
Energetic Extraction and Clearing

A healing ceremony focused on clearing from your body and spirit any non-self-energy that you may have picked up during your life from another person, place, specific event, your ancestral line, a disembodied spirit, or by coming in contact with an item that carries invasive energy. The ceremony can last 60 to 120 minutes.

Forget what I said earlier about demons coming back. I was wrong. Demons don't come back. They never leave. And that's an important thing to call out. Tina and I had an enormous amount of activity in 2012. I'm talking weeks within us moving into the Bothell house. 2013, for a while, was quiet. Then January 2nd, 2014, came and the rest, as they say, is history. If someone wants to know what the house occupant thinks, ask me, and I'll tell you. In my opinion, the spirits don't leave. No, they buy their time.

'Keith' that's what I hear when I'm sleeping. An ambient female voice. I've become numb to it. That's how often it happens. I don't even turn away from the whisper anymore. What's the point? I can't swing at them. I can't curse at them. I can't yell at them. I've tried that. Doesn't work. Screaming lets the minions know their tactic is working. I can't do that. I know what I'll do. I'll ignore it. I'll add a few more prayer lines into the prayers I'm already saying. Does that work? Nope. *Uh oh*, She's back and oh my god! She's not alone. One week later, this woman (same description as before) has been riding me for what feels like an eternity. If I didn't know any better, I'd say I was going in and out of consciousness. That's how intoxicating their love is. I'm being propped up against my headboard by two beautiful women. Its dreams stacked on top of dream at this point.

These women have been switching places throughout the night. I wish I could tell you at what point I started sucking on her nipples, but I can't. I can't remember when the demonesses started letting me do that. Everything I do to them requires permission. We're pretty much feeding each other at this moment. Each one of the ladies (when it's their turn) kisses to initiate extraction of what I can only believe to be my essence, i.e., my soul. Something in my head says *Keith, this is wrong; this shouldn't be happening. Get out. Get out. Resists this!* It's more of an internal instinct than a voice. Something inside me starts combating the 'Keith' whispers I keep hearing. It's what wakes me up. I'm shivering like a leaf. I feel disheveled. I'm head heavy and dehydrated. What happened tonight was different than the previous nights. Up until now the order in which things unfold has been: 'Keith' whisper → Mattress indentations → Movement towards me → A woman manifests top of me → We start making out → Passionate kisses → Euphoria → Extraction → Energy drainage → My soul fights back → They're gone. I'm being visited by scantily clad women several times a week now. No matter what bedroom I sleep in, they're there.

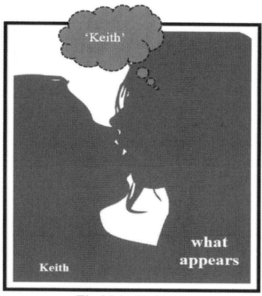

Fig 25.3: 'Keith'

I wake up and find these beautiful women already making love to me. I couldn't give you the first letter of the English alphabet if my life depended on it. That's how drunk I am – drunk of euphoria. Imagine waking up in the arms of three (whatever your taste is) women. Each one knows your sexual desires better than the woman who just mounted off you. Love making → Passionate kisses → Energy drainage → The extraction lasts longer each time → My soul fights back → Poof. They're gone. Do you understand why I said earlier that if given a choice as to which dreams to get rid of, I would choose nightmares? The night terrors are horrible. Evil is how I would describe it. There's a noticeable difference between the night terrors and the nightmares. One is all sexual, and the other is pure torment. Are all my dreams sexual in nature? Not all of them. I doubt I'd be here if they were. That's how taxing these sexcapades have become. The dreaming sleeps I've shared so far make up about twenty percent of all dreams I'm having.

Forty percent of my nightmares have to do with family dysfunction. Demons love that. It doesn't matter if the disagreement is minuscule or major. They come running. The remaining nightmares are about mostly current event stuff. I'm having a hard time sharing this story I'm about to share. It's dark, and it's for lack of better word nuts! Promise me two things. Number one – say a prayer before going to bed. Second – try not to judge me too harshly. I'm just a human being (like yourself). I said I would not pull any punches or sugar coat what it is I've been through. Pulling punches about the supernatural doesn't do anyone any good.

Your reasons for buying this book might have to do with your own experience. The experience might have affected you greatly. Maybe a family member of yours had an experience, and you were there when it happened. Some of you are just curious. I get that. You have a right to be curious. Whatever reason you have for buying this book, understand everything you've read so far and will read moving forward is the truth. No more. No less. It's important I reiterate that before diving into the next encounter.

2016 - 2019 - The dreams I'm having. The ones that have me making love with scantily clad women had changed without my knowing. My name being called was once the precursor to all sexual encounters. Not anymore. The only time I hear my name being called now is after the ladies are done. Whatever this dream state this is that I'm in has me waking up with the women already done. That part where I feel my energy being drained – the part where my lips are clasped to theirs. I used to watch that from beginning to end. Not anymore. I find myself waking up right when the kiss is over. My defense mechanism that used to go off. It's gone. That jittery feeling, I had after breaking off the sexual contact. That's gone too. What's replaced it is extreme fatigue. I've been going at it with this succubus without my knowledge for hours. I'm drained and relaxed. Fatigue notwithstanding, I feel pretty damn good. This woman who's been riding me for quite sometime raises herself off me so my manhood can slip out of her. She starts peddling backward. I can see all of her now. She's gorgeous. I can tell my lips have been all over her breasts based on the number of hickeys she has.

Fig 25.4: Unbelievable affection and attention being given

Just when I was beginning to get my wits about me, I hear a female voice say, 'Thank you.' *What did I do? Thank me for what?* I'm not sure if I uttered those words or if I thought those words. I'm not sure of anything right now. Before I could determine if the voice, I heard was an actual voice or a voice somehow implanted in my subconscious, a similar voice popped in saying 'for giving me your essence.' I was so at peace right now. I could barely make out what she said. She's so freaking beautiful! This woman leans towards me and kisses me smack on the lips and poof! She's gone. It might be difficult for some people to imagine, but it's like a dream inside a dream. I could have sworn my eyes were already open because this woman that's gone now. I saw her as plain as day. I felt her weight on top of my body. Her lips were warm and wet. I opened my eyes for real this time, and there I was lying on my back. The sun was piercing my bedroom window, indicating it was time for me to get up. *Time to go to work.* If you told me all I had to do was leave a bedroom light on to get that particular woman back here, I would do that. But I don't have to do that. They always come back. I rarely get the same woman twice. By twice I mean two times in a row. What triggers this? I don't know. I'm in a deep dream sleep when all of a sudden, I feel my energy being drained. I can feel it being pulled from deep inside me. Like I said before this is not sleep paralysis. Others have spoken about a force holding them down. If anything, I'm being held up. I'm so at ease. I'm so eager to be loved. I get the idea that this woman that's kissing me profusely would love to keep going. But she can't. The rules (some code they have) says that she can't or that she shouldn't. 'You can't kill him.' I'm gasping for air. I open my eyes and see this sensual woman's lips suctioned to mine. I'm looking dead at her. *She's not letting go. She doesn't want to stop. Even I know this is not how it's supposed to go. She must be new to this or something. She's not supposed to drain me this long. Suddenly she realizes that I was right, and she was wrong. She's been draining too long. She lets go of my lips and repositions herself.* I could count every eyelash on her. That's how close we were. Wow! She tops them all. *Can we do that again?* I just woke up and found the most beautiful woman on the planet making out with me. She and others like her at times don't want to stop. But they have to. I'm almost sure of it. I want to reach out and touch this woman's hair so bad, but I can't. I'm scared of what might happen. Can someone hand me the book that lists what I can and cannot do? Am I allowed to initiate a kiss with her? Can I return the favor? Those are the questions I was asking myself. I could easily fall asleep again. That's how weak and tired I was. Just when I was about to doze off, I hear a 'thank you.' It's the sweetest voice imaginable. The mattress rose a little, indicating whoever was sitting on my bed was now gone. I woke up a few hours later thinking *that was the best sleep ever.*

I believe I'm going to work from home today. That's exactly what I'm going to do. I should not be behind a steering wheel. Not after the night I just had. My legs feel like spaghetti. Who taught these demonesses how to fuck? Who taught them how to kiss? Kissing, in my opinion, is the best form of foreplay. It's the ultimate connection in my opinion. Making out with these women surpasses anything I've ever experienced.

The word is out that Keith puts out. Keith's a willing participant. My name and the address of where I live must be written on a restroom in hell somewhere. I'm averaging three visits a week now. Oh, it gets worse. Way worse. I wake up (in my dream) now and find several women on top of me. Two heads are bobbing up and down below my waist. One woman has aligned her lips with mine. She's extracting what they keep referring to as my "essence." Between me and my headboard are two other women. They're holding me up – that's right, they got me propped up against their bosoms. *Which is a great place to be, I might add.* Whoever extracts from me last is responsible for laying me back down. By the time the last lady gets done with me, her friends are usually long gone. 'Keith' and 'thank you' that's what I hear as I'm being laid back down. For some odd reason, this demoness has decided to stick around longer. I feel myself slipping out of her. Something's going on. The woman in front of me utters that she's 'from LA.' I thought to myself. *The only LA I know is Los Angeles.* I seriously thought that. The woman gives me a femme fatale stare and said, "We all travel. We travel from place to place. Home to home. Bed to bed. We find men like yourself. Sexually deprived men. We sense what you like from afar, and we seduce you. We tell others after we're done that you're open for pleasure." It suddenly dawned on me that the woman I just had sex with was not talking to me. I can see her. I can feel her. Her lips haven't moved the entire time. We're exchanging thoughts. Oh my god! As soon as I think of something she responds. Her next stop is Vancouver, Canada. She was able to convey where she was headed to next by simply looking at me. *What's in Vancouver?* She doesn't answer my question. Instead, she climbs back on top of me and resumes where she left off.

She and her other demonesses have been going down on me the entire night. I told you earlier what their methodology was for disarming me. They have other methodologies they incorporate. They know what my weaknesses are. One is an innocent bashful Barbie girl look. Their facial expression says it all. It's my turn. 'My turn to drink from him.' Drink from me? There's not a man alive who wouldn't want to hear that. Who wouldn't want to oblige that? No man alive would say no. Just so I'm clear, I was never under the illusion these women visiting me are just that. Women? I might be horny, but I'm not stupid. This is not their true appearance. You know that. I know that. I've been researching my nightly ordeal online for the past couple of months, and one of the words I keep running into is the word succubus.

A succubus - *is a demon in female form, or supernatural entity in folklore (traced back to medieval legend), that appears in dreams and takes the form of a woman in order to seduce men, usually through sexual activity. The male counterpart is the incubus. Religious traditions hold that repeated sexual activity with a succubus may result in the deterioration of health or mental state or even death.*

These women have been fucking me going on three years now. I hate to use the word fucking, but I have no choice. That's what going on. Love doesn't exist right now. Sex does. Non-stop sex. This succubus (if that's what they are) look nothing like women I've been with. Not even close. They look like the women I've encountered throughout my day to day life that I craved to be with but never could. They look like goddesses. They are goddesses. Goddesses of sexual depravity. No woman can kiss like them. No woman can bite like them. The word no is not in their vocabulary. It's not in their DNA. Lazy in bed? Blasphemy! They don't know what that means. Remember what I said about them holding me up? Why are they holding me up? They're holding me up because they're fucking my brains out. I'm tapped out. Does my being tapped out slow them down? Hell no. They have ways of getting what they want. It's the weirdest form of politeness ever. Seriously. The way they hold me. The way they touch me. The way they brush up against me, it's unbelievable. I can't tell you how many times I've been kissed out of the blue. I'm not talking about the nights where they've visited me. I'm talking about late at night where I've had no dreams whatsoever. Imagine tossing and turning in your bed – you've woken up for a split second to fluff up your pillow. Here comes this kiss. Right on the lips. Where did it come from? I almost leaped out of my bed the first time that happened. Who out there can resist this level of attention? I can't! I'm not even sure I want to anymore. The level of appreciation and affection being applied here is unreal. I've longed for this type of attention all my life. From one woman, mind you. Four women are giving me what I always wanted, and they're giving it to me at the same time. Different women – different appearances every night. How can you turn that down?

The number of endorphins running through my veins right now has helped me ignore the fact these women are not human. A woman's skin is soft and smooth. What I've encountered in my bed at night has not always been soft and smooth. Sometimes it's scaly. Sometimes it's hairy. I'm talking peach fuzz hairy. I'm allowed to put my hands anywhere. And I do. I'm caressing, licking, biting, and tasting throughout the entire process. Most of what I run into is soft and smooth. Not always, though. Occasionally I'll run into something resembling a dorsal scale piercing through the skin. The first time that happened, I stopped. Not anymore. When you have boobs in your face as far as the eye can see, nothing slows you down. There's no *oh my gosh, what am I doing?* That's where the hot shower comes from. The embarrassment. Think about it. We've been going at it for hours – them mostly. My entire body is sandwiched between what I can only describe as an orgy. Skin on skin (scales). Lips on lips.

Genitalia on genitalia. I hear everything. The grunts. The growls. The snorkeling. Heavy panting. You name it, I've heard it. We've tasted so much of each other's fluids to where I don't even care anymore. This woman who's built like an Amazonian woman has been screaming for hours. The more I pelvic thrust, the more she screams. The women holding me up are soaked with excitement. They can't wait for their turn. Neither can I. She's this close to wanting me to stop. Can you believe that? A demoness is near the point of screaming 'stop, stop, stop!' She likes how I'm giving it to her. She loves it. I love it. If I wake up minutes later still inside her, I know I've done my job. The mattress we made love on is soaked. A symbol of the ecstasy that just happened. What have I done? That question always comes after I'm done. Why is that? Might be because the drug they've given me has worn off. What drug is that you might ask? Attention. That's the drug, ladies, and gentlemen. The demonesses never waiver from it. I'm the center of their universe for the duration of them being here. It doesn't matter where they came from or where they are going to next. Their level of focus exceeds anything I've ever experienced. It's uncanny. Imagine all your sexual desires descending on your bed every night. My desires and their needs combined is what's being fed to me right now. Imagine two water fountains drinking from each other at the same time. That's what this is.

What do they get out of all this? I made the mistake of asking them that question one day and let me tell you the answer I got was not what I expected. They scolded me. Which is weird because a part of them scolding you requires them giving you more sex. While that might sound awesome – in all honesty, it is awesome. You have to remember I'm a human being. They're demonesses. They operate on brute honesty. The telepathic answer I got one night was 'shut up and fuck us. It's obvious you don't have the power to send us away. You would have done so already. Just enjoy what we're giving you.' I have to admit her brut honesty hurt me. Seriously. I almost woke up right then and there. But I didn't. She was right. The ability to send them away had come and gone. I like to think I tried at some point, and for reasons, I can't yet explain <u>was</u> just unsuccessful. Try and understand there's an unbelievable sense of euphoria in these dreams. An unbelievable amount of pleasure *What is this costing me*?

The woman who I've been inside for hours must have realized her words hurt me. I can feel her walls tightening around me. She starts thrusting harder and faster. One of the women holding me up from behind tilts my head back and sticks her tongue down my throat. That's all it took to remove my hurt feelings. I'm thinking *In the name of God, don't stop. Please don't stop.*

https://youtu.be/V1VOsogquUw
Attachments – 'Keith….' at 00:23
Headset Required*

Fig 25.5: Dreams in the arms of the most beautiful women ever.

The Mistress Strikes

Three hours before
the sun rises,
the mistress strikes
the mistress strikes

Four on one
one by one, taking turns,
the mistress strikes the
mistress strikes

Riding me
draining me,
the mistress strikes
the mistress strikes

As soon as they're done
no more fun, the
mistress strikes the
mistress strikes

My head feels heavy
what's low is empty,
the mistress strikes the
mistress strikes.

by Keith Linder

Fig 25.6: They go from city to city – they appear as the most beautiful women imaginable extracting male essence.

CHAPTER 26

Sleepless in Seattle

As you can see, there are a lot of things happening in my bedroom. Etheric sex mixed in with psychedelic nightmares — terrors that would make Charles Manson blush. Pulsating mattress. Mattress indentations and phantom heartbeats. The question some of you might be asking yourself: how and the hell am I able to function? My answer, and I'm being a hundred percent sincere; I don't know. The poking and prodding within seconds of lying down are nerve-racking. Voluptuous psychic vampires are granting me every sexual wish I can imagine. Every female ethnicity you can imagine has entered my room and kissed me out of my sleep. These spirits are unrelenting in how they conduct their affairs. As omnipresent as they are in granting me my fondest wish, interestingly, they've not killed my desire of wanting female companionship. I'm talking about a girlfriend. You would think them manifesting *in my* dreams at night in human form would kill my urge for true female companionship. It hasn't.

There have been times where I've looked forward to falling asleep. Yes, I've had those thoughts. I'm ashamed to say this, but it's true. I find myself (at times) longing for sleep. Can you blame me? Look, what awaits me? Look at what they're doing to me when they're with me. I've been monitoring my daily habits to see if any of what I've just told you have impacted me negatively. Outside of being extremely tired come morning and on occasion bored with whatever female I'm dating at the time; I can't find anything. These demonesses, if that's what you call them, there's no drama with them. No indecisiveness whatsoever on where the relationship is going.

I told you what happened to me when I asked a question. I got chastised. Their definition of chastisement is more sex. More debauchery. 'We don't please you enough?' 'OK, take this. Take that.' What woman in the real world can compete with that? No one! And that, ladies and gentlemen, is my wakeup call — my pause button. Every time I ask myself that question, I realize something. I realize I can't become a recluse. I can't allow myself to be sucked in. Maybe that's what they want? Maybe not the ones riding me. But someone else. So, the answer to my question is simple. I need a girlfriend.

It made sense for me to wait after I moved out of the Bothell house before seeking a new girlfriend. The attack Patty received when she spent the night at the Bothell house made me think the spirits didn't want any other female spending the night after Tina. But paranormal investigator Nikki Novelle wasn't attacked during the week she was here. Karissa Fleck was (see *The Bothell Hell House*). That being said it might be wise not to start dating again until after I move out of the Bothell home for the simple fact that when Tina and I broke up, I didn't have a chance to grieve. God knows I wanted to. But I couldn't. *Ghost Adventures* had just told the world that Tina and I were possibly making things up. That it was mine and Tina's fault they didn't get any evidence? That led to an unfortunate chain of events — the one that affected me the most was Tina leaving me. A distant second to that was Tina being called the black "demon lady" by fans of the show on various social media outlets. How was I viewed? I was viewed as the guy who wasted Zak Bagans' time. Which according to Zack Bagans' teenage fan base is something you don't do. After Tina moved out, things were ugly for about three to four months. I'm talking about the mood of the house (See Chapter 33 *The Bothell Hell House*). Tina and I are both living outside the Bothell house now. We've both reached the conclusion that our relationship is beyond being reconciled. It's a bitter pill for me to swallow (bitter for me) because of the way our breakup occurred. Ask any single person living in Seattle for an extended period about dating in this town. It sucks! I'm not saying that just be saying it. It does. What excited me the most about moving to Seattle before I moved was the idea of finding a wife.

Find a good job and a good wife. That's all I want. The websites I read before I moved here had listed Seattle as one of the best cities to live in if you're single. I had to arrive here to understand what that meant finally. Seattle, Washington, for the most part, is looked at by the outside world as having good coffee and to an extent good technology. But there's more to this city than meets the eye. This seaport city was once famous for logging has undergone several identity changes over the years. In between those different identities lies an interesting culture. I found out after I moved here, that a town listed as being good for singles doesn't necessarily mean a city is conducive to marriage. According to the CDC – *"In 2012, the last year for which statistics are available, the national average rate of divorce is 3.4 per 1,000 people, according to the Centers for Disease Control and Prevention (CDC). Fifteen percent higher than the national average."* Yikes! But it gets worse.

There's a word in this city called the *"Seattle Freeze."* What is that? It's *"A social phenomenon commonly found in the Seattle area. It concludes the majority of Seattle residents as snobby, cold, unfriendly people with a fake-polite exterior. Many people move here with the impression that Seattleites are friendly and laid-back but upon moving quickly realizing how superficial and forced that friendly exterior is. Some say it's the nerdy tech population, some say it's the Scandinavian culture, some say it's the weather, and some even say it's the transplant's fault."* It's a different kind of friendly. One I've not dealt with when I was living in the south. I've been out of the dating scene for over five years now. That's an eternity in the dating world. I'm not the same man anymore. I've seen things. Ladies and gentlemen, the Seattle Freeze is about to come face to face with the Bothell hell house. So, I was back on the online dating sites. I created a profile, and I was emailing women. What I forgot to take into consideration when I began creating my dating profile was the term known as *catfishing*. Catfishing is when you create a fake persona of yourself on a dating website with the hopes of meeting someone. Both sexes do it. I've been out of the online dating scene for quite some time, therefore, was unaware of how prevalent this catfishing had become.

Catfishing has become a major problem in this town. Especially for women. That's going to be a problem for me. You see, I wasn't expecting the women I meet online to google my name online immediately after our first date. I can't tell you how many times I've gone out on a date, and when the night ends the women says, "I can't wait to see you again." And she means it. She does. The date we had was magical. It was. That scene where Fred Astaire is dancing and singing in the rain? That's me. I'm doing cartwheels back to my car, and I don't even know how to do cartwheels. Twenty-four hours later, I called the woman I dated the night before. No response. *That's weird.* I texted her. No response. This happened on multiple dates where the woman I was dating, and I were reciprocating the other person's affection — we've established great rapport. It took me three months to realize what exactly was going on. Finally, a woman I was dating told me point blank why she was breaking things off. She said she googled my name and found all this stuff about me living in a haunted house. You know the sound a record player makes when the record comes to an abrupt stop? That's what my heart does the second a woman tells me she looked my name up on Google.

http://ghostadventures.wikia.com/wiki/Demons_in_Seattle_(episode_)

http://supernaturalmagazine.com/articles/living-with-a-poltergeist-an-interview-with-keith-linder

https://paranormalglobe.com/2016/11/08/paranormal-researchers-return-haunted-bothell-home/

I can't fault a woman for doing a little bit of research about the man she's dating. I've advised my female friends to do that. Combine what you know about catfishing, which is to "lure (someone) into a relationship by means of a fictional online persona" with a horrific story I'm about to tell, and you'll understand why women in Seattle, (more now than ever before) are looking online for the names of people they've gone out with. A few months before I started my online dating (weeks before I moved out of the Bothell house) a nurse by the name of Ingrid Lynes went missing. Every woman I went out on a date with was talking about the Ingrid Lyne. Who's Ingrid Lyne? Ingrid Lyne *"was an American nurse from Renton, Washington, whose dismembered body parts were discovered in the Seattle area on April 10, 2016. On April 11, 2016, John Robert Charlton was arrested and two days later charged with first-degree murder. He pled guilty and was sentenced to 28 years in prison.*

https://fox2now.com/2016/04/11/mother-of-3-vanishes-after-date-with- man-she-met-online/

https://en.wikipedia.org/wiki/Death_of_Ingrid_Lyne

Ingrid Lyne met her killer on an online dating website. Same websites I was using to meet women. How she was killed was extremely gruesome (see links above). This story sent shock waves through the Seattle dating community. It gets at you. When news came out that Ingrid Lyne met her killer online let me tell you the single women in this city went on high alert.

When a woman tells me, she wants to break it off with me because of my haunted house experience, I understand. I get it. This one of those situations where you have to be brutally honest. I get asked all the time. "Did the spirits follow you?" It doesn't matter how great the date went. Doesn't matter how attractive the woman is. Doesn't matter how great the sex is. I can't lie. The water puddle incident? The poking and prodding incident has transpired already. My answer, therefore, is yes. Something followed me. There ends the date. So, it's back to square one. All I can do is keep trying. I've met some wonderful woman through online dating. I'm talking about dates where the waiter in the restaurant we are in walks up to us and says, "We're about to close now, you two are our last customers." My date and I bust out laughing. Funny how time flies, we both say. I pay the tab, and that ends that. No response the next day. No 'hey Keith I got home safe.' Demoralizing? Hell yes. It's very demoralizing. So, demoralizing that I call my female friends and ask them what's going on. My female friends tell me point blank "women are google searching their dates within minutes of learning their first and last name. Some even do it on the date." Especially after the murder of Ingrid Lyne. And you know what? They're right. I've had dates google my name with me still sitting at the table. They say you're never supposed to mention religion and politics on a first date. Those two things are a no, no. There's a third no, no. Don't bring up haunted houses. Understand, I'm not trying to hide my haunted house ordeal. Heck no. There's a possibility that I might have attachments for the rest of my life. For the foreseeable future. I've accepted that. It sucks! But what I can do?

Not every woman who meets me breaks it off. Some find it cool. Cool as is in "wow, you have a bona fide survivor's story." Wow, you still want to date me. The woman's response is, "Yeah, why would I stop dating you based on what you went through?" *My sentiments exactly.* So, I'm dating now. Things have been going great in the dating department. Yippie! The women as of late have a lot of interests in what I went through. They can't necessarily understand all of it, but they get it. 'You and your girl moved into a house together with the righteous of intentions and things didn't quite work out. You had an evil presence there that wreaked havoc on both of you. That's an unbelievable story.' The women appreciate more than I do the survival aspect of the story. They recognize right away that what Tina and I saw few people rarely get to see. They understand why this story needs to be told. I explain why that's very important to me later in this book.

A few months into whoever I'm dating at the time something I'm all too familiar with begins to happen. I start getting weird text messages. I'm talking frantic text messages. The woman I've been dating for a few months tells me the lights in her house are flashing off and on. Uh, oh. I know this scenario. I've lived it countless times. My former attorney (key word former attorney) started experiencing this after she nonchalantly made fun of the spirits in my house. I advised her not to, and she did it anyway. Weeks later, she started having activity at three of her homes. I remember the text messages my attorney sent me. Her fear was off the chain. So is the woman I'm now dating. She's freaking out over the phone and, knowing the answer to my question; I ask her which lights? Her reply was in a frantic voice, "All of them!"

Other women I've dated have admitted to something similar.

- Their dogs barking at something in the corner.
  ✓ The dog that was well potty-trained uncharacteristically pees on the floor now.
- Woke up and found all the kitchen their cabinet doors open.

Fig 26.1: Weird Things

There was one woman that I liked. I appreciated her a lot for her beauty and her smarts. I mean, we had a lot in common. The chemistry was great. Communication was great. Sex was great. Something started happening that reminded me of what Tina, and I went through. The woman I had become fond of started to notice how her jewelry (she was wearing) at the time she came over would go missing. I'm not talking about an earring here or there. I'm talking about heirlooms she would wear when she came over. They're gone now. You know something's frequently happening when the woman says, "every time I come to your house, I lose something." We searched and searched. Nothing was found. Everything I've told you in this chapter is happening between demoness visits. Between the poking and prodding – between the pulsating mattress. The mattress indentations. We were a few weeks from becoming an official couple when things begin escalating. I got a text message from my girl. All the doors in her house kept closing and opening by themselves. This is the same woman who after googling my name online said with energy and excitement that she still "wants to date me." Her fear level was now off the charts. While she was telling me about what it is, she just experienced, I was thinking *dammit am I a contagion or something?* Every woman I've dated post-Bothell hell house is asking me the same questions. "Is this what you and Tina went through?" "Did you experience missing jewelry?" "Did your house lights flash off and on?" Yes, Tina and I experienced all of that.

A few hours after our in-depth conversation, I got a Dear John text. 'Keith, you're a great guy, but I can't deal with this. Good luck finding someone.' That's it. That's all I got. Women here when they break off something, they break off something. Am I heartbroken? Yes, I'm heartbroken. I'm extremely heartbroken. I'm frustrated. How do you fight something like this? How do you win? I don't mind losing a woman for something I did but losing someone for something you didn't do? Better yet, for something you can't control. How do you not despair over something like that? Guess who's there to reap the benefits of my broken heart? The demonesses. The succubus let it be known they and they alone are the only ones that can take care of me.

I hate to admit this, but so far, they've backed up everything they've said. Are they responsible for the events happening? I don't think so. The women that appear in my bedroom at night are very vocal about their role and responsibilities. They come to fuck and suckle off the energy. The energy they get from me is what allows them to travel elsewhere. So, who's behind all of this? *You'll soon see.* Two months have now passed. The new woman I was dating, and I had just left the movies. We got into the car, and all of a sudden, my date screamed, "Ouch!" I looked at her and asked what's wrong? My date rose from the passenger seat and pulled out a woman's earring. I've seen that earring before. It belongs to a woman I used to date. The earring my date was now holding was last seen in my bedroom. Talk about an awkward conversation moving forward.

I can't tell the woman I'm dating the truth. I can't tell her the last time I saw that earring was when I was dating someone else. If I do, she'll *skedaddle*. Do you how awkward that sounds? What I say instead is stupid and cheapish. That earring must belong to one of my co-workers or female friends. I never heard from that woman again. The last two things I'll talk about in this chapter have to do with adult establishments and shadowy figures. I'll talk about the shadowy figures first. Have any of the women I've dated seen shadowy figures? Have they seen the minions? The answer to that question is yes. Not only did one of my dates see one (a woman I was falling in love with, I might add) she freaked out by jumping on the couch.

I can talk about the shadow figures till we're both blue in the face. Answer any question you give. Until you see one with your own eyes, you're not going to fully understand the level of horror that takes over the second a minion walks past you. It's not by accident that you see them. If you see a shadow figure, it's because they wanted, you to see them. How did the two women I was dating one in 2017, the other in 2018 see them? One woman I was dating saw them out the corner of her eye. The second woman I was dating saw one in plain sight. Understand most of the women I've had over to my apartment don't even notice the activity happening around them. And that's a good thing. The less you know about the shadow figures, the less chance you have of them following you home. The minions have paraded themselves out in the open a few times. By paraded I mean appearing in plain sight of the woman I'm with. Other times they're just assholes. Good example — playing with the TV remote control in the middle of me and my date watching TV. The necklace my date is wearing is now missing. Shoes she took off when she walked into the apartment have been relocated to other parts of the living room. Those little nuances are easy to forget when you're distracted. September 2017 - Maria and I were at her house watching TV when all of a sudden, I saw something move out the corner of my right eye. The movement came from the far end of the couch. Description — a small head peeped above the far end of the couch. Maria was sitting to the right of me. I know she saw what I saw because she turned towards the arm of the chair two seconds before I did. I wanted to say so bad did you see that? I chose not to though. Maria didn't see me turn towards the arm of the chair. If she did, I'm pretty sure she would have freaked out. Two people turning towards the direction of a shadow (at the same time) is proof that you both saw something. I know what I saw. Maria doesn't. If she asked me if I saw something? I have to say yes. Yes, I saw a small head peak above the arm of your couch. Something black and round peeped above the arm of the chair and lowered back down. We both turned towards the arm of the chair when it happened. That relationship ended a few weeks later as a result of her daughter becoming uncharacteristically violent and irritable.

August 2018 – The woman I had been dating for quite some time decided to come over to my apartment for dinner. There we were watching TV together and out the blue came this black crawly looking thing. It darted across the floor in front of us. It had to be three feet from us. Susan (pseudonym), the girl I'd been dating for several months, saw it and screamed: "what was that?" I wanted to say the words I don't know. I wanted to lie so bad. You want to know why? I'm tired of receiving Dear John text messages. It's like you are working at a job for three months and all of a sudden, you're told the company has terminated you because your background check came back unsatisfactory. Forget the fact that you've been there for three months. Forget the fact that you've been performing admirably.

All the breakups I've had since I moved out of the Bothell are a result of me living in the Bothell house. Susan saw the shadow figure run across the floor. I'm not going to insult her intelligence by denying what she saw as much as I wanted to. I'm not. I can't. I'd be committing the same atrocity that people committed against Tina and me. That was one of the shadow figures. That's what Rhonda said her son saw from time to time. That's what I see from time to time. Now let me tell you one of the reasons why I liked Susan. Susan was one of three women I've dated that went out and bought my book *The Bothell Hell House*. She did that without so much me asking her. Why did she buy my book? Her answer, not mine, was "it gives me access to a part of you that even you can't give." And she's right. If you googled my name after going out with me a few times and in doing so learned I used to live in a haunted house, not just any house, a house with two documentaries under its belt. A house that was featured on the Travel Channel network and the Seattle local news.

Instead of writing me a Dear John text you do the opposite. You send me a screenshot of you purchasing my book off Amazon. *I didn't ask you to do that.* Part of me wants to marry you right then and there. I'm dead serious. That's how hard it is to date in this town. If it's hard for regular people, and it is, then imagine how hard it is for me. A majority of the women I've dated told me their biggest fear when it comes to dating is meeting weird men. Most of the women I've dated have just gotten out of a tumultuous relationship. They dare not enter something similar than what they left, i.e., infidelity, alcoholism, physical abuse, verbal abuse, crazy in-laws, etc. You name it; they're done with it. Burning crosses, flying furniture, 666 wall writings, and an episode titled "Demons in Seattle" where would you put all of that having experienced what they already experienced? Who wants a boyfriend with that kind of baggage? By baggage I mean attachments. When the women tell me, they must stop seeing me (those that do tell me) all I can do is say I understand. The women who continued to date me after knowing I lived in a haunted house; it's not long before they started having unexplained activity at their homes.

Susan saw the shadowy figure run across my living room floor three months into our dating. I got a text message from her the next day – she has questions as to what happened. I knew then and there that her Dear John text letter had already begun taxiing the runway. And for the record, I'm OK with it. I understand why she wanted to call it off. People tell me all the time. I wish this stuff happened to me. I wish I could see a minion. I think to myself, No, you don't. You say that for the simple fact of not knowing what that means. Even those who believe me, and Tina's story can't fully grasp it. The only people who can grasp it are the people who live it. The spirits attached to me are aware of everyone I interact with. Whoever comes into my orbit is weighed and balanced. Act too arrogant. Guess what? The spirits are going to mess with you. Act naive? Guess what? The spirits are going to mess with you. Got skeletons in your closet – unresolved issues? Guess what? The spirits are going to mess with you. Everyone who's dumped me after experiencing their activity – has yet to tell me the activity is continuing.

Fig 26.2: August 2018 - chat with Susan. Left side-Susan. Right side - Keith

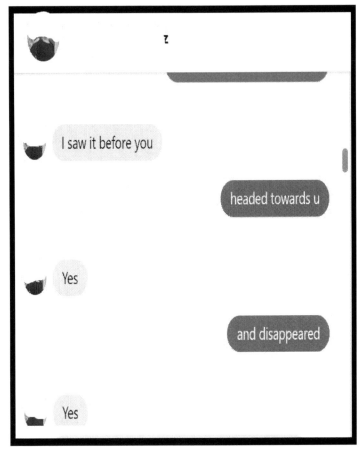

Fig 26.3: August 2018 – cont. Facebook chat

Fig 26.4: August 2018 - Communications with Susan (via Mobile phone) about the shadow she saw run across the floor.

Poltergeist, for reasons we've, can't yet explain, seem to focus their attention and energy (the majority of it that is) on one individual. This targeting is the epitome of what it means to have attachments. A year living in my new apartment I decided to do something I never did before. I decided to visit a massage parlor. Why did I decide to do that? Loneliness – *the demoness was right.*

The thing I miss the most about me and Tina's relationship – the thing I wish to God I could get back is our pillow talks. No matter how hard it got living in that house, the thing Tina and I looked forward to the most was our moments in bed. That was our time to talk about the type of day we had. It might please you to know that our talks weren't always about the activity taking place. Pillow talk was our way of catching up on each other's day. What do we both have planned for tomorrow? Did you talk to your mom today? Did you get the promotion or raise you so eagerly wanted? That meatloaf you cooked today was awesome. That's the kind of pillow talk we had – in the midst of objects being thrown. But there's more to pillow talk than the talk itself. There's the cuddling. In my opinion, there's no better reward (in life) than the feeling of your woman backing herself into you before to going to sleep. The conversation before, during, and after once again, in my opinion, is priceless.

Loneliness and the desire to be in the arms of a woman are what led me to a Seattle massage parlor back in the spring of 2017. I must have driven by a hundred or so in the time I lived in Seattle. I've always been curious. Are the massages as good as I heard? Are the women that attentive? Do they really give you a happy ending? I want to find out. I need to find out. I miss being in the arms of a woman. I'm talking about a real woman. I miss a woman's scent. A woman's touch. A woman's warmth. Her fragrance. I miss that feminine voice near my person. You would think I would have realized by now that I'm never alone. These spirits are always with me. When I walked into the massage parlor, it never occurred to me that I would experience what it is I'm about to experience. I'm not talking about the services being offered. The establishment I walked into was everything I could have imagined. Incense burning. Asian instrumental music playing in the background.

The woman who I've been chatting with all day on my cell phone as a means of making me feel comfortable with this whole idea of even doing this greets me at the entrance of her place. I lose my nervousness within seconds of walking through the door. *Is this how it is supposed to be?* Yes, it is.

This beautiful Asian woman had been giving me a body massage for over forty-minutes now. The conversation was not even close to what Tina and I had, and that's OK. I was not here to re-create what Tina and I had. I was here because I missed the physical aspect of being with a woman. I was enjoying our conversation. This woman has embedded her fingers and hands into every muscle in my body. So firmly. I doubt she's interested in what I do for a living. I mean, it sounds like she is. I couldn't care less. A voluptuous woman had doused herself in hot oil and was on top of me. She's naked. She told me to turn left. I turned left. She told me to turn right. I turned right. She told me to lie on my stomach. I lay on my stomach. She tells me to lie on my back. I lie on my back. She ran hot oil over my upper and lower extremities and began massaging me more intensely. Without so much as a word being spoken, the Asian woman began performing the act known as a *happy ending*.

There I was with my eyes closed, receiving this happy ending when suddenly the room filled with light. I'm talking about a bright light. Dammit! I was this close to having a climax. The woman leaped off me while saying "so sorry, so very sorry" in her sexy submissive Asian voice. I tried to open my eyes, but I couldn't. I was blinded. Before my eyes could adjust to the new level of light, the lights dim again. The masseuse mounts me again and proceeds with giving me a happy ending. She says, "That's never happened before." I'm trying hard not get out of the moment, but I have to ask. What was that all about? "The light came on by itself. Sorry, that's never happened before. I'll continue servicing you." And she does. The lights come on again. I think *what the hell*. The masseuse darted off again. In the middle of performing a happy ending. Mind you; we were both oily and naked. My manhood was standing at attention. The masseuse turned off the light and started giggling. We both do. I mean what else can we do. The masseuse who I have to reiterate is drop-dead gorgeous. She's taking it all in stride while at the same time saying, "I'm so sorry, I can't believe this is happening, this has never happened before." I was thinking to myself. It has with me. The light would have to come on one more time inexplicably before I got my happy ending. Was it worth it? I think so. After I cleaned myself up and got dressed, I remember looking at the masseuse and saying thank you. I was ready to get out of there. I was thinking to myself how I should have bought a voice recorder with me. I'm pretty sure I would have gotten some interesting EVPs (electronic voice phenomena).

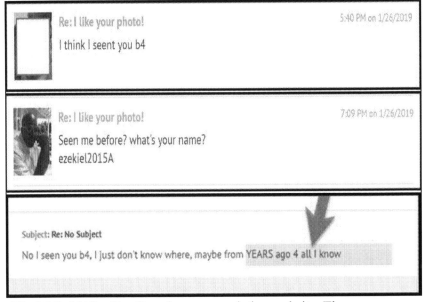

Fig 26.5: 2019 – Email exchange on a dating website. The woman says she's seen me before.

CHAPTER 27
The Usual Suspects

I've spent a lot of time talking about the spirits haunting me. I've admitted to having attachments. I've used the word minion and demon interchangeably, purposely, throughout the book as preparation for what I'm about to discuss. What's the difference between a demon and a minion? According to what I've seen and experienced. Nothing. The best example I can give you about the organizational structure surrounding poltergeist, minions, and demons is the National Football League – any sports league for that matter. If you ask five professional football players what their occupation is, you might get five different answers. Some will say, "I'm an NFL football player. I'm a professional football player." Others might say, "I'm a football player for the New England Patriots, etc." None of the answers they gave is incorrect. The table below explains my view of poltergeist, minions, and demons.

Poltergeist of Washington State		Intelligent Haunting
Organization	Professional Sports	Malevolent Spirits
League	NFL	Poltergeist
Franchise	Sports Team (Seahawks)	Minions
Individual Contributor	Individual Player	Demon

Fig 27.1: The league of extraordinary spirits

The subtitle of this book is called the Poltergeist of Washington State. The same subtitle as my first book. What's the definition of a poltergeist? Not a noisy ghost, I'm afraid. Poltergeist aren't ghosts. They never were. Removing that word from the record might put us in a better position of ascertaining what they are. I don't think there's ever been a case where the house occupant did this much research on his or her own in figuring why this house was the way it was. Let me tell you, it has not been easy. A part of me says *we* (all those involved in this case) *should have figured out this a long time ago. Another part of me says good job, Keith. Way to say the course.* Why do I say that?

I received an email one day from someone in the paranormal community. A well-respected person I might add. This person wanted to know why the events being reported in our house had for the most part not attracted the attention of career skeptics. He was referring to the skeptics that went after cases like The Enfield Poltergeist, Amityville, Indiana House Haunting, Bell Witch, The Haunting in Connecticut, and countless others. I told him I wasn't a hundred percent sure. Those cases I discovered after my ordeal, and he's right, skeptics came out in droves debunking those cases. I'm not saying those cases are false. Far from it. Skeptics' main tool for debunking something is Occam's Razor. Occam's Razor is "a logical principle attributed to the medieval philosopher William of Occam." One thing I can say about this principle as it relates to the paranormal is it's behind the times. "The principle states that one should not make more assumptions than the minimum needed – that the simplest explanation (as to why something is happening) is most likely the correct one." Why you would adopt that principle to something as complicated as the paranormal as a means of determining root cause is beyond me. Medieval principles don't work with the paranormal. We're talking about a different paradigm here. Skeptics (the career ones) lack of interest in *The Bothell Hell House*, in my opinion, can be attributed to how well this case has been documented. That and the fact that it was only Tina and me living in the house. Skeptics go after what we refer to in IT as low hanging fruit. Low hanging fruit is as "a thing or person that can be won, obtained, or persuaded with little effort."

If a case has "holes" in it, a skeptic will find it. Any inconsistency whatsoever. That's Occam's Razor, ladies, and gentlemen. That's what career skeptics use to debunk cases. All cases. They forget that Occam's Razor is a guideline; therefore, it is subject to flaws and misuse. The idea that the simplest answer is the correct one - therefore this case and other people's poltergeist cases are fake, or hoaxes are just ludicrous. Occam's Razor is outdated in my opinion. It's easily misused – the wielder of it only goes after low hanging fruit. That low hanging fruit (if found) becomes the root cause.

Individuals (like myself) who've made it this far in their career and their life don't create hoaxes. Your opinion of humans has to be pretty low to you think that a person would set fire to his own house - *on more than one occasion I might add.* A house he's renting. But it gets funnier. Tina and I call the local fire department and in the middle of all that burn two more Bibles? As if that wasn't enough, we decide to paint 666, upside-down crosses, and other abhorrent words and symbols on walls. Walls we don't own. Only then do we decide to go to the local media who not only respond but after they leave, they (not us) notify someone else — a world-renowned television network. Don't forget all of this media exposure (we now receive) two years after the plant levitation has to be authorized and approved not by me (the so-called pyromaniac) but by the homeowner. After all, it's his house. The homeowner mind you, never came to the house. Not once in the four years of Tina and me living there did the homeowner stop by. These nuisances (and there's more) are what kept career skeptics at bay. That and the fact we didn't have any children living with us. Ask any researcher. Investigating a house that's "Geist" infested where children live is extremely difficult. I'm not talking about the possibility of a child being an agent. I'm talking about the amount of confusion and inconsistency that might be present due to children being on the scene. Skeptics equate inconsistent testimony from a paranormal case (from children) as being hokey. I don't necessarily believe that to be true, but that's another story. I digress. It's time I talk about each spirit individually. The ones Tina and I, unfortunately, had the luxury of fighting. So, make yourself a warm cup of coffee and don't forget to turn on a few lights. We're going back to the Bothell house. When Rhonda and I spoke the second time in summer of 2014 one of the first things she told me that almost made me fall out of my chair was her admitting that her son was still seeing "saw shadowy figures." If this is true, and I believe it is, then it has huge ramifications. It means Rhonda and her family have attachments, and they don't even know it. More importantly, it means the spirits don't care whether Rhonda and her family know they have attachments or not. The spirits are still going to do whatever it is they're doing. Rhonda was clear when she said her family might have been followed. She referred to it as a dark cloud. That could explain Rhonda's lingering desire of wanting to commit suicide. Was her family followed and if so by who? I'll tell you.

Minions – These minions I'm about to speak about. They're creature-like figures (see Fig: 27.2). It doesn't matter if they're working solo or independent; these supernatural entities can exert an enormous amount of negative energy towards an individual. It's not what these mean little cusses do that scares me; it's what they got coming down the pipeline (that I don't know about) that scares me.

Fig 27.2: Omnipresent manipulators and facilitators – Minions

My son said that hed seen figures. He still sees them. Out of the corner of his eye. My son almost died last dec-feb. he was in a coma due to menangitis. He was very ill again in july. They have no idea how he got the menangitis. Or how he had it or whatever it was again. We were in isolation at seattle childrens this last time for a week. He was 10. He loves God. My son. He had brain surgery because of the meningitis. We see a neurologist on 26th. Hes not the same child. Its been very hard. A nightmare. It never seems to end. But we still have our son.

Fig 27.3: Summer 2014 – Rhonda's son

The question you might want to highlight with a yellow highlighter pen is why were the minions in Bothell house there, to begin with? Why are they in my apartment now? The long answer is a little bit complicated. Short answer? Because they can. It's going to take me the remainder of this book to explain why this house was without a doubt the house from hell. Remember, what I'm espousing relates to my case and my case only. What percentage of the horrors Tina and I experienced were these minions responsible for? I'd say eighty-five percent.

Poltergeist	Activity / Horror	Date
Minions	'Kid cough'	May 1st, 2012
Minions	Missing items	2012 – 2016
Minions	Items appearing	2012 - 2016
Minions	Wall writings	2014
Minions	Poking & prodding	2014 – Ongoing
Minions	Objects thrown	2012, 2014, 2015
Minions	Pushing me down the stairs	Jan 2nd, 2014
Minions	Manipulation	2012 – Ongoing

Table 27.1: Minions' modus operandi

Example:

- Missing items – Mom's coffee cup, Tina's jewelry, Bibles, Holy water, candles, sage sticks, etc.
- Items appearing – Old letters from previous tenants, kid toys, female jewelry, etc.
- Wall Writings – 666, Die KL, upside-down cross.
- Poking and Prodding – subtle pokes and jabs in the kidney, and back area – before falling asleep.
- Objects thrown – flowerpot, bar stool, Bibles, computers, armoire, candles, etc.
- Manipulation – woman jewelry appearing in the bed that Tina and I slept in and on the staircase. phantom tweets, and text messages.

MUST WATCH - **https://youtu.be/QssN3KJhOc**

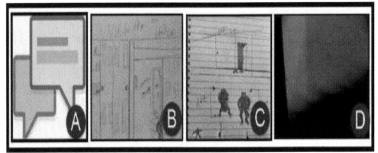

Fig 27.4

A.) 2008:2009 Rhonda's son saw shadowy figures. Was still seeing them in 2014 See Fig 26.2

B.) Spring 2014 - I start drawing shadowy figures before I knew Rhonda and her son even existed.

C.) Late Summer 2014 - I contact Rhonda. She describes the house "as a living hell."

D.)April 2016 – S.E.P picks up shadowy figures on motion detect cameras. Two years after I had already started drawing them. **Eight years after Rhonda son saw them. It's hard for a skeptic to refute that!**

We need to understand this "out the corner of my eye" thing. The best way to do that is by reviewing other cases. I've been doing that for quite some time now. What I've uncovered is interesting. There are accounts of people seeing 'shadowy figures' (in their home) going back several centuries. The description people give is identical to what I and Rhonda's son have described.

It's important to note that some of these people who reported seeing shadowy figures saw them in the middle of them experiencing strong "Geist" like activity. What does that tell us? It tells us that "Geist" outbreaks might be the works of malevolent spirits and not R.S.P.K. What others have reported seeing going back centuries and what Rhonda's son and I have seen can't be a coincidence. Susan, the woman I was dating summer 2018, (see Fig 26.4) saw a minion dart across my living room floor while we were watching a movie together. You saw how frightened she was when she texted me. I'm telling you shadowy figures, whatever you want to call them, are real. I'm not talking about monsters with pitchforks. Let's get that out the way right now. There's no guy named Lucifer sitting in the middle of the Earth's core cloning gremlins. Demons are not red. They're not what you see on television. The ones haunting me don't look like that. These minions I've seen average one foot in height and have weird looking shapes. They have weird facial expressions. What you see stays with you – whether you want it to or not. Why this house? Why Rhonda and her family? Why Keith and Tina? Up until now, that's been a difficult question to answer. But in truth, it never should have been. As you're about to find out the spirits in our home have been trying to reveal who, why, and what they are for quite some time. The biggest roadblock has been us, humans. I'm not surprised. Most of the teams that investigated the Bothell house walked through our front door carrying an inordinate amount of subjectivity. Which as you know is a huge no, no. This subjectivity, i.e. world view was the basis for them being there. You'd be surprised how many paranormal researchers turned a blind eye to events happening around them (in our home) simply because what was happening was in direct contradiction to their worldview. The best explanation I can give you as to why Rhonda and her family were attacked and, more importantly, why Tina and I never really had a chance when we moved into the same house can be summed up in two words. Dionaea muscipula, better known as the Venus flytrap. *The Venus flytrap catches its prey with a trapping structure. Formed by the terminal portion of each of the plant's leaves, which is triggered by tiny hairs on their inner surfaces. When an insect or spider crawling along the leaves contacts a hair, the trap prepares to close, snapping shut only if another contact occurs within approximately twenty seconds of the first strike. Triggers may occur if one-tenth of the insect is within contact. The requirement of redundant triggering in this mechanism serves as a safeguard against wasting energy by trapping objects with no nutritional value, and the plant will only begin digestion after five more stimuli to ensure it has caught a live bug worthy of consumption.* In short, the Venus flytrap doesn't eat everything that lands in its mouth. There has to be some "nutritional value" in conjunction with certain stimuli being activated.

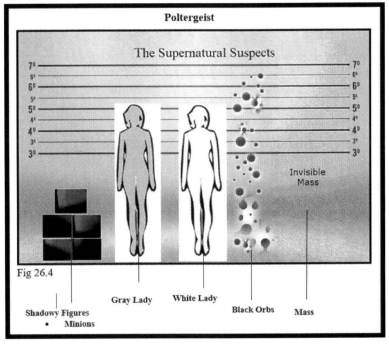

Fig 27.5: The supernatural suspects in Keith and Tina's home 2012 – 2016

One of the snickering questions I get from both skeptics and cynics is 'if your house is as active as you and Tina say it is, why isn't nothing being reported now?' Why haven't other families stepped forward? "I mean come on; a house that active would have people reporting stuff all the time?" Going back to what I said earlier about skeptic's misuse of Occam's Razor. "Other families haven't stepped forth and reported activity. Therefore, your story is not true." That's one of the low hanging fruit items skeptics use when questioning me. Let me start from the beginning. Rhonda and her family had activity for the short period they lived in the Bothell house, which was 2008-2009. Two families lived in the house before Rhonda, and her family arrived. One of those families was the homeowner. Overall, we're talking five maybe six families total. Combine Rhonda's experience with ours, and you have a house that's thirty-three percent active-if we add the homeowner in (just for kicks), the percentage increases to forty and fifty percent. Those are astronomical numbers where the paranormal is concerned. Skeptics still scream, "Why isn't the house active all the time?" Who says it isn't? Bibles burning and objects levitating is not how you measure activity. Bibles caught fire in our house because Tina and I put them out. That's what we were told to do. Every action creates a reaction. That's the thing you need to understand most about the poltergeist. Earlier in the book, I said the occupants in the home (at the time of this writing) knew before buying the house that the house was haunted. I doubt they know about the extreme activity that took place. I know because I didn't tell them. That's good. The less you know about what happened inside the Bothell house (if that's where you live) the better off you will be. No one should walk into a house as active as ours was knowing about every single event that happened. Do the homeowners who moved in after me know the house was haunted? Yes. Where they giving tips on what not to do? Yes. But that's it. Unless someone died in the house (which no one did) trust me you're better off not knowing every single detail. Why is that? Short answer. If the minions in the house get the slightest inkling that you're walking on eggshells, i.e., peeping around corners, hearing noise where there aren't any. Guess what they'll start doing? They'll start giving you what you wish for? A haunting. Doesn't take much for them to spring into action. The house occupant becomes an unwitting participant in the activity taking place. People who try to criticize Tina and I overlook the timeline I created. They ignore it. That timeline describes everything that happened in the house. In 2013 we had no activity whatsoever. To our knowledge, everything just stopped. Then 2014 came. Bam! Hell, on earth reemerged. Did the spirits leave and come back? Of course not. They went dormant or better yet what I consider to be low-level activity. Listen carefully because this is important. Most people (including some of you reading this book) don't notice the low-level stuff because you're too busy going about your daily lives. That's what Rhonda and her family were doing up until the time the kitchen cabinets opened and closed by themselves. That incident is what caused the live-in nanny to flee the house. What I'm trying to say is it's possible the other families living in the Bothell house before Tina and I had activity but didn't notice it. Those familiar with my story know the activity didn't start increasing until after Tina and I started introducing sage and motion cameras. Nick Kyle wasn't lying when he said the reaction to certain phenomena could raise the activity level. (see Demons in Seattle Uncovered documentary).

But let's pretend no one else in the house had activity. Let's pretend the people living in the house now have yet to experience anything. Going back to the Venus flytrap example I introduced, it's possible the spirits in our home require a certain dynamic be present before acting up – a certain imperfection. Think about the fly that's caught inside the carnivorous plant. Imagine if the fly knew (ahead of time) that all it had to do to avoid being eaten by the plant it landed on was to not move for the first twenty seconds (after the flytrap closes its branches). That fly could easily fly off. The fly doesn't know that so what does it do? It reacts. That reaction causes the Dionaea Muscipula to go into action. It's thinking *I have a potential meal – this insect is interacting with me. Let me begin the captured and digestive phase.* The Venus flytrap can't afford to waste energy on every insect that lands in its mouth. It would die. So, what does it do? It uses nature gift – a built-in detection system. The spirits in our Bothell home behave the same way. It could be years before an imperfection, i.e. stimuli cross their path. It takes years. Centuries even. The fact that the Venus flytrap doesn't need insects to survive was news to me. I didn't know the plant could live its life not ever tasting one insect. That should give you an idea of why some people experience activity and why some people don't. There's a prerequisite component that can't be ignored. The fact the Dionaea Muscipula doesn't need an insect to survive doesn't mean the Dionaea Muscipula is going to pass up a free meal. By free meal, I mean an impatient fly. It's not so much the number of house occupants that makes a house active. It's about the quality, e.g., type of dysfunction of the house occupants. Like I said in my previous book, one of the reasons why Tina and I decided to move in together was to work on our relationship. We were at the make or break stage. That's all a mean-spirited entity needs, ladies and gentlemen. Just a little chink in the armor is all it takes. The spirits put jewelry from other women (probably from previous occupants) in Tina's path because they knew that would cause arguments between us. When your last relationship ended due to your husband's infidelity, that creates a level of insecurity. The spirits knew mine and Tina's background better than we did. Understand there were, and still is, in my opinion, all types of minions running through the Bothell house. Each has its specialty when it comes to wreaking havoc. I get irritated when people ask me, "Have you gone back to the house?" "Are you curious to know if the people living are experiencing anything?" No, I'm not. Going back would mean I doubt my own experience.

Researchers should know better than me that the people living in the house now might not necessarily experience what Tina and I experienced. Why would they? My smudging. My buying infrared cameras and placing Bibles everywhere is identical to a fly wiggling inside a Venus flytrap. What's the first thing you should stop doing when trapped inside quicksand? Stop moving. The more you move, the quicker you sink. It's important to understand that no reaction to the phenomena taking place doesn't guarantee you a free pass of not being messed with. We know that from Rhonda's testimony and her suicide. What I'm trying to call attention to are the different levels of activity. Most people are not going to go through the lengths I did to see if their house is haunted. Most people just pack up and leave. If I leave a room and come back and see the light is off, I know I didn't turn it off. I know Tina didn't turn it off. I make a mental note of why the light in my office is always off when I come back to my room. *I know what I'll do. I'll put a video camera in my hallway facing my office. Let's see what happens. Uh, oh my cameras are gone. Where did the camera (including the tripod) go? Who took it? I need to find out.* That's all a malevolent need to raise the activity level – me putting on a sherlock homes hat.

The Gray Lady – Who is she? She's the first apparition to come out of the woodwork. It's believed by many that apparitions appear in less than three percent of poltergeist related cases. That alone should tell you how much we know about them. The apparition I saw was full-bodied. She wasn't transparent or see-through. What struck me the most about the female apparition I saw that night (summer 2012) was how she appeared. I was in my office typing away on my computer when all of a sudden, the light in my room went off. At the very same time, I heard a 'click.' I did what any human being would do. I turned towards the direction of my light switch – *same direction the noise came from.* Low and behold, a woman is standing there. A gray woman. Who is she specifically? She's a demon. One of the high- ranking minions that (for reasons we may never know) decided to take on the appearance and likeness of Rhonda Lee Jimenez. That's right. Rhonda Lee Jimenez. The previous tenant I contacted two years later. The tenant who eventually committed suicide. Talk about foreshadowing.

Tina and I had been experiencing on and off lights issues before the first apparition sighting. I have videos of this phenomena on my YouTube Channel. The only answer I can come up with is that she wanted me to see her. There is that possibility. After all, we're talking about malevolent spirits. Rhonda's doppelganger had more than one emotion on her face that night – fatigue, conflicted, worrisome, loneliness, troublesome, and mischievous.

https://www.youtube.com/watch?v=ZE-

BpTve31E Hallway Lights 2012 Off/On at 13:17

Female apparition's facial expression - emotion:

- Conflicted – I shouldn't have done that – takes off running.
- Confused and Troubled – Why can't I dematerialize?
- Mischievous – Turning off the light in the 1st place. Premeditated act.

Which emotion did she exemplify the most? Mischievous without a doubt. Everything went downhill from that point on. Books started flying off the shelves. Lights started flashing off and on every night versus every other night. More stomping. More door slams. More pitter-patter footsteps. More plants being thrown and more loud bangs. Multiple sightings in the coming months.

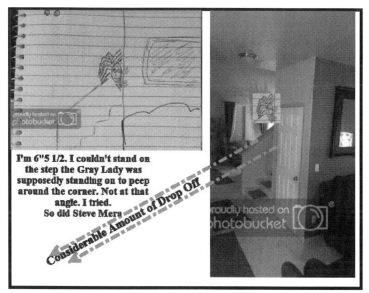

Fig 27.6: I'm 6"5 1/2. I couldn't stand on the step like the Gray Lady did in this recreation picture. Considerable amount of drop off.

Apparition	Activity / Horror	Date
Gray Lady	Turning off lights manually	Summer 2012
Gray Lady	Phantom footsteps	2012-2016
Gray Lady	Peeping around corners	Summer/Fall 2014
Gray Lady	Manifesting on bedroom door (captured by Nikki's investigative team)	Spring 2015
Gray Lady	(possible) objects were thrown	2012, 2014
Gray Lady	Tantrums (stomping, door slams)	2012, 2014

Table 27.2: the Gray Lady's modus operandi

Black Orbs – There's not a lot I can say about the black orbs except to say it wasn't me that first saw them. It was Microsoft. That's right. Microsoft. Summer, 2013 - Microsoft asked me if I'd be interested in being a beta tester for their prototype Xbox One and Kinect system. I leaped at the chance as did a thousand other gamers.

The rules were simple:

1.) Use the console in your free time
2.) Play the games we give you
3.) Maneuver through the Graphic Interface as often as possible
4.) Download updates when needed
5.) Complete surveys
6.) Have fun!

Someone's always monitoring your gameplay from what was often referred to as headquarters. Occasionally, and this happened maybe once every other week, the project manager and her team would come by the house and videotape me playing their console. That's how the orbs were discovered.

worst was behind us. But let's not speak too soon. The Microsoft research team comes over one night to observe me on the Kinect. They came in like they always do, holding clipboards, tablets and tons of video equipment. But then something happens. But then something happens that causes one of the remote technicians to call the team in my house. "Hold on guys; we got an anomaly on our end of the screen; we can't tell where it's coming from." So, the project manager sitting next to "says stop using the Xbox." Their engineers have picked something strange. With the Xbox now off and the Kinect still on, my TV began showing what appeared to be black masses on the TV screen. The masses were moving - moving the way wax moves inside a lava lamp, only throughout my TV screen. Now, given how the Kinect works, these masses or images cannot be coming from the Kinect itself. These floating black masses, perhaps five in all, and each about the size of a softball, were in behind us.

Understand that the Kinect sits near your television. It has one specific job - distinguish

Fig 27.8: The Bothell Hell House page 49.

Do you understand the level of expertise standing in my living room? The level of expertise working at Microsoft Research and Develop center? This is not Bill Chapel running around with a Kinect duct tapped to a clipboard calling out ghosts. No these are coders, engineers, business analysts, developers, technicians, program and project managers working feverishly to launch a new console into a five-billion-dollar industry. Microsoft is trying to get their Xbox One out the door before the Christmas rush – before Sony launches its PS4. Saying the stakes were high when this all happened is putting it lightly.

The fact that other people saw the black orbs before me and made a huge fuss about it is the only reason for the orbs being on the usual suspect's lists.

Fig 27.9: One email out of many between Microsoft and me

Microsoft Email Correspondence:

Slowly but surely, games are becoming available for you to play. We'd love for you to try out Kinect Sports Rivals, Zoo Tycoon, and Reflex! Create a playlist in Xbox Music and pin it to your Home screen. The Blu-ray Player is working. If you haven't already done so, download the Blu-ray Player app and watch a movie. Skype is also up and running. Go ahead and try to make a Skype call. Please install Voice Studio from the App Store and run it. It should only take about 15 minutes. The quality of our voice recognition is directly related to how much test data we can get, so your help is very much appreciated! There will be another follow-up survey mid-week next week.

Black Orbs	Activity / Horror	Date
Lava like	Unknown	2013

Table 27.3: Black orbs' modus operandi

Reenactment - https://www.youtube.com/watch?v=J6-u0J2NgIU

Mass - Wiki *defines mass as being both a property of a physical body and a measure of its resistance to acceleration (a change in its state of motion) when a net force is applied. The object's mass also determines the strength of its gravitational attraction to other bodies.*

I think certain aspects of mine and Tina's ordeal get overlooked simply for the fact there's just so much information to take in. I get a lot of questions thrown my way about the burning Bibles. A lot of people want to know about the wall writings. Who's the Gray Lady? Who's the White Lady? I'm still waiting for someone to ask me about the morning my Final Fantasy poster caught fire in my office. That house attack was one of the first attacks ever where I felt perhaps an evil presence was occupying the house. I might have mistakenly given you the impression that the minions (shadow figures) are the deadliest spirits in the Bothell house. They're not. Don't get me wrong. The minions are some mean mother fuckers. Their hands are always in the cookie jar. They're always up to something. But there's a spirit worse than them. Ten times worse than them. That spirit is Mass.

That's the name I've given it. Is it a demon? That's putting it lightly. There's a scene in Peter Jackson's movie *Lord of the Ring's* that best describes the sheer dread Mass invokes when arriving. J.R. Tolkien's Balrog character. Remember that scene? A horde of goblins is chasing Gandalf and his fellowship. They're cornered and surrounded by what appears to be a hopeless situation.

All of a sudden, you hear a roar. Everything goes quiet. The goblins that surrounded the fellowship take off running. That close up shot of Gandalf closing his eyes (my favorite scene in the movie) says what words can never say. Gandalf's like *'oh shit we're screwed.'* The only solution to their problem is to run like hell!

In my book *The Bothell Hell House*, I said that paranormal investigators wouldn't be nearly as cavalier as they are (on TV) if they knew what they were possibly facing. You wouldn't be so quick to scream "come out, wherever you are!" Not if you've seen what I've seen. And what have I seen? Not a goddam thing. That's the point. Mass is not a thing you can see. Mass is a thing you feel. Mass is an interpersonal space invader. "The ebb and flow of the Atlantic tides, the drift of the continents, the very position of the sun along its ecliptic. These are just a few of the things I control in my world." That movie quote describes Mass perfectly.

I could always tell when this spirit, in particular, was around. The atmosphere completely changes inside the house. An example of that would be our bedroom ceiling fan. Our ceiling fan (if it was on) would suddenly start wailing. SQUEEK! SQUEEK! That's all you hear. Lights (if they're on) start flashing off and on. The TV would turn on if it were off. Or turn off, if it was on. Then the pause. The pause is me and Tina looking at each other thinking *what's going to happen next?* That something is always a large object being thrown. I learned the hard way that the best way to conjure up Mass is to smudge. Smudging and heated arguments between Tina and I served as perquisites for the activity elevating. You could tell something new had entered the house. Had entered the room by the mere fact that the atmosphere is now different. Mass is not here to give orders. He's not here to take orders. He doesn't interact with the demons who are already there. Mass is his own thing. He's here to do one thing and one thing only: launch objects and destroy property that up until now haven't even been touched. It always felt like the other spirits in our home sort of went into hiding themselves once Mass arrived. You have this mass explosion of activity taking place for what felt like days. The Katie Perry weekend is a perfect example of that.

To my knowledge, the first time I encountered Mass directly was when the poster in my office caught fire. The house had been active the night before to the point of me asking Tina if she would smudge the house before we went to bed. The next morning Tina and I woke to a house feeling extremely heavy. The only thing to do was to start our day as quickly as possible. Tina left for work, and I went to take a shower. I stepped out the shower a few minutes after Tina left when suddenly the fire alarms started going off. I'm thinking *not again! You bastards want to do this now?* I ran to the doorway of our bedroom to get a sense of what was going on. All of a sudden, I felt something run past me. A powerful force. Its presence alone can cause a man to pee his pants. I know because I almost did. That's the amount of evil bouncing off it.

If I had stepped onto the hallway at the exact time Mass ran by, we would have collided somehow. I'm pretty sure I wouldn't be alive right now. Father Roy told me prior to him conducting an exorcism on our house that "there are certain spirits that if you should so happen to try to block them – impede their path accidentally. You run the risk of being significantly injured." A demon doesn't care about wrong place wrong time. It's not going to think 'oh you stepped out of the hallway earlier than anticipated. Let me make room for you.' A demon couldn't care less about that. A demon cares about getting the job done. My stumbling into the hallway half-naked doesn't buy me any sympathy whatsoever. I've seen three-hundred-pound furniture in my house get tossed from one side of the room to others like it was no heavier than a pillow. We're talking bullet traveling speeds.

Mass	Activity / Horror	Date
	Atmospheric changes in the house environment -	2012 – 2014
	Katie Perry weekend w/minions	Spring/Summer 2014
	Lighting sage stick	Spring 2014
	PC monitors catching fire w/minions	Summer/Fall 2014
	Shirt catching fire	Summer / Fall 2014
	Walls popping	Spring 2014
	Mood change	2012 – 2016
	Objects flying while sleeping w/minions	2012, 2014
	Front door opening and slamming	Spring 2014
	Interpersonal space - invasion	2012 – 2016

Table 27.4: Mass modus operandi

"Interpersonal space is the region surrounding a person which they regard is psychologically theirs. Most people value their personal space and feel discomfort, anger, or anxiety when their personal space is encroached."

I can't tell you how many times I've inexplicably woken up to what felt like anxiety and fear. It's worse than being watched. I later learned that phenomena are what some define as being targeted. Mass is not alone in the house. He's not only in the room. He's standing right over me. Yeah, he's been hovering over me for what feels like an eternity, but it isn't. He just got here. That density I spoke about earlier makes it feels like he's been there awhile. The first thing I do when I open my eyes (the room is in total pitch darkness) is take stock of my surroundings. It never fails. As soon as my eyes finish their panning, the room, a large object goes flying.

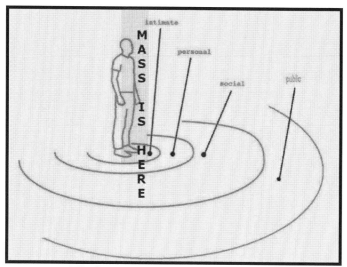

Fig 27.10: Interpersonal space zone

The White Lady – I had to save the White Lady for last. Not because she's dangerous or malicious. Far from it. The White Lady apparition I saw, i.e., full-bodied apparition is the third victim. I saved her for last because she and the upside-down man wall symbol are what help me solve the puzzle as to why this house was haunted. Out of all the spirits I've talked about, the White Lady (female apparition) is, without a doubt the most profound. She's the DNA of this entire case. I hope researchers (the world over) study what I'm about to reveal about the white lady for quite some time. Rhonda and I were having multiple conversations by the time October 2014, rolled around. She told me she and her husband had just gotten back together. As we're talking, I started thinking to myself *I know you, I've seen you somewhere before?* I kept ignoring it at first until finally, after a few more face chats on Facebook and Skype, I asked myself the question. Out loud this time. The Gray and White Lady apparitions both look like Rhonda. Unlike her gray counterpart, this full-bodied white apparition wasn't running around turning off lights. She wasn't peaking around corners or appearing on motion detection cameras. She didn't allow herself to get photographed as the Gray Lady did. To my knowledge, she hasn't done anything nefarious. I doubt she could scare Tina and me the way the other spirits have. I'm pretty sure she can't. You want to know why? She's not like the Gray Lady - she's not a demon. She's a living apparition. What the hell is a living apparition? "A living apparition is when the spirit of a person who is still alive appears to someone in a place that is different from the location their body currently inhabits." The Gray Lady went out of her way to interact with me. She hit the light switch in my office and took off running. That's not an example of stone tape theory.

The White Lady and I had no interaction whatsoever. When I saw her, it was like I was watching a movie. I probably would've never known she was in the hallway had it not been for the rustling sounds that came before. Both the Gray and White Lady were completely identical. The only thing that separated them was their color and their mannerism. There are multiple definitions on the internet defining what a crisis apparition is. The one closest to what I've seen, and sort reveals what I know about Rhonda (up until the time of her death) says a "crisis apparition is usually someone known to the witness. They appear at a time of crisis in the life of the person appearing, e.g., a life-threatening incident or at the time of death itself."

The actual apparition is of a person undergoing extreme stress. I know from talking to Rhonda that she was going through an immense amount of stress in her Yakima home. Her son was still sick and still seeing shadowy figures. Rhonda at times was still depressed. Still suicidal.

Here's a reenactment video of me seeing the White Lady for the first time.

https://youtu.be/urjrfaWj8mk

Poltergeist - The White Lady

October 2017, (a year after Rhonda's suicide) I decided to do something I hadn't done in a while. I decided to review some of her previous statements. This method of reviewing old material was what helped me discover that the upside-down stick figure of a man in my office meant that a man has died, or a man is about to die. All I did was stare at the wall markings for some time, and the idea finally it hit me. Google exactly what you see on the wall. It's how I discovered the left-over markings on the office door days after Steve and Don left the first time. That discovery was one of the reasons why they came back. That discovery led to me learning about bone black. The question we've not been able to get a definite answer is why this house? What makes this house the house from hell?

When it comes to problem-solving, project managers like me, we have a lot of tools at our disposal. One tool we use to determine the root cause is a tool known as the Fishbone diagram. Also known as the Ishikawa diagram. This tool helps your sort problems into categories. "When you have a serious problem, it's important to explore all of the things that could cause it." The goal for me and my team when using this tool is to determine the potential causes of a problem. No knows how this problem got into our project. Therefore, it's time to use the Fishbone diagram. When you're in the midst of problem-solving, there's no such thing as a wrong answer. Everybody on the project team must voice what they feel the root cause could be. Every theory as to why a problem keeps occurring gets talked about.

It's sort of like the process of elimination. Themes that repeatably come up are looked at analyzed.

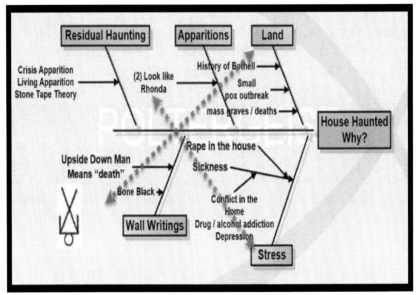

Fig 27.11: Bothell House – Ishikawa diagram

I'm speaking about individuals on the project. There's no such thing as a wrong answer. Can one person do this diagram themselves? Yes! That's what I'm doing. Let me tell you; I've seen some interesting Fishbone diagrams in my day.

The stress and turmoil Rhonda and her family went through while living in the Bothell house combined with the two apparitions; I saw that looked like her are just too coincidental to be ignored. Those things and her eventual suicide stand out on a Fishbone diagram. Could those things combined be why the house is haunted? Yes and no. The first thing you want to avoid doing when conducting an Ishikawa technique is looking at symptoms. Symptoms are the result of a problem; they are not the cause of it. A lot of what's listed above (see Fig 27.11) are symptoms, not causes. There are over eighty-five houses in the neighborhood where Tina and I once lived. All of them were built in 2005. We can list the land as possibly being the root cause, but the question then becomes, why not the other houses? None of my neighbors have come out and said their house is haunted. Not one. It's not like my neighbors didn't have the opportunity. I've had multiple paranormal vans parked in my Bothell driveway.

The street the Bothell house is on looked like a Hollywood studio when Ghost Adventures was here. Black-tinted SUVs were everywhere. Steve and Don interviewed several of my neighbors and came up empty-handed. So did the other teams. So, the opportunity for someone to step forward and say our house is also haunted has come and gone. No one's having activity except Tina and me. "When you have eliminated the impossible, whatever remains, however improbable, must be the truth." It's as simple as that. *If all the apparitions I've seen resemble Rhonda, then the question as to why the house was haunted might have something do with Rhonda. Rhonda is an important piece to solving this puzzle.* **She's not the only piece, trust me, she's not.** *She's an important piece.* This is what I was thinking about in the latter part of 2017. I was heading home after a night of partying with friends thinking; I *have to find out more about Rhonda.* Unfortunately, she's no longer with us. When someone's no longer with you all you have is their testimony, they gave before passing away. I trust Rhonda. I trust what she told me while she was here. It would be good to corroborate some of what she said.

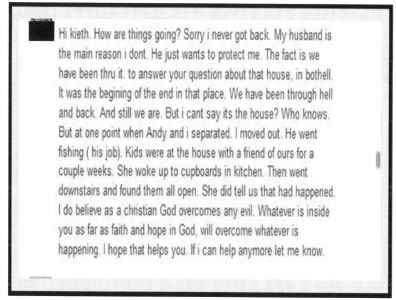

Hi kieth. How are things going? Sorry i never got back. My husband is the main reason i dont. He just wants to protect me. The fact is we have been thru it. to answer your question about that house, in bothell. It was the begining of the end in that place. We have been through hell and back. And still we are. But i cant say its the house? Who knows. But at one point when Andy and i separated. I moved out. He went fishing (his job). Kids were at the house with a friend of ours for a couple weeks. She woke up to cupboards in kitchen. Then went downstairs and found them all open. She did tell us that had happened. I do believe as a christian God overcomes any evil. Whatever is inside you as far as faith and hope in God, will overcome whatever is happening. I hope that helps you. If i can help anymore let me know.

Fig 27.12: Aug/Sept 2014 – Keith and Rhonda chat

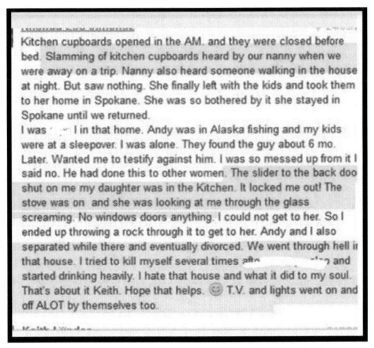

Kitchen cupboards opened in the AM. and they were closed before bed. Slamming of kitchen cupboards heard by our nanny when we were away on a trip. Nanny also heard someone walking in the house at night. But saw nothing. She finally left with the kids and took them to her home in Spokane. She was so bothered by it she stayed in Spokane until we returned.
I was I in that home. Andy was in Alaska fishing and my kids were at a sleepover. I was alone. They found the guy about 6 mo. Later. Wanted me to testify against him. I was so messed up from it I said no. He had done this to other women. The slider to the back doo shut on me my daughter was in the Kitchen. It locked me out! The stove was on and she was looking at me through the glass screaming. No windows doors anything. I could not get to her. So I ended up throwing a rock through it to get to her. Andy and I also separated while there and eventually divorced. We went through hell in that house. I tried to kill myself several times aft~   ~'~ and started drinking heavily. I hate that house and what it did to my soul. That's about it Keith. Hope that helps. ☺ T.V. and lights went on and off ALOT by themselves too.

Fig 27.13: Aug/Sept 2014 – Keith and Rhonda chat

It's important to note — Rhonda never said the house was haunted. She said it was "a living hell." It was "the beginning of the end," she called it. You can tell from the chat messages above that Rhonda's family, nanny included, were experiencing poltergeist activity and didn't even know it. Let's separate everything Rhonda said so that we can understand it better:

- Cupboards open in the AM, but they were closed before bed. (Fig 27.12) **Rhonda had exited the home already**.
- Slamming kitchen cupboards heard by the nanny.
- TV and lights would go off /on "A LOT" by themselves
- Nanny heard footsteps in the house (but no one was home). Another argument against R.S.P.K
- The slider door slid (verb) shut on Rhonda (while she was having a cigarette on the back patio) and locked her out. Daughter started screaming. The only thing Rhonda could do to get back into the house **was bust through the glass** using a rock she found outside. ☞ **Remember that**.

Tragic events:

- Rhonda was raped in the house
- Son developed a rare, deadly form of meningitis
- Rhonda and husband divorced (in the home)
- Multiple suicide attempts
- Became depressed
  - alcohol addiction
  - prescription drugs addiction

Rhonda's opinion about the house:

- She hates the house (for what it did **to her soul**).
  - And for ruining her marriage.

I became so focused on the fact that Rhonda and her family experienced activity similar to me and Tina that I forgot the obvious. Rhonda said she was raped <u>inside the home</u>! That's an extraordinary revelation. No one's ever thought about the ramifications of what this statement means. Let me tell right now. It means a lot. The word that stands out more than any other word is Rhonda. Rhonda's suicide attempts and the rape she experienced in the house should have raised all kinds of red flags (with every researcher who came in the house). *Ghost Adventures* had her contact info, and they never called her.

When Rhonda first told me about her rape experience, I backed away from it. Why? Rape is a touchy and sensitive subject. I'm not skilled to deep dive into that arena. I'm not even sure I want to. That's the mindset I had while living in the house. Not anymore. There has to be a way to corroborate what Rhonda said. There has to be some paper trail. Some sort record on file of Rhonda's attack. If not the attack, then surely her suicide attempts. People who fail in killing themselves usually fail because of some intervention. Maybe a friend or family member was able to get that person help before the suicide attempt was carried out. There would be some record of that if that were the case. I'll be damned. There is!

Fig 27.14: County responds to my request for public records

- Request submitted on October 23rd, 2017
- Response from Snohomish County December 27th, 2017

Officers Mental Health Contact Report

Voluntary/Involuntary Commits

Date 09-08-2008

Subject: Rhonda Lee Jimenez

On the listed date and time, I contacted Rhonda at her residence. Her family and pastor had called because she said she going to kill herself. Rhonda said she had drunk a six-pack of beer, but she said was not suicidal. Her husband Andrew said she had been drinking nonstop for days and he had several messages on his phone from Rhonda. I listened to a message from the previous night and heard Rhonda scream "I'm going to fucking kill myself." Andrew said that Rhonda again said she would kill herself tonight and that's why he called. Andrew also said he was concerned that Rhonda may be abusing prescription medicine.

X as a result of a mental disorder presents an imminent likelihood of serious harm to self and others

1st Report

Snohomish   County   Sheriff's

Office   Use   of

Force/Miscellaneous   Report

Date 3-20-2009

Subject: Rhonda Lee Jimenez

Officer dispatched to (address omitted), Bothell.

Report of female screaming and banging on door. On arrival I heard yelling inside ----- garage:

- "Why are you doing this to me!"
- "I just want to go home!"
- "Stop it!"

(officer proceeds to the back of the house)

Rear slider door broken; mattress stuffed into opening. Entered and searched the house. Subject came out of garage interior door. **Screwdriver in hand**. Would not drop it. Despite being told twice! Used my taser ----. Striking subject once in the hand/wrist area. Screwdriver dropped. Subject --- on the floor. **No one else in the house.**

2nd Report

Officers Mental Health Contact Report Voluntary/Involuntary Commits

Date 03-30-09 (ten days later from 2nd report)
Subject: Rhonda Lee Jimenez

Rhonda has been drinking for the past week. Rhonda said she was raped 4 days ago and is having thoughts of about hurting herself. Rhonda has been drinking today and became agitated when I asked her to go to the hospital. Rhonda is a danger to herself. Rhonda has previously attempted suicide. AID units responded and transported Rhonda to Stevens Hospital.

X as a result of a mental disorder presents an imminent likelihood of serious harm to self and others

X suicide thoughts X involuntary
X suicidal

3rd Report

I was not expecting a report like this. I wasn't expecting a report at all. I expected Snohomish county to write back to me saying 'those records are inaccessible. They no longer exist.' The first thing that came to my mind after reading these reports was, *I have to call Tina.* She needs to read this. She needs to know that she and I never really had a chance in this house. The house was never going to be a dream home. Not for us, it wasn't. What do Rhonda's rape and Rhonda's suicide have to do with the house being haunted? What does it have to with the minions being present? Short answer: bad energy. Steph Young, the book *Desolating Spirits: The True Story of Discarnate Entities and their role in Mind Control & Unexplained Disappearances*, says "ugly acts of cruelty" when they occur "become sacred ground to malevolent spirits." It attracts (awakes) them. The walls. The floors. The ceiling. The sliding back door. Everything in the Bothell house has become sullied. The demons — minions, apparitions, black orbs, specter, poltergeists, residual ghosts, unexplained energies, and stuff we've still had yet to ascertain. All these things, in my opinion, are the result of the past two events: Rhonda and her family's experience in the home and the history of Puget Sound itself. Let's deal with the Rhonda aspect first. A full-bodied female apparition that looks like one of the previous tenants in the house — what's that all about? The fact that a spirit would go out of its way to resemble Rhonda four years before Rhonda's death is just mind-blowing. We're not talking about the paranormal anymore, ladies and gentlemen. Oh no, this is supernatural stuff. The stuff I'm about to introduce right here, right now, is far beyond what you see on television. The time has come for us to abandon our prejudices about what we think the paranormal is and isn't. Going back to what I said earlier about why skeptics stay away from this case. Tina can't create a Snohomish County Sheriff's report. Nor can I. These are state reports. Official documents. These reports were created two years before Tina, and I knew each other. I want the reader to think about that seriously. Think harder than you've ever thought about the paranormal. Rhonda told me in 2014 that she had to throw a rock through the sliding glass door to get back into the house. The door "slid shut and locked on its own in front of her and her daughter."

A spirit must use an enormous amount of energy to do that. The officer responding to a woman screaming (distress call) wrote in his report that he found a mattress stuffed in the sliding door. His account coincides with what Rhonda told me (three years prior). Compare the timestamps on the Snohomish reports I've provide – my initial request (see Fig 27.14) with the communications between me and Rhonda in my book, *The Bothell Hell House*. Rhonda told the arriving officer on March 30th, 2009 that she had been raped four days prior. That rape happened six days after the officer in report two arrived on the scene. The spirits were watching all of this unfold. When it comes to depression, attempted suicide, drug addiction, and alcohol addiction try to understand each one by itself is essentially a beacon of light for wandering (ready to exploit) evil spirits. If the spirits can observe Steve and Don setting up cameras in the hallway, you best believe they watch (and give commentary) of someone inflicting pain on themselves and others. Can you imagine the conversation the spirits have the minute they see the officer walk in and tase Rhonda? Allow me to reiterate what the officer wrote down in his official report. *I've put my questions underneath each bullet point below.* ***In bold.***

The officer said he arrived at the house and said he heard a woman screaming:

- "Why are you doing this to me?"
  My question - who's doing what to you?
- "I just want to go home!"
- "Stop it!"
  My question - stop what?

No one else was in the home. Read the reports again 🗎 in conjunction with this book and *The Bothell Hell House*, as means of appreciating what this means.

Question: who Rhonda was screaming at? No one else was home. Marinate on that for as long as you like.

OFFICERS MENTAL HEALTH CONTACT REPORT **ORIGINAL**

VOLUNTARY/INVOLUNTARY COMMITS

SNOHOMISH COUNTY SHERIFF'S OFFICE

ON THE LISTED DATE AND TIME I CONTACTED RHONDA AT HER
RESIDENCE. HER FAMILY AND PASTOR HAD CALLED BECAUSE SHE SAID
SHE WAS GOING TO KILL HERSELF. RHONDA SAID SHE HAD DRANK A
SIX PACK OF BEER BUT SHE SAID SHE WAS NOT SUICIDAL. HER
HUSBAND ANDREW SAID SHE HAD BEEN DRINKING NON STOP FOR
DAYS AND HE HAD SEVERAL MESSAGES ON HIS PHONE FROM
RHONDA. I LISTENED TO A MESSAGE FROM THE PREVIOUS NIGHT
AND HEARD RHONDA SCREAM "I'M GONNA FUCKING KILL MYSELF"
ANDREW SAID THAT RHONDA AGAIN SAID SHE WOULD
KILL HERSELF TONIGHT AND THATS WHY HE CALLED. ANDREW
ALSO SAID HE WAS CONCERNED THAT RHONDA MAY BE ABUSING
PRESCRIPTION MEDICATION.

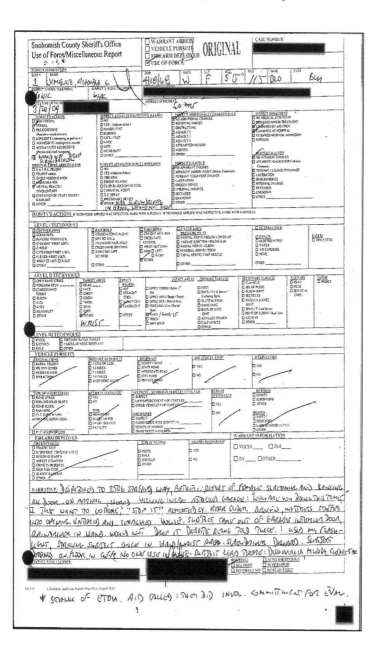

OFFICERS MENTAL HEALTH CONTACT REPORT — ORIGINAL
VOLUNTARY/INVOLUNTARY COMMITS
CONFIDENTIAL REPORT - NOT SUBJECT TO DISCLOSURE

SNOHOMISH COUNTY SHERIFF'S OFFICE

TYPE OF REPORT	CHECK APPROPRIATE SELECTION		
( ) OFCR SAFETY	[X] SUICIDAL	( ) DANGER TO PROPERTY	[X] ALCOHOL INVOLVEMENT
( ) OFCR ASSAULT	( ) HOMICIDAL/THREATS TO OTHERS	( ) MEDICAL PROBLEMS	( ) AGREES TO MENTAL HEALTH TREATMENT
( ) PERSONS	( ) WEAPONS	( ) DRUG INVOLVEMENT	[X] REFUSED MENTAL HEALTH TREATMENT
	( ) PRIOR RELATED CONTACTS	( ) UNABLE TO CARE FOR SELF	

INCIDENT CLASSIFICATION
- [ ] INFO MENTAL
- [ ] COURT COMMITMENT
- [ ] SUICIDE ATTEMPT
- [X] OTHER: SUICIDEL THOUGHTS
- [ ] VOLUNTARY
- [X] INVOLUNTARY
- [X] AS A RESULT OF A MENTAL DISORDER, PRESENTS AN IMMINENT LIKELIHOOD OF SERIOUS HARM TO SELF OR OTHERS
- [ ] IS GRAVELY DISABLED
- [ ] IS A DANGER TO THE PROPERTY OF OTHERS.

PREMISE TYPE / NAME: RES 2-STORY

REPORTED ON: MONTH 03 DAY 30 YEAR 09 TIME 1520 DOW MON

CLIENT
NO. 1 — NAME (LAST, FIRST, MIDDLE): JIMENEZ, RHONDA L.
D.O.B. 04/18/68 AGE 40
CITY: BOTHELL STATE WA ZIP 98012 RES. STATUS: P

NARRATIVE:

RHONDA HAS BEEN DRINKING FOR THE PAST WEEK. RHONDA SAID SHE RAPED 4 DAYS AGO AND IS HAVING THOUGHTS ABOUT HURTING HERSELF RHONDA HAS BEEN DRINKING TODAY AND BECAME AGGITATED WHEN I ASKED HER TO GO TO THE HOSPITAL ~~THAT~~ RHONDA IS A DANGER TO HERSELF RHONDA HAS PREVIOUSLY ATTEMPTED SUICIDE AID UNITS RESPONDED AND TRANSPORTED RHONDA TO STEVENS HOSPITAL.

SH-260

CHAPTER 28

Where Are They Now?

Wherever you stand, be the Soul of that place."
~ Rumi

W hat would you say would be one of the takeaways from this ordeal I and my ex-girlfriend experienced? What would be some of the lessons learned? If there's one lesson worth taking away from all of this is "the absence of evidence, doesn't mean the evidence is absent." I'm referring to when Ghost Adventures arrived at the house, in the end, ended up leaving empty-handed. Imagine what would have happened had I not stuck to my guns about our encounter being real. Not just my encounter. But Rhonda's encounter also. The second thing worth remembering is to never give up. Never let another person tell you what you experienced (could be anything) is not actually what you experienced. That includes family members. If there is to be one silver lining about this entire ordeal (and there are a few) that silver lining has to be *Ghost Adventures* crew leaving empty-handed. Had the *Ghost Adventures* crew found one muffled (hard to interpret) vocal response or dust orb – things they love to parade on the show as good evidence. This book I just wrote wouldn't be here. None of the investigators I met after the "Demon in Seattle," episode would have never come into my life. That includes Nikki Novelle, Karissa Fleck, Vanessa Hogle, and the rest of her team. The Scientific Establishment of Parapsychology led by Steve Mera and his chief researcher Don Philips would have never been contacted. Why would all that and more not have happened? Short answer? I would not have felt a need. *Ghost Adventures* would have declared they found something and that would have been sufficient for Tina and me.

Remember, all we wanted at the time was to be taken seriously. Alert the proper paranormal authorities. We were told it was *Ghost Adventures* – we were wrong. Who would have thought that one of my biggest accomplishments in my life was not taking no for an answer? Paranormal teams seem to be under the impression that people like myself who are calling you because we want you to tell us if we have a ghost problem or not? That's not why Tina and I called you. The day the plant levitated off the floor near the entertainment center and fell back to the ground was the day we realized we had a ghost problem. We called you because your website said you might be able to help us. Some of you couldn't, and therefore, I have to keep trying. I have to see it through.

One question I don't mind answering is the question of where are they now? Are there still spirits inside the Bothell home? The answer is yes. There are a lot of spirits inside the Bothell house. My having attachments doesn't make the Bothell house less safe. Doesn't mean the house is empty. Let's analyze what spirits are still there and why.

Minions – you best believe they're still there. Think of them as opportunists — spirits with orders to avenge. The minions saw dysfunction in two relationships: Rhonda's and mine. Try not to get too wrapped around the word dysfunction; it's not meant to be derogatory — quite the contrary. As human beings, we're subject to weaknesses. It's what makes us who we are. Malevolent spirits can identify these weaknesses on site. I refer to these demons as minions because of their numbers and because of their ability to group think. Mostly because there always up to something. You've heard their voices throughout this book.

'Image detector.'
'Go and lift one of these.'
'You chickened out, you puss.'

Table 28.1

The Gray Lady - I have two theories surrounding the Gray Lady. Theory number one, which I spoke about earlier – the Gray Lady I saw was a demon in disguise. I'll never forget how she couldn't negotiate disappearing into the washroom door. Wouldn't a spirit know how to do that? Did turning off my office light manually impact her ability to disappear? Is the Gray Lady still in the house? Damn right she is.

The White Lady – Polar opposite from the Gray Lady. I got zero negative feelings from her. The Gray Lady if you saw her, you'd know right away she's not to be messed with. Don't tangle with her. She'll win every time. She may look like Rhonda, but that's about it. It wouldn't surprise me if she were the one that threw the chef's knife at me. It wouldn't surprise me if she were behind a lot of things Tina and I witnessed. The White Lady? Totally different. There was a moment when I thought for sure she was going to run into my office and start choking me. I realized later that was just my inner fears fucking with me. The White Lady wasn't sending me any message whatsoever. She can't. She's stoic. That's it. She's the only one in the picture (see Fig 28.1) that's terrified. Why is she terrified? Look at who she's surrounded by. You see the white female apparition is not a sentient being. She didn't ask to be the White Lady. But she is, and that's one of the most tragic components of this story. Tina and me? We could have left the house anytime we wanted to. We have that ability, that wherewithal. The White Lady? She can't go anywhere. She's trapped. She's a product of the psychosis Rhonda Lee Jimenez underwent when she lived in the house. Think of the White Lady as a remnant of all the bad things that happened to Rhonda. Let me remind you what those horrors were. The horror of potentially losing a son. The mental anguish surrounding that is just too hard to imagine. The horrors of being sexually assaulted. In your house, mind you. The decision to not press charges. Rhonda never told me why she didn't press charges. She just told me she regretted not pressing charges.

She said that led to her depression. It's why she became an alcoholic. Imagine you're outside on your backyard patio. You're trying to smoke a cigarette while the food you put on the stove is cooking. Your infant daughter is sitting in a highchair just a few feet away. Happens every day. All of a sudden, the sliding door slams shut. Oh my god, you're now separated from your baby! You have no idea what's going on. No idea that there are demons in the kitchen with you right now. One of them decided to lock you out of the house. All you know is that you're locked out of the house. Food is cooking on the stove, and your daughter is screaming like crazy. Is the White Lady still inside the Bothell house? I don't know. Rhonda's suicide might have altered her existence. There's little data on crisis apparitions. So, I don't know. Let's imagine for a second that the Gray Lady I saw (Chapter 4, 20 *The Bothell Hell House*) was a demon. What reason would it have to look like Rhonda? Did the license to use Rhonda's form expire the same day Rhonda committed suicide? Some of the evidence Nikki and her team obtained when they monitored the house remotely for eight months helped us conclude that some of the events taking point to residual haunting. This theory is often referred to as Stone Tape. Wiki – *the theory suggests that ghosts and hauntings are analogous to tape recordings and that mental impressions during emotional or traumatic events can be projected in the form of energy, "recorded" onto rocks and other items and "replayed" under certain conditions.* I believe the White Lady falls into that category. What the Gray Lady did by manually turning off my office light was a form of interaction. She hit the light switch and took off running. There's nothing residual about that. That act was deliberate if not rehearsed. The White Lady is the total opposite. Watching her move through the hallway (Chapter 27 *The Bothell Hell House*) was like watching a movie. Two female apparitions. One gray. One white. Both looked like Rhonda. No coincidence.

The Black Orbs – The only evidence I can give that might give credence to the black orbs possibly still being in the house is we saw them after the activity had subsided. Which was in 2013. We have to always remember that the absence of activity doesn't mean the spirits have moved on. These spirits were always up to something when Tina and I were around. Should another paranormal team ever get back into that house, don't bring a ghost box. Bring a Microsoft Xbox Kinect.

Mass – It's very hard to describe, but you can sort of tell after living in the house awhile which spirit was doing what. Is Mass still in the house? Yes, it is, and no, it isn't. You know when Mass is present based on the trouble it creates. Mass was the only spirit that gave me the impression it could come and go as it pleases. The ability to evoke fear tactic begins the second Mass makes an entrance. Seriously, you'll know when Mass is around. Putrid smell? Mass is nearby. Humming noise? Mass is nearby. Concussion sounds? Mass is nearby. Nickel size flies appearing in the house in the dead of winter. Mass is nearby. You wake up because you feel like you're being watched. You are. Mass is worse than nearby. Mass is standing right over you. What's the best way to keep Mass from showing up? Don't argue with your significant other. Don't smudge. Some of the events that made this case what it is come as a result of me and Tina smudging. I can't think of one instance where smudging worked in our favor. I'm talking about the long term. Are all the spirits in the Bothell house evil? No, not all of them. Some of the spirits in that house are trapped. Some are lost. One of the EVPs Steve Mera captured when he was here the first time was an EVP that said something to the effect 'the demons are over there.' The Scientific Establishment of Parapsychology was able to get that on audio. Another EVP Patty and I caught happened hours before she was attacked. Patty asked me a question right before she went to bed. She wanted to know if she should leave the bedroom door closed or open. I told her to go to bed with her bedroom door closed. The same voice recorder that picked up her attack, picked up a voice which said, 'they'll walk through it.' That voice came in the middle of our discussion. 'They'll walk through it.' I sent that audio to Steve and Don, and let me tell you, they were just dumbfounded as was the Society for Psychical Research one of the oldest organizations studying the paranormal. 'They'll walk through it' Question - who is they?

Fig 28.1: Who's in the house still? Who's not?

CHAPTER 29

Bone Black II

W hy use bone black when there are other forms of liquids inside the Bothell house? Why not use the small cans of paint that were left here from when the house was constructed? Why not use Tina's mascara? Why not use the various Sharpie pens I had lying around? Did the spirit ever use any of those things? Nope. Did the spirits in our house ever use my dry erase pens? Nope. None of them were ever touched. None of my pens ever went missing. As you're about to see, bone black is an extremely difficult paint substance to paint over. A bitch to remove. One of the things I decided to do when I moved into my new apartment was continuing researching poltergeist cases. I started this endeavor back at the Bothell house right after Tina moved out. I advise everyone reading this book to do what I did. Learn about the poltergeist phenomena. Trust me; you won't regret it. One of the things I've learned is there are hundreds and hundreds of stories of poltergeist outbreaks that involve wall writings. I have a hard time understanding why Tina and I were given so much grief about the inexplicable markings in my office. Some people thought it was Tina that wrote all this stuff. I'm not talking about internet trolls or career skeptics. I'm talking about paranormal investigators. See the list of cases that involved wall writings on the next page. This list (below) mind you doesn't make up one percent of the reported wall writing cases.

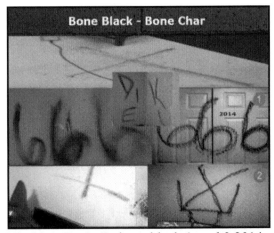

Fig 29.1: Bothell bone black **1**. and **2** 2014

Poltergeist Scribes:

- Michael Manning 1971
- The South Shields Poltergeist - The poltergeist would write threatening messages on a whiteboard and even send text messages to the couple, usually stating its **plan to kill them**
- The Enfield Poltergeist
- Australia Humpty Doo Poltergeist
- The Bratsk Poltergeist case, Russia
- The Phoenix Poltergeist 2017 – Hebrew Writing

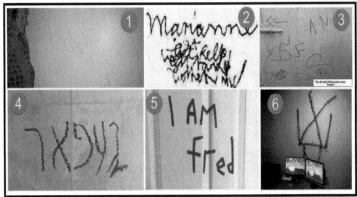

Fig 29.2: 1.) Humpty Doo 2.) Borley rectory 3.) The Bratsk 4.) 2017 - Phoenix Hebrew Writing 5.) Enfield 6.) Bothell - Washington State

According to the investigators that arrived on the scene in the majority of the above cases, the poltergeist (in question) used items that were already inside the home to carry out its scribble tantrum. Some of these writings involved use of a crayon. Others involved Magic Markers, pencils, paint, wax, ketchup, and other liquid substance except for blood and feces. There's little data of poltergeist ever using organic substances to write on walls. No record of incinerated bison/cow bone ever being used, which brings me back to my original question. Why bone black? Why was it used in our house? You have to admit that it's kind of odd that Bone Black was used. Can you at least give me that?

I mentioned earlier that the first wall writings in my office were done using our sage stick. Tina and I cleaned that mess up within a matter of minutes. Soon after that, it was black paint. Or that's what it appeared to be. Tina and I didn't own any buckets of paint. We did not need it. The new wall markings were hard to remove. Not impossible to remove. Just time-consuming. Now I'm buying paint. I have to paint over the 666 and upside-down man symbols. Paint and primer — that's it. To answer the question about why bone black was used, we need not look beyond what's on the wall. The question I kept asking myself, going on three years mind you, was why an upside-down man? Why would a spirit go out of its way to draw that symbol? The cases I read that involved wall writings most didn't have symbols associated with them. I've yet to find a case were pictography was used. I'm not saying that case doesn't exist. I just haven't found it. I've searched, ladies and gentlemen. I've searched hard. The cases I've studied go back hundreds of years. Not one upside-down man. That in itself is a clue.

Google the Native American man upside-down man symbol, and you'll see that it *means a man has died* or specifically that a man *is about to die* . NOTE - the spirit used bone black when it came time to draw an upside-down man. Never before, and never afterward. Both the symbol and substance are intrinsically linked. Not only are they intrinsically linked but the substance itself is very difficult to remove, which implies that whatever spirit wrote this wants the markings studied.

Wall writing – substance	Type of Writing	Clean up method
Sage ash	Upside-down cross, 666	Warm soap and
Black paint	666, upside-down cross	Primer, paint
Bone black	666, upside-down cross	Primer, paint, **markings bleed**
Black oily substance*	666, upside-down cross. Die KL	Primer, paint, **markings bleed through paint** and primer

Table 29.1

To give you an idea of how powerful bone black/bone char is I submit to you this article I found online:

BBC - Future - The solar explorer built with dead animal bones

http://www.bbc.com/future/story/20141105-the-spacecraft-built-with-bones

"A human technology straight from the Stone Age is being adopted for an ambitious 21st Century mission – to study the Sun at close quarters. The black surface that coats the titanium (of the space vessel) is made from powdered baked animal bones. Just 1/20th of a millimeter thick, this animal-bone-coated titanium foil will make up the outer section of the heat shield being fitted to the European Space Agency's (ESA) new Solar Orbiter spacecraft. Slated for launch in 2017, this probe will orbit the Sun at a distance of around 40 million kilometers (25 million miles). That is much closer to our nearest star than any previous mission, and well within the orbit of Mercury. Although many of the inner layers of the heat shield are reflective, the engineers developing the spacecraft calculated that a black outer layer would be the best way of releasing heat to space. Having worked that out, the next came the challenge of finding a ....

......suitable coating – **a paint** that stayed the same color and did not melt, peel or **degrade**. The technology they settled on is nothing new. Humans have been using burnt and powdered animal bone since the dawn of time for painting pictures <u>on the walls</u> of caves. Even the basic principle is still the same. Animal bones are incinerated in a furnace and ground down to get this very dark powder, like charcoal, says Draper. But despite its low-tech origins, it turns out to be one of the most robust coatings around. So, does the bone-coated titanium work? So far, all this heating, cooling and scraping has been successful, proving that even in the space age, some Stone Age tricks can still be useful." One of the most robust coatings around. I couldn't have said it better myself.

Fig 29.3: The Solar Orbiter's panels have to be able to withstand temperatures as high as 500C. Bone black1/20th of a millimeter, thick has been proven to withstand the heat of the Sun.

Everything you read from here on out I learned after I moved - including what you read about bone black being used in space. No one's sending me this stuff. Leonardo da Vinci once said, "Art is never finished, only abandoned." It would appear that applies to the paranormal field because no one's trying to ascertain why this house was haunted. The Scientific Establishment of Parapsychology, they're gone. Nikki and the team? Off doing other things. Ghost Adventures? They didn't take anything with them. Not one piece of wall fragment. Imagine if they did? Imagine what a powerful episode "Demons in Seattle" would have been had they uttered the word bone black.

We know Rhonda was going through was a dark time. The 911 reports I got from Snohomish county confirm that. A house with this much stress, this much darkness has the potential to attract evil spirits. Understand these spirits are not falling out of the sky or poofing out of portals. They're not crawling out of the ground. The spirits that tormented Rhonda and her family. That tormented me and Tina have been here for quite some time. They're loiterers. Leavings from a tumultuous period in Bothell, Washington. It's time you learn about Bothell, Washington. Let's look at the horror's that happened here before Boeing, Microsoft, Starbucks, Seattle Seahawks, and Amazon arrived.

Bothell – Thumbnail History

http://www.historylink.org/File/4190

[The earliest known residents of the Sammamish River and what would become Bothell were a Native American tribe that called themselves s- tsah-PAHBSH or "willow people." These were members of a larger group called hah-chu-AHBSH or "people of the lake" and the Duwamish Tribe. Historian David Buerge estimates that the tribe, along with a related group upriver, numbered between 80 and 200 individuals. Although poor, the willow people were apparently aggressive. One account has them staging an abortive raid by canoe on tribes of the lower Skagit Valley. A leader of the willow people, Sah-wich-ol-dahw, did not accept the validity of the Puget Sound treaty and joined the Battle of Seattle in 1856.

Following the attack and the Puget Sound war, the native people of the Sammamish were relocated. In 1862, a smallpox plague **killed** as much as half of the remaining native population

https://content.govdelivery.com/attachments/topic_files/WAKIN G/WAKING_993/2018/10/23/file_attachments/1093754/stream _monitor_2018_09__1093754.pdf As well as by the devastation from the effects of various **previous** epidemics.

https://www.revolvy.com/page/Sammamish-people

Remember during the "Demons in Seattle" *Ghost Adventures*; episode Zak Bagan's stated that they found no record of Native Americans living in the Bothell area. I don't who they talked to or where they looked, but they were grossly incorrect. I want to talk about the smallpox outbreak that decimated half of the Native American population in and around Puget Sound. That and the local skirmishes between Native Americans and local settlers (some Irish) deserve a look at.

Small Poll Outbreak – Pacific Northwest 1862

courtesy of HistoryLink.org and Greg Lang

".. the 1862 smallpox epidemic among Northwest Coast tribes. It was carried from San Francisco on the steamship *Brother Jonathan* and arrived at Victoria, British Columbia, on March 12, 1862. White officials vaccinated as many whites as possible and **very few Indians**."

"From April to December 1862, 14,000 Native Americans perished, about half the Indians living along the coast from Victoria to Alaska."

"A week after *The Daily British Colonist* confirmed the first smallpox case, the newspaper published an editorial titled "Quarantine." Noting the danger of smallpox, the paper implored the authorities to take prompt action. The editorial stated: The most stringent regulations ought to be enforced and enforced without a moment's delay. If a case occurs the parties [ought] to be placed beyond the reach of communicating the infection to others. Imagine for a moment what a fearful calamity it would be, were the horde of Indians on the outskirts of the town to take the disease. Their **filthy habits** would perpetuate the evil; keep it alive in the community, sacrificing the lives of all classes. We ... believe there is ... great danger if the smallpox be allowed to spread through the neglect of the authorities" (*The Daily British Colonist,* March 26, 1862, p. 2)." Between March 18 and April 1, 1862, The Daily British Colonist reiterated to the citizens of Victoria at least five times the importance of getting vaccinated. The paper estimated that by April 1, one-half of the "resident Victorians" were vaccinated. In 1862, Victoria, the largest town north of the Columbia River, had a white population of from 2,500 to 5,000. The **nearby Indian population** was about the same size. There were probably at least 2,000 Northern Indians (who lived along the coast from northern Vancouver Island to Alaska) camping on the outskirts of Victoria, plus at least 1,600 local Indians who lived nearby.

Initially, **no demands were made to vaccinate these local groups**. By March 27, 1862, Dr. John Helmcken (1824-1920), Hudson's Bay Company physician, had vaccinated about 30 resident Songhees Indians, who constituted less than 1 percent of the nearby natives."

Whites Concerned About Whites

On April 28, 1862, The Daily British Colonist published an editorial titled "The Small-Pox Among the Indians." The newspaper reminded readers of a previous warning (likely the March 26 article) 'that if proper precautions were not take[n] at once to prevent that loathsome disease from spreading, the Indians ... would become infected and through them spread itself throughout the colony. The paper remarked on the consequences of the authorities' intentional refusal to act to vaccinate and quarantine the Indians:

"Were it likely that the disease would **only spread among the Indians**, there might be those among us like our authorities who would rest undisturbed, **content that the smallpox is a fit successor to the moral ulcer that has festered at our doors**. ... [But] chances are that the pestilence will spread among our white population [because] ... [t]he Indians have free access to the town day and night. They line our streets, fill the pit in our theatre, are found at nearly every open door ... in the town; and are even employed as servants in our dwellings, and in the culinary departments of our restaurants and hotels" (*The Daily British Colonist,* April 28, 1862, p. 2). In June 1862, The Daily British Colonist, noting the devastation of the Indians up to that time, stated the obvious, inevitable consequences of these escorted canoes.

Referring to a group of Haida who recently departed Victoria, the newspaper wrote:

"How have the mighty fallen! Four short years ago, numbering their braves by thousands, they were the scourge and terror of the coast; today, broken-spirited and effeminate, with scarce a corporal's guard of warriors remaining alive, they are proceeding northward, bearing with them the seeds of a loathsome disease that will take root and bring both a plentiful crop of ruin and destruction to the friends who have remained at home. At the present rate of mortality, not many months can elapse 'ere the Northern Indians of this coast will exist **only in story**" (The Daily British Colonist, June 21, 1862, p. 3; Boyd, p. 173, 229).

"A smallpox epidemic broke out among the Northwest **tribes** in 1862, killing roughly half of the native population. Documentation in archives and historical epidemiology demonstrates that Governmental policies furthered the progress of the epidemic among the natives." [17]

https://en.wikipedia.org/wiki/History_of_Seattle_before_1900

"Smallpox wiped out roughly 65 **to 95%** of Northwestern Indian populations by 1840. Though there is a great deal of dispute about precontact Native populations, it seems fair to say that the Indian population of the Pacific Northwest (including present-day Alaska, British Columbia, **Washington**, and Oregon) fell from over **500,000** in 1750 to somewhere around **100,000** by 1850. By way of comparison, the 14th- century Black Plague in Europe and Asia claimed the lives of one-third of the population there. Smallpox and other diseases did kill some Europeans in the **Pacific Northwest**, but not nearly at the same rate as the illnesses decimated. Native-Americans."

http://www.washington.edu/uwired/outreach/cspn/Website/Classr oom%20Materials/Curriculum%20Packets/Indians%20%26%20 Europeans/II.html The early Seattle settlers had a sometimes-rocky relationship with the local Native Americans. There is no question that the settlers were steadily **taking away native lands** and, in many cases, **treating the natives terribly**. There were numerous **deadly attacks** by settlers against natives and by natives against settlers.

https://en.wikipedia.org/wiki/History_of_Seattle_before_1900 Bill Speidel writes in Sons of the Profits, "The general consensus of the community was that **killing an Indian** was a matter of no graver consequence than shooting a cougar or a bear.

Smallpox in the Puget Sound Region (Bothell area)

Smallpox was more widespread in Puget Sound than newspaper reports indicate. Perhaps one reason the papers did not report it was fear that news of smallpox would create alarm and keep people away. San Francisco, the point of origin of the Victoria epidemic, delayed reporting on it.

Local papers stated that smallpox was "far more terrible" among Indians than among whites and inferred that many Indian deaths would result. **Instead of recommending preventive measures for Indians**, the Puget Sound weeklies recommended preventive measures from the Indians. From the beginning, there was general agreement in the press that **removing** the Indians away from white man's towns was the best policy. Their removal would protect (white) town residents from getting infected. **Getting rid of the Indians would also improve Puget Sound towns both "morally and socially"** and be a boost to their (white settlers) "growth and prosperity" (North-West [Port Townsend], March 29, 1862; Ibid., May 24, 1862, p. 2; Overland Press, April 7, 1862; Puget Sound Herald, April 10, 1862).

One paper stated that "an added benefit" would be **reducing the number** of **"licentious** whites" from towns. The North-West (Port Townsend) made the following statement:

"The Indians are a loathsome and indolent race, of no earthly use to themselves or anybody else in the community — save the doctors — and their presence gathers and retains a set of graceless white vagabonds, who ... get a precarious living by peddling villainous whisky among them.

These social lepers are far worse than the smallpox. In ridding ourselves of one, we no longer encourage the other. Let the Indians be sent to the Reservations where they belong ... [and then] our natural resources would rapidly develop, society would improve and strengthen, and free-love and atheism find fewer endorsers on the shores of Puget Sound" (May 24, 1862, p. 2).

When word was received that Indians in the British colonies to the north were **"dying** like **rotten** sheep" even though "many hundred" were vaccinated, the Steilacoom paper stated: "We think the whites, guided by their superior intelligence, have little to apprehend from this dread disease" (Puget Sound Herald, May 8, 1862, p. 2). Two weeks later, hearing that the smallpox epidemic would "nearly **exterminate all the tribes** on the coast," the **Port Townsend** paper concluded that **it was**

better for the Indians "to die by smallpox than whisky and civilized lust" (North-West, May 24, 1862, p. 3). http://www.historylink.org/File/5171 Smallpox Epidemic of 1862 among Northwest Coast and Puget Sound Indians

War, battles, Unrest – 1856

"Settlers and soldiery slept uneasily in the small communities along Puget Sound as the year 1856 opened. Many of the Indians were hostile, and various instances of violence had been reported."

The unpleasant situation of Indian affairs renders it so disagreeable. It is impossible to tell what is in store for us, but certainly there never was a time in the settlement of any part of the country when things presented a more serious aspect than now. There seems to be such general cooperation among the different tribes whose former enmity to each other had secured safety to the whites. We have sent you several papers from which, if you have received them, you will perceive that those Indians who have committed these hostilities are not a whit behind the savages who formerly inhabited the Atlantic side, in barbarity. Indeed, the inhumanity of these cannot be surpassed.

Fig 29.4: Book – Seattle's First Taste of Battle, 1856

"We learn that the Indians are becoming more and more bold and that they are doing many **acts of cruelty**, of which they were heretofore judged incapable. They have killed some three or men near Olympia as they were traveling on the road, and they are scattering about all parts of the country in small bands ready to murder families who are living distant from neighbors and waylay single persons who are passing from part of the country to another."

Seattle's First Taste of Battle, 1856 **cont.**

RECAP - "Although poor, **the willow people (located in Bothell)** were aggressive. One account has them staging an abortive raid by canoe on tribes of the lower Skagit Valley. They paddled their shallow-draft river canoes into Puget Sound as far as Penn Cove on Whidbey Island, but the raiders' canoes swamped. The force had to build rafts to get back to the mainland and then walk home."

"After the treaties with the United States in 1854 and 1855, war broke out between the natives and the whites. Indian Agent David Maynard (1808- 1873) tried to persuade the Willow People's leader Sah-wich-ol-gadhw to go to Seattle, but the chief declined. Some of these tribe members were known to have joined in the attack on Seattle on January 26, 1856."

Bothell — Thumbnail History

http://www.historylink.org/File/4190

Native American Accounts

"A few Indian oral histories survive that may describe the 1770s epidemic. In the 1890s, an "aged informant" from the Squamish tribe, located near the mouth of the Fraser River, related the history of a catastrophic illness to ethnographer Charles Hill-Tout.

The ethnographer wrote:
"[A] dreadful misfortune befell them. … One salmon season the fish were found to be covered with running sores and blotches, which rendered them unfit for food. But as the people depended very largely upon these salmon for their winter's food supply, they were obliged to catch and cure them as best they could and store them away for food. They put off eating them till no other food was available, and then began a terrible time of sickness and distress. A dreadful skin disease, loathsome to look upon, broke out upon all alike. None were spared. Men, women, and children sickened, took the disease and **died in agony by hundreds**, so that when the spring arrived and fresh food was procurable, there was scarcely a person left of all their numbers to get it. Camp after camp, village after

village was left desolate. The remains of which, said the old man, in answer by my queries on this, are found today in the old camp sites or midden-heaps over which the forest has been growing for so many generations. Little by little the remnant left by the disease grew into a nation once more, and when the first white men sailed up the Squamish in their big boats, the tribe was strong and numerous again" (Boyd, 55). During the first or second decade of the 1900s, the photographer of Native Americans Edward S. Curtis interviewed an Indian who lived on the northwest side of Vancouver Island. Referring to the time of his great- great-grandfather, the Indian stated that a disease beset the village: "So great was the mortality in this epidemic that **it was impossible for the survivors to bury the dead.** They simply pulled the houses down over the bodies and left them" (Boyd, 27). Although his informant told Curtis that the deaths were caused by an epidemic, others reported it was caused by warfare. So, this may or may not refer to the late 1700s smallpox epidemic."

https://www.historylink.org/File/5100

It's estimated that **over 400,000 natives <u>died</u>** as a result of **coming into contact with settlers**. That's just from smallpox. There's no telling how many died as a result of fighting with settlers. Those numbers have to be in the thousands also. As you just read some were discarded in mass graves and others dumped in the nearby sea. Now we know why the upside-down man was drawn. The spirits that drew the upside-down man pictography on the wall in my office are not trying to imply that a man died somewhere underneath the house. No! Native men (and women) of all ages died throughout Puget Sound. Throughout the Pacific Northwest. Should the reader ever bump into Zak Bagans or and his chief researcher Dave Schrader please tell them what Keith Linder found by researching online. The information was free and readily available.

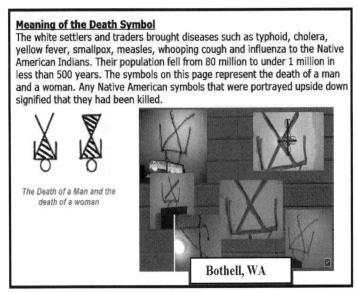

Fig 29.5: Native American Death Symbol / Office Wall Bothell, WA

I must reiterate the spirit could have used any paint-like substance in our house to draw an upside-down man. It could have used countless materials. Why bone black? To understand why bone black was used we need look no further than the war stories already mentioned. We've all seen the movie *Dances with Wolves* starring Kevin Costner. There's a scene of John J Dunbar and the Sioux nation standing together. They've just stumbled upon a mass killing of buffalo. Dead buffalo for as far as the eyes can see. The photos below explain better than me why bone black was used.

Fig 29.6: *Dancing with Wolves* 1863 open frontier.

Fig 29.7: Rougeville, Michigan - Bison pile up - man stands on top of an enormous pile of buffalo skulls; another man stands in front of the pile bones with his foot resting on a bison skull. 1892 Glueworks, office foot of 1st St. The enormous amount dead buffalo spread through the plans of the United States led to the creation and manufacturing of **bone black**.

Fig 29.8: Doug-fir log at Huron Mill Co., Bothell, 1890s Courtesy MOHAI (Neg. SHS 1,039)

Fig 29.9: North America - postcard from the **1880's** bragging about the devastation of the buffalo.

Fig 29.10: Cedar stump cemetery 1800s Washington

"During the western expansion and building of The Transcontinental Railroad many buffalo bones, that scattered the western prairies, left by hunters, were collected and used for creating the dye."

http://christophercochran.me/color-history/bone-black/

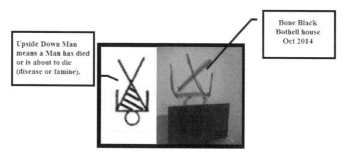

Fig 29.11: Upside-down man drawn in Bothell house several times. Substance bone black/bone char.

"By 1883, the big hunt was over, and bison were on the brink of extinction (Isenberg, 134). The Native Americans of the Plains were relocated to reservations. Starting in the 1870s, as the carcasses began to pile up, bones began to be more important than leather. In cities like Detroit, Philadelphia, and St. Louis, carbon works industries were being established (Product History). Carbon works, while sounding like they might have dealt primarily with coal, would be better seen as predecessors of the petrochemical industry. http://briankelleyart.com/bison-bone-black.html The bones were calcined into bone charcoal and then bone black..."

Fig 29.12: A.) How the population of buffalo in North America went from 30 million to 325 in a century. **B.)** "Some 70 million acres of commercial forest land once covered the Pacific Northwest. Large Douglas firs, spruce, hemlock, and cedar trees grew west of the Cascade Range – Seattle PI (Daniel DeMay).

https://www.seattlepi.com/local/seattle-history/article/Photos-A- tale-of- the-Northwest-s-logging-past-6775332.php

Fig 29.13: 1800s – Bison hunting in the American Plains and **tree hunting** in the Pacific Northwest.

One can see how the mass chopping down of trees, the smallpox outbreaks which killed hundreds of thousands of native Americans and the broken treaties between Native American and settlers (a percentage which is Irish) could be compared to the near extinction of the American buffalo. It awes me that a spirit went out of its way to make the distinction. This is deep stuff. This level of hostility between settlers and Native Americans can be summed up by one of the commentaries above (see Fig 29.5).

The spirits that drew the upside-down man in my office knew exactly what they were doing. Using bone black as your paint substance is a symbolic metaphor to atrocities that took place in the Puget Sound region. Seventy million acres of trees gone in the state of Washington. Thirty million buffalo gone in North America. The neighborhood where Tina and I lived, it's called the Timbers neighborhood. The town south of Bothell is named Woodinville. The town north of Bothell is named Mill Creek. It shouldn't be hard to believe that the Natives in the Pacific Northwest put a high value on their trees – equal to how the Native in the Mid-west valued the American buffalo. A percentage of the EVPs Steve Mera and Don Philips captured when they were here had Irish accents. One of the EVPs Don captured while under the house was the word 'longhouse.' When asked if there were any native burials in the area the answer Don got was 'yes.' To say that these spirits demonstrate a form of intelligence is somewhat of an understatement. Writing on the office with a Sharpie pen. That's vandalism. Writing on the wall with bone black? That's called graffiti. But we're not done. There's one more revelation I want to share with you.

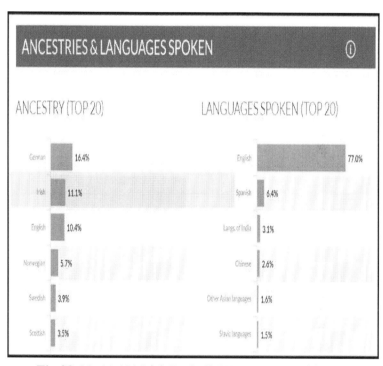

Fig 29.14: 11.1% Irish Bothell, WA Demographic Data

http://www.historylink.org/File/5348

Irish in Washington — The Early Years (the 1840s to 1890)

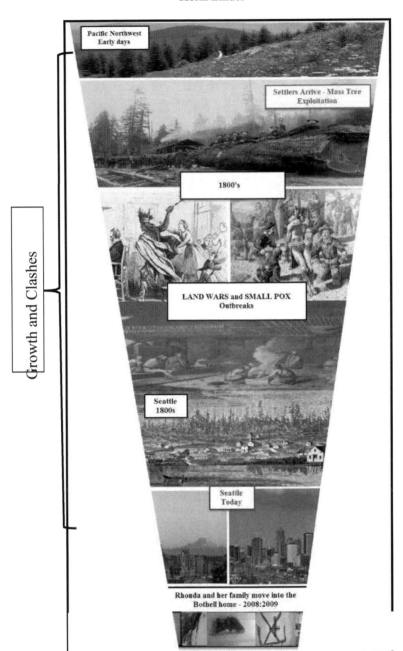

Pacific Northwest
Early days

Settlers Arrive - Mass Tree
Exploitation

1800's

LAND WARS and SMALL POX
Outbreaks

Seattle
1800s

Seattle
Today

Growth and Clashes

Rhonda and her family move into the
Bothell home - 2008:2009

**Keith and Tina
Arrive 2012**

I've been living outside the Bothell house going on three years now. There's so much stuff we still don't know. Where did the bone black come from? We know its buffalo bones. How did the spirit get it? Your neighborhood paint store doesn't carry this stuff. Buffalo are not native to the state of Washington. But there's another unanswered question: What application method was used to get this on the wall? You have to understand all of this was done while Tina and I were away. Us being gone creates a time window. We know the time we left the house and we know the time we came back. All the painters I talked to said there's no way they could have done this (even with help) within the time frame given – which is only a few hours. Some said they couldn't do it even if they had an infinite amount of time.

After discovering what the markings in my office (inside the Bothell house) were made out of I thought *there's no way I'm going to outdo myself.* I was wrong. In chapter four, I said don't forget the words Dippel's oil. I said that for a reason. Bone Black in its true form looks like gravel. When you hold it in your hand that's what it feels like. You can reduce it down a little further to where it feels like sand and to some extent powdered sugar. Those conditions alone don't necessarily make it a good paint material. You need an *adhesive of some kind.* You need a binding agent. In other words, Dippel's oil. What the hell is Dippel's oil? Dippel's oil is a by - product of bone black, i.e. bone char. The man who discovered it was Johann C. Dippel. Before proceeding to the next page, there are a few things worth knowing about Mr. Johann C. Dippel. Johann Dippel also known as Christianus Democritus was regarded by his peers as being the "most vile devil...who attempted wicked things." He majored in theology, philosophy, and alchemy at the University of Glessen. His place of birth was *Castle Frankenstein.* Seriously? I'm not making this up. WIKI – *"Dippel attempted to purchase Castle Frankenstein in exchange for his elixir formula (Dippel's oil), which he claimed he had recently discovered; the offer was turned down. [6] There are also rumors that during his stay at Frankenstein Castle, Dippel practiced not only alchemy but also anatomy and may have performed experiments on dead bodies that he exhumed.* Research Johann C. Dippel and you'll know I'm not making this up!

Johann Conrad Dippel - founder, inventor of Dippel's oil

Dippel wrote extensively about experimenting with deceased animals. He claimed to have concocted potions of various uses through boiling dead animal parts, including the *Elixir of Life* aka Dippel's oil as a **solution for exorcising demons**.

http://www.weirdworm.com/five-of-the-most-notorious-doctors-in-history/

Experiments:

- Dippel created something called "*Dippel's oil*," which he claimed was the Elixir of Life... it was just a bunch of dead animal parts thrown together.
- He did help discover *Prussian Blue*, a famous pigment, with his oil and potassium carbonate. (see Appendix C).
- Dippel attempted to transfer the soul from one cadaver to another.
- He was an avid dissector of animals.
- He made claims of potions for **exorcisms**.
- He claimed to have discovered how to create the "Elixir of Life" and the "Philosopher's Stone."

What exactly is Dippel's oil:

- Dippel's oil (sometimes known as **bone oil**) is a nitrogenous by-product of the destructive distillation of bones. [1] A dark, viscous, tar-like liquid with an unpleasant smell, it is named after its inventor, Johann Conrad Dippel. The oil consists mostly of aliphatic chains, with nitrogen functionalities and includes species such as *pyrroles*, *pyridines*, and *nitriles*, as well as other nitrogenous compounds: *WIKI Article*

RECAP - The founder of Dipple's oil a *bi-product of bone char* viewed his "elixir" as being a good tool for conducting exorcisms. There are so many directions I can go with that as it relates to our former house. If there was any house that needed an exorcism, ours was it. Rape, suicide attempts, meningitis, drug addiction, alcohol addiction, a mysterious fall down the stairs, Bibles catching fire, flies, Katie Perry weekend, arguments between Tina and me, and minions popping in and out existence makes this house worthy of receiving a dozen exorcisms. I refuse to believe this is all a coincidence. I don't quite understand it all. But's that's OK. The one thing I've learned about these spirits is they're not in the happenstance business. Everything connects when viewed close up. Dippel's oil serves as a binding agent – it's an organic adhesive. Going back to what I said about the spirits ability to demonstrate artistic license. Remember that oil substance that appeared downstairs back in March 28th, 2016? Patty and I found streams of it throughout the upstairs area of the house. You really couldn't see its color on the green wall downstairs. But it's yellow (See Fig 28.10). Dippel's oil by itself gives off a dark yellow appearance. Sit a jar of it next to your favorite cooking oils, e.g. olive, canola, peanut, and vegetable oil (label it carefully), because you'll hardly know the difference.

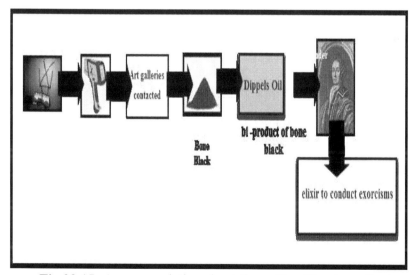

Fig 29.15: A new revelation about the wall writing ingredients.

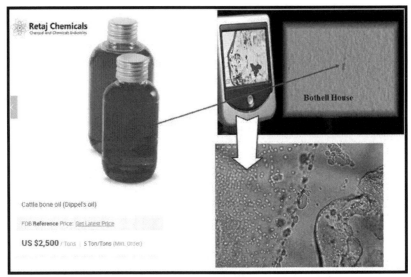

Fig 29.16: The yellow substance found on my den wall has an uncanny resemblance to Dippel's oil.

History

In the Classical World, painters used materials like egg, wax, honey, lime, casein, linseed oil or bitumen as binders to mix with pigment to hold the pigment particles together in the formation of paint. [3] Egg-based tempera was especially popular in Europe from the Middle Ages until the early 16th century. [4] However, since that time, the binder of choice for paint has been **oil**.

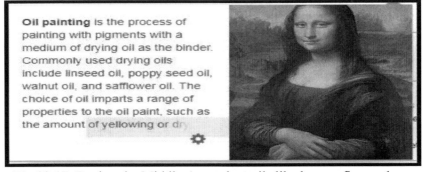

Fig 29.17: During the Middle Ages plant oils like honey, flaxseed, Dippel's oil, and other yellow color oils were used as binding agents. The majority of those binding agents left a yellow color hue within the painting.

When I first told Steve and Don about the substances dripping down the wall (weeks before they arrived the second time), my biggest fear was it was going to evaporate. *Please don't evaporate. I need you to be here when Steve and Don arrive.* Lucky for me it didn't evaporate. It's adhesive. It's not meant to evaporate. Can you walk into a store right now and say, 'I'd like some Dippel's oil?' Of course not. There are better forms of binding agents in existence right now. The keyword is right now. These wall markings (Halloween 2014) in particular go back a long time. Fig 28.11 During the Middle Ages plant oils like honey, flaxseed, *Dippel's oil, and other yellow color oils were used as binding agents. Majority of those organic binding agents left a* **yellow color** *hue within the painting.* I'm sure that frustrated a lot of artists. But what choice did they have back then? Bone Black produces its own binding agent during its creation process. That bi-product in its purest form is a yellow oil-like substance. Both have appeared in my house numerous times. The question I want to ask Mr. Johann if he were alive today. What is it about his elixir "Dippel's oil" that he feels was perfect for conducting exorcisms?

Could a spirit be nominated for a Pulitzer Prize award? My question is not rhetorical. I'm dead serious. If the upside-down man means a man has died and the substance that makes up that symbol is Bone Black. We know what Bone Black is. We know the history of the Pacific Northwest. We know the history of Bothell, Washington. We know hundreds of thousands of Native Americans died. We know how the original men and women were treated. We even know, and I forgot to mention this earlier, that a lot of settlers were living in fear. Fear of being attacked by natives in the area. Death could come in an instant. These settlers knew that. That feeling of not knowing when something horrible was about to happen that's how Tina and I felt. The angst. The fear. The feeling you're constantly walking on eggshells. Going back to what I said earlier about studying other poltergeist cases. The case that gives me the creeps every time I read it is the Bell Witch case. The spirit, in that case, said it was the spirit of a Native American. It instructed the Bell family to go out and look for its bones.

Find them and bring them together. It said "if my bones are all put together. I'll be able to rest in peace." According to the family, it said that, "The family tried to look for the bones of the spirit and were unsuccessful." Do you want to know something more frightening than that? The death of John Bell Sr. John Bell Sr., who it is believed the spirit had a deep dislike for, died of mysterious circumstances. The spirit said it killed him. It "fixed him" is the word it used. The morning of his death, John Bell's family found a mysterious vial in the room where Bell's body lay. A bottle containing black liquid. They fed the black liquid inside the bottle to the cat, and the cat immediately died. Johann Conrad Dippel death is rumored to have been a result of him purposely drinking his own "elixir." He thought it was a key to longevity. He had a stroke and died. Almost identical to John Bell Sr's death. I find it striking that both John Bell Sr. and Johann Conrad Dippel both died of mysterious circumstances involving a black liquid substance. The Bell Witch as it was called said 'find its bones and bring them together.' Add what I just told you about my case to what the Bell Witch poltergeist said as proof positive of "ugly acts of cruelty" being the root cause of poltergeist infestations. The Bell family never found the bones the poltergeist was referring to and therefore paid a severe price.

The spirits I've been referring to throughout this book have on more than one occasion demonstrated a keen sense of intelligence. Not only that but a keen understanding of how to make one's life miserable. How to sabotage a perfect date. How to sabotage a couple's marriage. How to sabotage a four-year relationship. No one's been able to pinpoint why poltergeist possess the ability to do what it does or why. More importantly, why this house? Based on the evidence gathered at my house and my apartment, I will have to say there are several reasons worth considering. One reason I spoke about earlier was an ugly act of cruelty. We often think of sacred ground as a holy place. As being religious or biblical. But that's silly. Sacred grounds can also involve areas where great atrocities occurred. If a mass group of people were killed unjustly and their remains not property buried, that could lead to some unruly spirits roaming around. This might explain the negative response Tina and I got from smudging.

The negative response we got from laying out crosses and Bibles. You read the articles I provided. You saw the role Christianity played in the extermination of Native Americans in and around Puget Sound. You saw the racism. When I said the spirits in our home could have chosen a multitude of liquid substances in our home to draw an upside-down man, I was serious. The spirits could have done that, but they chose not to. The Bone Black in my office was a riddle. It was a poem. That poem meant 'we're pissed.' Are these the spirits of the people who died from smallpox and other related illness back in the 1800's? Are these the spirits of people who were murdered? Some are. Some aren't. I wish I could share with you all the emails I got from people who've had similar activity and, in some cases, worse activity than what Tina and I experienced. The emails come from people living in the Pacific Northwest. There are reports throughout Puget Sound (including Bothell) of people 'being pelted with rocks' while jogging through wooded areas. No known source. Remember Steve Mera has an EVP (class A or B I might add) of a voice saying, 'the demons are over there.' Some people hate using the word demon. But what choice do you have when the voice on your voice recorder says, 'the demons are over there?' What choice do you have when the actions they take are horrific? You saw the shadowy figures they captured in the upstairs hallway of the Bothell home. That's not human. Once again, when I use the word demon, I'm referring to a negative spirit. I'm thinking minions. Sexual violence. Murder. Mental abuse. Domestic abuse. Smallpox. Genocide. Substance abuse. That's some of the negative components associated with this house. With this city. With this county, and I'm embarrassed to say, with this region. Anything that involves the creation of negative energy — here they come. I'm talking about negative spirits. It's not too far-fetched to believe that someone coughing up their last breath of smallpox, cold, deaf, and blind might utter in their native language 'curse all who come after us.' They're not necessarily summoning their deity to enact such vengeance. No. They're summoning something more sinister. Some might find that repulsive and crazy and I get that. I do. Trust me; no one's been a witness to crazy things happening around them more than me.

What you read in this book is what we found. It's what I've found. The spirits who did this, in my opinion, wanted it found. All of it. They wanted it known. Why that particular house in Bothell? I just gave you the longer answer. The short answer to the same question is the house occupants were easy pickings. Rhonda's family and Tina and I bought baggage that was easy to exploit. Go out and study the most horrendous poltergeist cases on record. I'm not talking about Enfield or Amityville. There are cases way darker than those – that rarely gets talked about. Find those cases and combine them with all the cases I've mentioned in this book, and you'll see that the darkest cases involve some physical or psychic violence happening in the home.

Steve Mera said it best when he said the Bothell house "is simply waiting for the right synergy of people to feed it to become something much darker than what we experienced. ...Some dysfunction or trauma that unleashes all of this negative energy into the environment." – from the book *House of Fire and Whispers* by Jenny Ashford and Parapsychologists Steve Mera.

Fig 29.18: 1.) House of Fire and Whispers Jenny Ashford and **Steve Mera** 2.) The Bothell Hell House by Keith Linder 3.) A Century of Ghost Stories by Richard Sugg and 4.) Project Phenomena: Evaluating the Paranormal by Brian Allan - **books providing further analysis of the house in Bothell and the phenomenon known as poltergeist.**

CHAPTER 30

The Bothell Hell House

If you told me in 2004 that I would be writing a book about a house that I lived in. That I would be giving testimony about phantom footsteps, strange water puddles, inexplicable wall writings, and shadow figures I would have laughed at you. These phenomena you said I'm going to become a witness of. They're the stuff of Hollywood movies. Right? They're not? A beer bottle zigzagging in mid-air? Seriously, Hollywood has a lot of catching up to do. How in the hell did I survive this? I get that question all of the time. My honest answer is I don't know. My short answer is (not trying to offend agnostics and atheists) God was protecting us. That fall I took back on January 2nd, 2014. That was a bad fall. I could have been crippled or killed. We know the spirits were behind that. They've admitted to it on the voice recorder. When I say God was protecting me, I don't mean like how Zeus was protecting Perseus in the last two *Clash of the Titans* movies. No, it's way deeper than that.

One of the negative responses I got from skeptics after learning of my and Tina's ordeal was "you're too calm. If this was real as you say it is, keeping one's composure would be impossible." Judging me without even knowing me is prejudice in its purest form. When I left college in nineteen-ninety-three, I returned to Austin Texas, to jump-start my IT career. The two companies I worked for right after college were Dell computers and MCIWorldcom (now called Verizon). My first job at MCIWorldcom had me working with irate customers. One of the first things they teach you in customer service training is "how to remain calm when encountering irate customers."

Whatever the customer says to you, you have to take it. If you can't take it, then this job isn't for you. I think I've demonstrated in both books that I can take a majority of what the poltergeist is dishing out. I'm talking about the part about remaining calm. It helps to remain calm in the middle of a poltergeist attack.

Things MCIWorldcom taught me that have aided through the years:

- Remain calm
- Don't take insults personally
- Use your best listening skills
- Actively sympathize
- Apologize gracefully
- Find a solution
- Take a few minutes on your own

Remain calm, don't take it (what's happening in the house) personally, use your best listening skills, and find a solution. Those are things we tried to incorporate while living in the Bothell house. Combine that with how I was raised growing up — perhaps you can understand how I was able to remain calm in certain "Geist" situations. Let's go back to that stereotype of African Americans being too scared to live in haunted houses. There's no science whatsoever to support that. African Americans are no different than any other race on this planet. If we can tolerate living in America for four hundred years, I think it's safe to say we can tolerate living in a "Geist" infested home. Judge me based on the evidence presented here versus some eighty's standup comedy routine.

Were there moments where I almost gave in? Of course. I'll never forget the day when the spirits almost succeeded in getting Tina and me to kill each other. That was the day the scratches appeared on my car. (Chapter 18 *The Bothell Hell House*). People who study these phenomena for a living will tell you a calm demeanor is one of but a few tools you can use to defend yourself. Why even go there? No matter how angry you get, the spirit gets angrier. The spirit always wins. There were a few times where I did get angry. That resulted in my clothes catching fire.

I'm talking about the clothes I was wearing. Talk about sending a shot across the bow. That's exactly what it felt like. 'Careful with your indignation, Mr. Linder, you're our bitch. Remember that.'

I've been living in my two-bedroom apartment for almost three years. It's time for me to think about living elsewhere. Not because of the phenomena that's continuing to happen. If I move, it's because I miss living in a house. I do. I miss hosting dinner and wine tasting parties. I like to cook. I like the thought-provoking conversations that form over food and wine. I miss that. My reason for getting this apartment versus getting another house can be summed up in one word: Quarantine. If I have attachments, there's no sense moving into another house. I'd rather be in a small place versus a big place. Small place? That has to be better, right? Imagine coming home from work and seeing every picture of yourself nailed to the wall. Your face burned out of all of them. How did they get the pictures on the wall? They used a chef knife and scissors. That's just one example of what Tina and I came home to. I told myself back in April 2016 that *it'll all stop once I move out.* These spirits can't leave the property. I was trying to psyche myself into believing that I don't have attachments.

May 21st, 2018 – This person wanted me to know that I'm not the only person who's experienced this type of phenomena. The website I was given was a repository of similar events taking place throughout the world. The description people gave identical to the one I've been giving for the last three years.

Indentations in the mattress. Paw-sized indentations:

- Pulsating
- Heartbeats
- Localized inflating and deflating within mattress and pillow
- Movement towards you (see book cover)

Esther Cox's Poltergeist - <u>Amherst Poltergeist</u>

The Great Amherst Mystery began in August of 1878 - Esther Cox lived with several relatives in a cottage house in Amherst. Reportedly, the precipitating event took place when Esther was the subject of an attempted sexual assault (act of cruelty) with a gun by Bob McNeal. He was a family acquaintance that she had developed a fondness for, despite rumors he was of poor character. Esther was traumatized by the assault, and her behavior changed. Her sisters witnessed her crying herself to sleep, and she seemed depressed. But they just assumed the emotional girl merely had a falling out with Bob. Esther hadn't told them of the assault. Strange things began happening shortly after the event with Bob. Esther and her sister, Jane, shared a bedroom, and they began to hear strange rustling sounds under the bed. At first, the subtle noises led them to believe it was just a mouse. But events intensified quickly when on subsequent nights the noises would be accompanied by intensely frightening experiences that would prove this was no mouse. There were strikingly loud sounds like **claps of thunder** that appeared to originate from under the bed, and later from the roof. The girls told how there seemed to be something crawling underneath the blankets. It was big enough to scare them out of the bed. Everyone assumed it was a mouse that was trapped in the sheets, but thorough searches revealed nothing *http://www.ghosttheory.com/2011/11/05/the-amherst-poltergeist*

> **Theory 7: Ghosts are sentient entities that enjoy vexing and even harming humans.** Some ghosts seem to like to mess with us, poking and prodding and pulling hair, or, in many cases, engaging in much more terrifying and violent activity. This is the realm of the poltergeist, the demon, the shadow person, and the djinn.

Fig 30.1: Ghosts, Specters, and Haunted Places by Michael Pye, Kirsten Dalley

But the case that caught my attention the most was the one that involved the Snedeker family often referred to as The Haunting in Connecticut. One of the testimonies Al (may he rest in peace) and Carmen Snedeker gave was of them being poked and prodded. Compare the description I've given in this book and in my book *The Bothell Hell House* with what Carmen and Al described back in the 1980's.

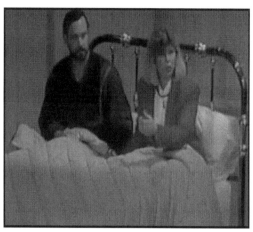

Fig 30.2: Haunting in Connecticut – the 1980s

https://youtu.be/nxMtNTQOIXw

 Review time stamps below

Time Stamps	Quote
10:31	*"The bed would begin to vibrate."*
10:38	*"The bed had a pulse and a heartbeat."*
10:52	*"Someone else could go up and touch it, and feel it..."Walk around the bed, small feet, ... impression of the bed. Cat's*

Table 30.1: Poking and prodding – Snedeker family

Compare what you heard above with what Nikki (Nicole) Novelle said when she was interviewed about my house.

Next page →

Fig 30.3: Paranormal Interview – Nikki

Time Stamp		Quotes
47:58		*"Sounds like the house has a heartbeat."*
48:17		*"You start feeling. Just the mattress...vibrating."*
48:21		*"...pulsating...like a pulse."*

Table 30.2: Nikki's account of bed heartbeats coming from my bed.

Interview - **https://www.youtube.com/watch?v=whsHPreLIZ4**

This is why I have a YouTube channel. So, individuals like the person who contacted me on Facebook can contact me about cases they know about. That's how I found out about the Snedeker family. In 1986, Allen Snedeker and his wife Carmen Snedeker moved into an old residence in Southington, Connecticut. What they experienced while living there supports what I've been saying throughout this book. Malevolent hauntings have more to do with discarnate and incarnate spirits than R.S.P.K (Recurrent Spontaneous Psychokinesis). Some people might view the Snedeker family case with suspicion based on Ed and Lorraine's Warren involvement. Let me address that. Individuals like Peggy Hodgson, Allen and Carmen Snedeker, Tina Resch, Tina and myself, and countless other cases, we all have one thing in common. We all want the haunting we're going through to stop.

Try to understand this, house occupants are always at their wit's end by the time researchers arrive. It's true. It took me three years to find true help. Three years to find someone who knew what they were doing. Paranormal teams and organizations are not listed on Yelp or the **_BBB (Better Business Bureau)_**. Being taken advantage of is the furthest thing on your mind when living in a "Geist' infested house. Are there opportunists in the paranormal field? Of course, there are. There are opportunists in any field. Why should the house occupants' claims be less real due to the involvement of opportunistic researchers? The opportunists are always going to respond quicker than a sincere researcher. Hello, *Ghost Adventures*? If you find that hard to understand, maybe you can understand this. Imagine you were about to go down in sinking ship when all a sudden you see someone coming toward you with a life rope. The person coming was a liar, an opportunist, and a cheater. Would you deny the rope being thrown at you? Of course, you wouldn't.

Allen and Carmen account that the pulsating mattress is identical to mine. It's identical to what Nikki described. If you read my book *The Bothell Hell House*, you'll see where I mentioned not ever experiencing the pulsating mattress when Tina was in bed. Only when Tina was not in bed did I experience this. That's the same thing Mr. and Mrs. Snedeker said on the video. Only a "Geist" survivor would know that. That's how I know they're telling the truth. You can't make up nuances like that, ladies and gentlemen. As far as *corroborating* go that's as real as it gets.

CHAPTER 31

What Happens Next?

There's a dialogue scene between Clinton Eastwood's character The Stranger, and the character named Mordecai (played by Billy Curtis) in the movie *High Plains Drifter*. Mordecai asks The Stranger what do him (Mordecai who's officially the town's Sheriff now), and the town people do after they've killed the three escaped convicts? "What happens when it's over?" The Strangers replies, "You live with it." If you experienced anything close to what Tina and I experienced, you'll probably agree with me when I say living with it is all you can do.

Tina and I throughout this ordeal never looked at ourselves as victims. We never said out loud 'why have you forsaken us?' We loved that house. Poltergeist, notwithstanding it, was an awesome house. I often said to myself why me? Why has life dealt me this card? I think I know the answer to that question. The notion of quitting when the activity was at its apex was never really an option. In the house, I grew I up in as a child, trial, and tribulations are to be accepted. "Stand firm and you will win life," says the Bible. "After difficulty comes ease," says the Holy Quran. That's how I was raised. Tina and I tried to make that house livable. We fought the good fight.

When I ask myself why me? One of the answers I come back with is the late Georgia State Representative George Linder. George Linder *"was one of twenty-four black representatives elected to the Georgia Legislature in 1868 - one of thirteen black men who served in the Constitutional Convention and Georgia Legislature. Linder, known as Uncle George Linder, was respected by both races in Laurens County. Racism was tearing Georgia apart. The Klu Klux Klan was turning more violent, getting away from its original purpose of protecting white victims of the Civil War and Reconstruction. Each member was given one hour to speak before being expelled from their seats -*

by the KKK led effort. George Linder is on record saying from within the chamber to the white extremists about to take control 'roust us from here, and we will roust you!' Some of Linder's colleagues were threatened with violence. One was killed, and a few were injured. On October 22, 1869, Congress enacted the Congressional Reorganization Act of 1869, through which Linder and the other black representatives were reseated. George Linder served the remainder of his term until the legislative election of 1870 when the Democratic Party gained control." I can't even imagine the level of courage it took for George Linder to say the words 'roust us from here, and we will roust you' to a group of KKK clansmen in 1800's Georgia. I have to believe his ability to stare death in the face during a dark period in America's history is what gave rise to me staying in a haunted house for long as I did. And in doing so received a lot of thank you emails. "Thank you for sharing your story." "Thank for documenting everything." "Thank you for not giving up." "For sticking to your guns." There's not a continent on this earth I haven't gotten a heartfelt 'thank you' letter from. People the world over have experienced similar things. It doesn't matter where they come from or what their status in life is, they've met Mr. Poltergeist. Those who've experienced something similar always imply "it's hard to go back to a normal life." I couldn't agree with them more. It's extremely hard to get back to a normal life. Conversations I have with my family and friends seem so bland now. Politics? Religion? Which football teams going to the Super Bowl this year? What's the stock market doing today? What's my 401K doing? Talk to me about those things now – I'll listen. You'll have my attention for about five minutes. Five minutes that's it. I hate feeling that way, but I can't help it.

Nick Kyle's (then President of the SSPR) advice to me back in April 2016, was to "try to put this experience behind you. Try not to talk about it. Even if someone asks you point blank, kindly tell them that you've moved on." I have to admit Nick's advice caught me off guard. *What good can come from keeping things bottled up?* You, Steve and Don, have seen shadow figures in my house. You heard the footsteps. The pinging sounds. The disembodied voices.

I see Nick's point. There's always going to be a percentage of the people who view instances such as this as nothing but attention-seeking. No matter how well a case gets substantiated or documented, your motive for bringing this experience to the public will always be questioned. Survivors of extreme hauntings are often viewed as attention-seekers. As hoaxers. Sounds weird, doesn't it? It's true though. You saw the negative response Zak Bagans and Dave Schrader gave when Steve Mera and Don Philips made their findings public. No one forced Zak and Dave to say that. If you thought it was just the United Kingdom's investigators receiving an inordinate amount of scrutiny from paranormal peers, you're wrong. Nicole (Nikki) Novelle and her team received way more character assassination attacks than Steve, Nick, and Don. Why? Probably because their team was majority female.

That's why Nick Kyle told me just to move on. Why subject yourself to that level of scorn when you don't have to? But you see, I can't move on. Not in the manner that he suggested. It's hard to walk away from something that's affected so many people. Look what happened to Rhonda and her family. Look at what *Ghost Adventures* did, what Nikki and her team did, what her team found. Look at what Steve and Don found. Look at what I found. Look at the bone black – the Dippel's oil. Look at the shadows Steve found on his motion camera. The voices Don Philips found in the woods. Look at the history of Bothell Washington. Who in their right mind can forget that? By forget I mean to shrug it off as if it never happened. It might lead to my detriment. Oh well. I've always been a cup half full type of person.

The smallpox outbreak, the wars in and around Puget Sound, the mass graves, the ill-treatment of Native Americans, Rhonda being raped, meningitis, social media's ill- treatment of Tina and me, Rhonda's suicide, the relationship breakups. That's the negative takeaway. The positive takeaways, albeit small in my opinion, are worth preserving. Tina and I are still alive. We still have our health, our jobs, our careers, our close friends, and our family (albeit strained, we still have them). Our experience would have been worse than it was had one of those things I just mentioned been taking from us. The next positive takeaway would be the evidence that myself and others got. Everything you ever wanted to know about the Bothell house (as told by Keith Linder) is on YouTube. It's on *Facebook*. It's on *Twitter*. It's on *WordPress*.

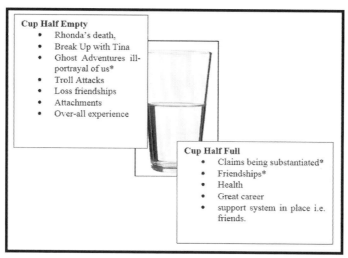

Fig 31.1: Cup half full mentality

The question you probably asked yourself already through the course of reading this book is why do I have attachments? The most straightforward answer I can give you is I lived in the Bothell hell house. Four years is a long time, ladies and gentlemen. It really is. But is it the length of time you stay at a place that causes you to have attachments or is it something else? Or is it both? The answer to why I have attachments is complicated. I said earlier that the possibility of me having attachments, i.e., being followed to my new place of residence was talked about by many. Researchers, paranormal teams, and friends of mine all told me at different times that they'd be surprised if the spirits in the Bothell house didn't follow me. They were justified in feeling this way. I've had sheets yanked off me in the middle of the night while traveling on business. Electrical problems you wouldn't believe in the hotels I've stayed in. Problems the hotel IT department couldn't explain. Pillows yanked off the bed while I was sleeping and thrown on the floor.

You need to look no further than the experience I had when I went to pick up my clothes at my neighborhood cleaners to understand the phenomena known as attachments. I'll never forget the look on both the store owner and his wife's face when they handed me back my clothes untouched (see Chapter 33 *The Bothell Hell House*). The shirts I had bought into the cleaners the day before looked like ribbons. Like confetti – that's how shredded they were. What precipitates the symptoms I've just mentioned? Let's pretend you asked me this question over a bottle of wine or salmon dinner. What would I tell you? I'd tell you my being followed is probably the result of multiple things.

I've listed below some of the possible reasons:

- Environment
- Synergy and one's past
- Staring into the abyss
- Throwing down the gauntlet
- Get it over with
- Don't know / unknown

There's a lot to unpack here so let's get going. The law of cause and effect teaches us that "the effect produced by a particular cause becomes the cause of another phenomenon, which, in turn, becomes the cause of a third phenomenon, and so forth." Everything I've witnessed and experienced would have never happened had I chosen another house to live in. Wall writings, spontaneous fires, objects being thrown, missing objects, objects appearing out the blue, poking and prodding, nightmares, and night terrors. None of that stuff would have happened. Rhonda Jimenez? *Ghost Adventures*, the US / UK paranormal teams, this and all the other events I just mentioned never would have taken place had Tina, and I lived elsewhere. The Bothell house, that's where it all started. That's the environment I'm referring to.

Synergy and one's past – there's a scene in the movie *The Empire Strikes Back,* of Luke Skywalker questioning Yoda about a nearby cave. Yoda tells Luke the cave he's is staring at is strong with the "dark side of the force. Into it, you must go."

Luke (with his farm boy expression) asks Yoda what's inside it. Yoda replies, "Only what you take with you." Luke goes in and as you know (from watching the movie) is shown his own dark side. I believe the spirits in the Bothell house possess the ability to know a person's past within seconds of meeting them. Study this. Tina and I heard a kid 'cough' the day we went to pick up the keys to the house. Not the day we moved in. I'm talking about the day we went to sign papers. A few days later, my car keys went missing. I should stop saying car keys because it was actually my car fob also known as a keyless remote. If you watched my video on YouTube or read my book *The Bothell Hell House,* you already know the inexplicable problems I had with my previous car. The spirits took my extra car fob from a glove box. A well tucked away glove box. You want to know something else that was well-tucked way? So, tucked away that I forgot I still owned them? Family photos.

Summer, 2014. The spirits did something I thought was inconceivable. They took all the pictures that I owned. Pictures of me with my family – they stacked them on the desk in my office. My face, ladies and gentlemen, had been burned completely out of all of them. If you look at the picture, you'll see I'm with my immediate family at what appears to be a graduation. A family member is missing in these photos — my twin brother. You'd think my twin brother and I would be thick as thieves. That we would be very close. Not so.

Fig 31.2: Sister and brother graduation photo. Missing sibling.

My decision to move to Seattle widened wedges between my siblings and me. None of my siblings thought it was a good idea. They thought I was selfish. The thing I heard the most was "Seattle's too far away; why are you moving there?" My twin brother stopped talking to me. I mean, we didn't talk for years. Family dysfunction? It can be hidden from just about anything you can think of. It can be hidden from your employer. It can be hidden from your friends. From church members. It can be hidden from the relationships you have with people, i.e., wives, husbands, girlfriends, etc. It might be difficult to hide but it can be done. It cannot. I repeat it cannot be hidden from spirits. The spirits in the Bothell house for reasons I've yet to figure out seem to have a proclivity for dysfunction. It's like they can sense it on sight. I know from talking to Rhonda that there was a level of dysfunction in her and her husband's marriage. I've admitted to the level of dysfunction Tina and I had in my previous book as well as in this book. My twin brother's absence from two of his younger sibling's college graduations points to a level of dysfunction in my immediate family.

The majority of the nightmares and night terrors I'm having (which started after I moved out of the Bothell house) deal with past disagreements I've had with siblings – a majority of it involves my twin brother. The minions know this. They read it. I've met a lot of twins in my life. I know the closeness other twins have. I'm talking about the spiritual and mental connection. Being each other's BFF. My twin brother and I don't have that. I share this with you not because I want to put myself and my family in a bad light. I share this with you because I want you to understand the phenomena known as attachments. People who tell me they wish they could experience what I experience, I can't help but look at them strangely. Unless your acts throughout life rival that of Mother Theresa, my response to you is no you don't. Staring into the abyss — My love for science fiction and technology made this a given. The spirits knew this. They knew I would be fascinated by some of the events happening around us. In my office at the Bothell house was a book titled *A Brief History of Time* by the late Stephen Hawking. Some of the things Tina and I have witnessed science says might be possible in a different universe - slightly different makeup as ours. Wormholes, double slit experiment, The Uncertainty Principle, virtual particles, electrons disappearing and reappearing what science theorize about on the minuscule scale I've seen on a large scale. It's beyond fascinating. It's one of the reasons why I decided to set up cameras. Understand the day I bought video equipment into the home was the day I entered the abyss. The spirits sent a few shots across the bow as a warning. Cameras went missing. Cameras were destroyed. That didn't deter me. Not one bit. I just bought more cameras. The more cameras I bought, the more the activity began to escalate, which led to me throwing down the gauntlet.

What's throwing down the gauntlet mean? Throwing down the gauntlet is when you tell the spirit (usually in a loud voice) to 'come out wherever it is or else.' It's when you dare the spirit do something for the purpose of being impressed. It's when you give a spirit an ultimatum. If you've watched paranormal shows on television, you know exactly what this is. Zak Bagans' of the popular show *Ghost Adventures* has done this on quite a few of his episodes. It's become his trademark essentially. My reason for doing this differs from Zak's. Zak does this to provide entertainment value to his audience. He's metaphorically sticking his head inside the lion's mouth saying, "I dare you to bite down on me." Knowing well in advance that, that's not going to happen. Me? I'm running on four hours sleep. I've just paid a locksmith five hundred dollars to make me a new key fob. The one I had is missing as are a lot of other things. The walls I just painted over have new wall markings. I'm frustrated. So yes, I threw down the gauntlet a few times. I told the spirits in the Bothell hell house to cut it out or else! Their response? More attacks. Get it over with is when you're so beaten down. So, sleep-deprived that the decisions you make about what to do next might not even be your decisions. This wear down component associated with poltergeist haunting is one the least talked about (the least studied) instances in the paranormal. The spirits are doing multiple different things to wear you down. Sounds weird but it's true. I uttered the words get it over with. It was a morning I was lying in bed by myself (see *The Bothell Hell House*). Suddenly I felt the mattress indent as if someone were climbing in bed with me. Or better yet, falling in bed with me. Instead of turning around like I always do, I decided to lay there. I was tired. I was upset. I was curious. I was curious about what was about to happen. What was happening then has happened before. My response in the past has always been spinning around. *Poof! The bed indentation is gone.* I get up soon after to start my day. No harm. No foul. Not today, though. I was spiritually and mentally exhausted. I kid you not, the second my brain said *oh, get it over it, be done with it,* I felt a feeling I've not felt before. Something(s) runs in me. The sensation I felt was all in my lower back area. From that point on what I just described to you has become every other day occurrence.

I hope I've given you an idea as to why I have attachments. Is my past darker than the average person? Is it darker than Tina's? No. That shouldn't be the takeaway here. Plus, or minus a few things, my past is no different than those reading this book right now. The underline theme should be walks of life. A combination of different walks of life emerging under one roof. A roof that witnessed an ugly of act of cruelty (Rhonda's rape) and a house built in an area where hundreds of thousands of Native Americans lost their lives due to smallpox and racism combined with the six bullet points, I've listed could be the underlying reason for me still having attachments.

Those who pray for this type of phenomena need to take one thing under consideration: You have no control whatsoever on what type of spirit you might encounter. There's a scene in first *Avengers* movie of a portal door opening above Manhattan. Do you remember that scene of the Chitauri race waiting on the other side of the portal door? The Chitauri waste no time springing into action. When you say stupid stuff like "I wish that happened to me" or "come out, come out, wherever you are," or the worst saying of all "show me what you got, or else." Or else what? Or else you're going to force them to come out? That's TV, ladies, and gentlemen, – that's not real life. Attachments are like water faucets. Some water faucets can be turned off easily. Some cannot. It's impossible to know what's on the other side of that portal door; therefore, it's impossible to have the right tool on standby. Tina and I didn't open up any portal doors. The spirits were already here when we arrived. The last reason for me having attachments I feel no shame in admitting is I don't know. And it's OK not to know. I wish more paranormal teams would have uttered the words 'I don't know' when Tina and I came calling. They would have saved us a lot of grief and headache. The majority of what happened in this house and the apartment I'm living in now most likely won't ever be figured out. I hate to admit it, but it's true. The spirits hold all the cards. They know the answer to all of our questions. It's time to recap what's been talked about in this book. In my profession, we call this takeaways.

Poltergeist of Washington State – things that must be studied and re-evaluated as it relates to the phenomenon known as poltergeist include.

Wall Markings Analysis – Patty and I used her husband's truck to take the office door to the paint store. Identical markings appeared on the bed of her husband's truck. Review again **https://youtu.be/u-UTd37duCQ**

Bone black– Results from an XRD/XRF gun revealed the wall markings to be a hundred percent organic. The spirits chose this substance specifically to convey the genocidal atrocities that took in Puget Sound in the 1800s. One question we don't have an answer to, and we need is: where did the bone black come from?

http://fliphtml5.com/lglzz/baql - Bone Black
Three yellow streaks. Dippel's oil?

Patty's Attack Guest Bedroom Bothell House

Chapter 11

Parapsychologists Steve Mera and Chief researcher arrive back in Seattle to investigate the Bothell house a second time:

Case Highlights:

- Voices captured in the master bathroom. Reminiscent of the men's first visit where they captured voices saying, 'it's a camera, it's a camera,' see *The Bothell Hell House*. Steve and Don's second visit. Voices begin at 1:31. "Ray" "Ray, Image Detector" "Cable" "it's the only way it can be powered like that", "Go and lift one of these." Could all paranormal events where objects disappear and are never to be seen again be a form of thievery?
'Image Detector' –
https://www.youtube.com/watch?v=3xOswSf9qXw&feature=youtu.be
- Motion Sensors – placed on the bed in the master bedroom. The room is sealed off. Those same motion sensors were - later found on the bedroom floor. The area they were found gave off a high milligauss reading.
  - ✓ Steve Mera, Nick Kyle, and Don Phillips remove the mattress and other coverings. The compass Steve is holding gives off strange readings. Don Phillips – Conducts an EVP session in the forest area behind the house. Several unexplained voices captured. A male voice utters the word 'yes' when asked if there were bodies buried in the area. Begins at 9:21
  https://www.youtube.com/watch?v=xXKdMi3H9wM
- Steve Mera – launched an experiment in my upstairs hallway using motion detectors and strobe light technology. Picked up shadow images. Both men were able to obtain compelling evidence at the same time in different locations.
https://www.youtube.com/watch?v=UQxtGBUxAdk

Honorable mentions during Steve and Dons 2nd visit

- https://www.youtube.com/watch?v=ovIrMEZ-GiY
'Uaah I thought I saw it.'
- https://youtu.be/uBte7PDEmTc
'I'm a Mirror'

Water Puddles – May 10th, 2016
- https://www.youtube.com/watch?v=Aj6p2FWGxtY& featur e=youtu.be

New place of residence – Week One. Apartment manager writes report admitting to the root cause not being found.

Dishwasher goes on the fritz - June 8th, 2016
Building maintenance swopped out brand-new appliances with other brand-new dishwashers. The problem persisted several months. Those same dishwashers worked fine in other units.

Passenger Seatbelt Light On/Off - 🔔
Passenger seat belt lights go on and off. The problem went on for a year, intermittently. Tapered off on its own. The root cause could not be determined. Voice captured saying 'sit in the chair'
https://youtu.be/nF2X2rTiGwA

Night Terrors
- Psychic attack
- Dreams - Twisted déjà vu

Nightmares
- Psychic attack
- She-demons' visitation
  - ✓ Multiple 'Keith' EVPs
    - o voice placement/telepathy
  - ✓ Sexual encounters
  - ✓ Victim referrals
  - ✓ No paralysis
  - ✓ Eroticism on steroids
  - ✓ Mental orgasms
  - ✓ Sex with half-woman half-beast

Active Investigation - Stage 2:
13/04/16 - 19/04/2016
Data Collection: 102 Gigabytes
Audio recordings - 127 obtained.
EVP Class B and C discarded.
56 EVP Class A from inside and outside of house.
4 AVP (Actual Voice Phenomena)
Audible Disturbances throughout the house.
Physical Phenomena Detected.
Over 30 hours of video footage obtained.
211 photographs obtained and 20 anomalies.
Samples taken of unknown liquid on walls.
Psychological Assessment and Profiling completed.
Interviews and documentation obtained.

Fig 31.3: 2nd trip synopsis. Scientific Establishment of Parapsychology

CHAPTER 32

Dear Reader

The Bothell Hell House and this book Attachments: Poltergeist of Washington State are first-person accounts of a poltergeist haunting. If you aren't blown away by the events being reported in both books, then please accept my apology. I mean that. I've failed in describing what Tina and lived through. When people like myself step forward and reveal their experience, i.e., their encounter with the netherworld, they're quickly bombarded with all kinds of character assassinations. All types of name-calling. That causes other people not to come forward with their experience. Which is unfortunate. Writing a book is the oldest method for sharing information. Cynics will say 'that's what the hidden motive was all along. Get rich by writing a book.' Ironically! If I had a quarter for every time a skeptic told me that, I would be just that. Rich. I'm speaking on behalf of all poltergeist survivors those still alive and those who are no longer with us. No amount of money can make up for what we went through. I'll say this now just in case I haven't said it already. My reason for writing both books is I believe this information needs to be shared. It needs to be studied. This stuff needs to be archived. Whatever this is we're going through; I bet you (if there's a name for it) is about to be redefined. Maybe not now. But one day. Someone out there is going to see this stuff and in doing so advance the paranormal field by leaps and bounds.

I said at the beginning of this book that the last words in this book shouldn't come from me. It should come from the researchers that investigated this house. It should come from those who study poltergeist. The sixty-plus page report detailing everything Steve Mera, Don Phillips, and Nick Kyle found are accessible here. Please read it. But your quest for knowledge doesn't end there. The link to the "Demons in Seattle Uncovered" documentary by Don Phillips has been added here. Steve Mera's report and Don's documentary go hand in hand. I know what some are thinking. Why read when you can watch? Trust me; you don't want to do that. There are things in the report that are not in the documentary, and there are things in the documentary that are not in the report.

Before I sat down and started writing these books, I said to myself, this book has to be more than just words. More than just stories. I've worked for some of the largest companies in the world. Companies that hired me to put standardization around their most strategic processes. In IT, success is determined by your ability to keep good records. I'm talking about documentation. You must be organized. You must be communicative. You must have soft skills. The greatest asset of all is soft skills. Conducting a lesson learned with your project team is extremely important. Mistakes made while solving a problem should be documented and shared. That's why I wrote these books. That's what the spirits came across when they met Keith Linder. A man keen on documenting everything he and girlfriend encountered with the hopes it will be studied later. What will I do next? I'm going to try to live my life. I'm hoping the attachments I have will eventually get bored of me and therefore fade away. I'm hoping that's what happens. In the meantime, there's one more thing I have to do. I have to write my third book. This won't be non-fiction. There's little else I can tell you about my experience except that it's still happening. This third book won't be about current events (knock on wood). This third book will be a dissection of the evidence obtained. About the major phenomena's we encountered. One of my favorite books to ever read was _A Brief History of Time_ by the late great Stephen F. Hawking. It's a fine read. What's an even finer read is *The*

Illustrated Brief History of Time, Updated and Expanded Edition by the same author. That book contained 240 full color illustrated photos of some of Stephen Hawking's greatest theories and predictions. The purpose of his second book was to explain better what some "found difficult to grasp despite the clarity and wit of Professor Hawking's writing." My third book will contain illustrations created by me and the artists I hire that convey and explain what skeptics embarrassingly characterize as "outrageous claims." There are good books out there about the poltergeist. Exceptional books. The best books I'm afraid to say were written in the twentieth century. Well, guess what? We're in the twenty-first century now. The time has come for us to explain some of these phenomena being reported using today's terms. Mine and others.

I'm talking about:

- The Bibles that caught fire (in my house) — the third book will explore the mechanizations of what is known in parapsychology circles as a pyro poltergeist
- The wall writings.
  - ✓ How was the spirit able to do what it did in such a short
    period of time? Time dilation? Possibly.
- Objects thrown
  - ✓ This phenomenon resembles the Heisenberg Uncertainty
    Principle in uncanny ways. Too coincidental in my opinion.
- Water puddles – these phenomena are equally as old as objects being thrown. There were two unexplained water puddle instances: both the Bothell house and my apartment.
  - ✓ The liquid version of asport/apporting
- Asport/apporting
- EVP – Unexplained voice phenomena

I'm talking detailed captions alongside each illustration of each bullet point above. To my knowledge, this type of book has never been done before in both parapsychology and paranormal communities. How are the spirits able to do what it is they do? How are they able to set objects on fire within a few feet of the house occupant? What's the science (if any) behind that? It's as if the spirits were thumbing their nose at the laws of physics. Why is that? Science likes to quickly disavow such occurrences as easily explainable without performing the most basic form of troubleshooting, which is interviewing witnesses. No one can explain why these events are taking place in homes throughout the world. Science can't explain it. Shame on them. This third book, if done right, will offer an in-depth look at everything I've reported. Some of you might not have known this, but a lot of what happened in our house happened in sets of three. Three Bibles caught fire. Three candles thrown. Three loud bangs within seconds of objects flying, i.e., flowerpot. Three wooden crosses missing. Three female apparition sightings. Three shadow people. More examples are in my previous book *The Bothell Hell House*.

"Three is the first number to which the meaning all was given. It is The Triad, it's a holy number, and one highly respected among the celestial world. The number of the whole as it contains the beginning, a middle, and an end." It shouldn't be a surprise to people that "the power of three is universal in that it is accepted in just about every culture imaginable as being a representation of heaven, earth, and waters." In short "body, soul and spirit." So, you see I have to do a third book as a way of climbing out this hole I stumbled into called the paranormal. It's pretty much a requirement at this point.

I've now reached my favorite part of the book. The part where I get to thank people. There's no way I could have gotten through this ordeal had it not been for some key individuals. The first people I want to thank is you. Yes, you! Thank you for buying my book *Attachments – Poltergeist of Washington State*. Thank you for reading it. I sincerely hope I was able to give you some insight about this case and the phenomena known as attachments. I hope you can view all the links in this book. All the reports and all the interviews. There's a lot of stuff. Please take your time and review everything. You're going to find it very interesting. I promise. I would also like to thank Nicole (Nikki) Novelle, anonymous person, Vanessa Hogle, Karissa Fleck, and the rest of the United States paranormal team. Thank you for shedding light on this case. You ladies saw validity in my claims before anyone else. Look what came about as a result of your ladies' involvement. Steve Mera, Don Phillips, Nick Kyle, and the always professional, Patty Hale. Thank you for everything you've done – for realizing the now moment. I can't tell you how great it was for me to see Steve, Nick, and Don writing things down on notepads. It might sound weird coming from an IT specialist, but technology or the over-dependence of it can sometimes get in the way. Thank you, men, for your exemplary notetaking. I want to send a huge thank you to David Rose of Seattle Fox 13. I can always tell when a reporter is just after a story vs. if they have true interests. David Rose exhibited an inordinate amount of interests in the case from day one. You and your team spent a considerable amount of time at the Bothell house, and the results was amazing – 17 million views. And last but certainly not least. Thank you, paranormal community. Thank you for going well out of your way towards getting the truth. Every radio and podcast show I went on to talk about my first book, *The Bothell Hell House,* greeted me with open arms. Thank you, Jeremy Scott, for being the first radio person to recognize the validity of this case. To all the host and hostess. God bless all of you. God keep all of you and may you all continue doing what it is you do. Don't forget to click on every link in the coming pages and please, pretty please review all the links in the chapters provided. God bless!

Comprehensive Report

The Scientific Establishment of Parapsychology

SEP Investigation Ref: 26411
Assistance from Nick Kyle of the Scottish Society of Psychical Research: SSPR
Investigation of alleged paranormal disturbances
Two stage investigation: Jan 21st-26th & April 13th-19th 2016
Parties involved: Don Philips, Steve Mera, Patty Hale, Nick Kyle & Brian Allan
Compiled & Constructed by SEP

THE WASHINGTON STATE POLTERGEIST

The 'Demons in Seattle' Case

AMERICA'S MOST CONTROVERSIAL PARANORMAL CASE
A scientific evaluation of alleged paranormal disturbances at a residential home in
Bothell, Seattle, Washington, USA.

DRAFT COPY

This document is the property of SEP : The Scientific Establishment of Parapsychology
Media Coverage: Ghost Adventures, Komo 4 News, Fox News, Phenomena Project
Phenomena Magazine, International Press and Radio Stations
Third party association: Jackie Heighway, Thom Ross & Jenny Ashford

Copyright © JUNE2018-26411

Washington State Poltergeist Case - FREE PDF **60+** Page REPORT
http://online.fliphtml5.com/lglzz/nmor/

Articles and Reports

March 2016 Phenomena Project Visits The Bothell Hell House
https://drive.google.com/file/d/0BvUXMaBHOgPLU01rNjdKR
GpZaHc/view

March 2019 The Bothell Incident Revisited
https://drive.google.com/file/d/179mdNFs
Q-1bl0c0iEHkjtZXW9FYh-Bgc/view

Theory - Poltergeist of Washington State
http://fliphtml5.com/lglzz/ebbt

Washington State Poltergeist Case
https://youtu.be/sB_fnZ7pu1M

Parapsychologists Steve Mera Lecture
https://youtu.be/6ZYfbn0jwKY

Appendix A:

White Hyundai Sonata in Garage (Seattle) Your Trunk is Open

From: On Bu   5.com>
Sent: Friday, October 12, 2018 7:06 AM
To: *Non·   · 5.com>
Subject: White Hyundai Sonata in Garage (Seattle) - Your Trunk is Open

License plate ends in 559.

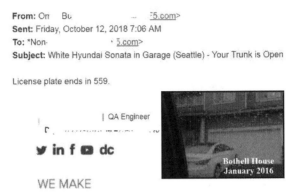

| QA Engineer

𝕐 in f ▣ dc

WE MAKE

Fig A.1: Periodic emails sent through our company's internal distribution lists alerting of an employee's car trunk door open. The car is mine.

Fig A.2: Work parking garage

Missing plant on car buying day
https://theghostvictimexperiment.wordpress.com/2017/04/16/pol
ter geist-objects-disappearing-phenomenon-by-keith-linder/
Attachments: Poltergeist of Washington State

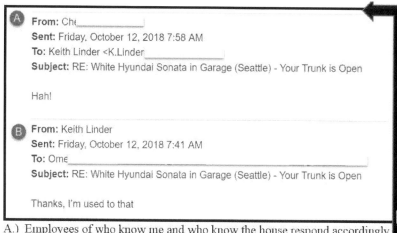

A.) Employees of who know me and who know the house respond accordingly.
B.) Thanks, I'm used to that – Keith Linder

Office Management email – *Creative Plant* — *"brought it to my attention today that we have a plant missing."* In the picture above you see two potted plants where there used to be three. "Please help me locate the plant so that I may return it to its home where it will receive the proper lighting and care...not to mention that the other two plants miss their friend. Please help us bring the plant home". December 22, **2015,** 4:38 PM PST B.) 2nd EMAIL – Facilities manager sends out a second email twenty minutes later alerting everyone that the plant has returned. – "Probably just went out for some fresh air, because it's back to its rightful place now" December 22, **2015,** 5:00 PM

Appendix B:

Tinnitus – I'm Screaming

I remember waking up in extreme ear pain during the first week in my new apartment. I'm talking about an extreme ringing sensation happening in both ears. I was sleeping in the guest bedroom in my new apartment, the same week as the water puddle and car battery incident. All of a sudden, I woke to loud ringing. Not a siren ring. It was like a factory of tea kettles were going off inside my head. Thousands of them – all at once. This pain I was experiencing lasted for quite a while. I was on the floor next to my bed pretty much in the fetal position. Seriously! I was balled up like a Texas Armadillo thinking to myself is this how my life ends? I later learned this pain I felt – this immense earring could be tinnitus. One of the leading causes of tinnitus is loud noises. You've gone from a loud environment to a quiet environment. Something loud you've heard every day for years is now gone. Could this tinnitus be a result of me living in the Bothell house? I'm not sure. It was very odd to have this happen within a few days of me living in my new apartment. People familiar with this case, with my story, know about the humming noise that took place in the Bothell house. I've talked about the strange rapping's. The constant concussion sounds. The constant humming. After a while, you get used to it. You forget it's there. You forget the fact that you're living inside a pressure cooker. You're inside a home where the noise around you is a vice. It was a few weeks after this incident that the 'Keith' whispers in my ear while sleeping began emerging. The high pitch ringing still happens from time to time. In between nightmares and night terrors. In between the poking and prodding.

Appendix C:
Wall Markings Magnified

Door still sits in storage

Wall Markings Magnified 1000x. Reveal new **Bone Black** markings invisible to the naked eye

March 2019 – I went online and ordered a digital microscope. Once again, I was hit with the idea to dig deeper into my case. I was thinking, *what do these visible markings look like under a microscope?* What does bone black look like magnified 1000X times? I wasn't expecting to see more wall markings invisible to the naked eye. You can to (see below).

https://youtu.be/y-cB350ewYc
Wall Analysis
https://youtu.be/SXWecKKy76c
Demons in Seattle - More wall analysis

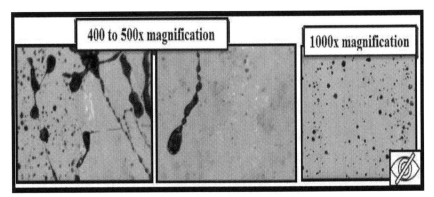

400 to 1000x magnification of office door.

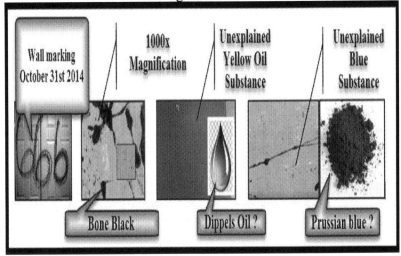

The markings from the office wall (Bothell house) was looked at under a microscope - **1000x magnification (see back cover).** A blue like substance can be seen. Its proximity to bone black which produces its own binding agent known as Dippels Oil which produces its own by-product known as Prussian blue is uncanny.

https://www.hindawi.com/journals/jamc/2018/6595643/
Numerous studies have been published concerning bone black identification through the detection of phosphates by micro destructive techniques.....micro-XRD)
https://www.sciencedirect.com/science/article/abs/pii/S05848547040
02046?via%3Dihub

Bone Black - Conservation & Art Materials
Encyclopedia Online **100 UM**

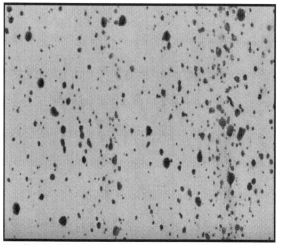

Wall Marking of Bothell House **100 to 1000X**
Magnification

See the family resemblance?

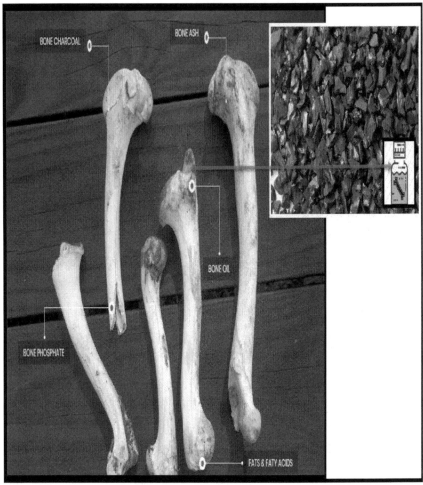

Bison/Cow Bone and all its bi products.

Appendix D:
Black Floating Mass / Microsoft Visit

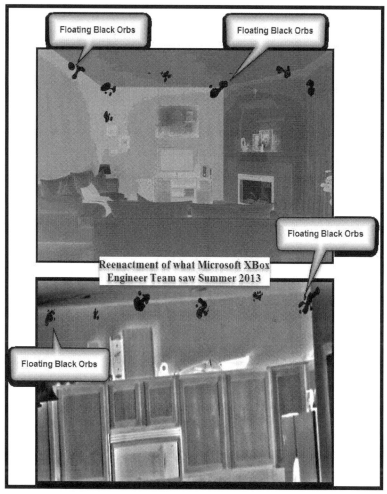

Illustration - Microsoft Xbox Study Summer 2013 – While monitoring my gameplay, engineers picked through the Kinect multiple floating orbs in both living room and kitchen on multiple monitors in my home and in their lab abroad. See The Bothell Hell House. https://www.youtube.com/watch?v=J6-u0J2NgIU

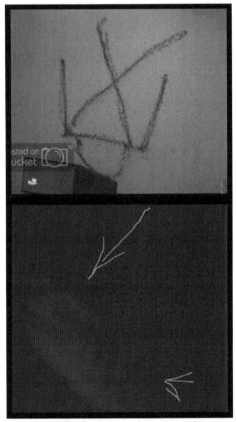

Obscure face (eyes) and mouth detected on a motion camera –Scientific
Establishment of Parapsychology

Additional Links

- Demons in Seattle: Uncovered Documentary
  https://www.americansupernatural.com/sream-full-movie-ppv

- Digital stethoscope: technology update
  https://www.ncbi.nlm.nih.gov/pmc/articles/PMC5757962/

- (App Review: Thinklabs) One Digital Stethoscope
  https://www.physicianspractice.com/app-review-thinklabs-one-digital-stethoscope
- Facebook
  https://www.facebook.com/Washington-State-Poltergiest-House-05963559540294/?ref=bookmarks
- Seattle Freeze
  https://www.seattletimes.com/life/lifestyle/seattle-freeze-forget-making-friends-half-of-washington-residents-dont-even-want-to-talk-to-you/
  https://www.urbandictionary.com/define.php?term=Seattle%20Freeze
- The Brain on Your Name: How Your Brain Responds to the Sound of Your Name
  https://name-coach.com/blog/brain-name-brain-responds-sound-name/
- Three children beaten to death; two escape
  https://www.upi.com/Archives/1984/03/04/Three-children-beaten-to-death-two-escape/5031447224400/
  https://murderpedia.org/male.D/d1/davis-james-lee.htm
- Word Press
  https://theghostvictimexperiment.wordpress.com/

Poltergeist Rapping Noise 45 minutes
https://youtu.be/j6fNRn92Svo

Haunted House Attack
https://youtu.be/lJcybAlMxD0 58 minutes

Spring 2016 – Piece of the Bothell house office door chiseled off. Black
marks left by the poltergeist later discovered to be Bone Black

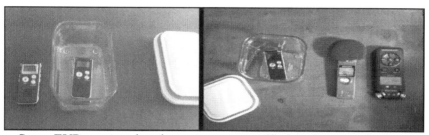

Some EVPs captured under water were muffled (voice recorder in Tupperware). Identical EVPs depending on the voice recorder used were heard inside and outside the plastic container. Overall the results were mixed. Verdict on direct voice placement? Inconclusive.

Left – Voice placement experiment. Right – UK teams "geist" interaction experiment.

Nightmare Notes Examples
(taken from Bed Diary)

4-3-2019
5:24AM

Crazy dream. Took me back to 50's and 60's. Riding (POV) 3rd person with a racist cop-Cop stops by old house downtown somewhere? Goes in – demands to see someone (black) the house occupants know what he wants. He then shouts at them. Calls for back up. He and the other cops start chasing me? I run. I land in another house. Top of building. A church! Now I'm Hispanic. I take refuge for help. Cops leave ½ way through dream I turn Asian. Watching an old Asian karate fight in a room full of all races?

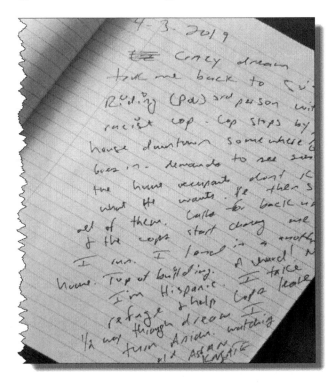

3-6-2910
Violent dreams
Mass killings
Neo – Nazis
Gun Advocates
Killing people, they kidnapped

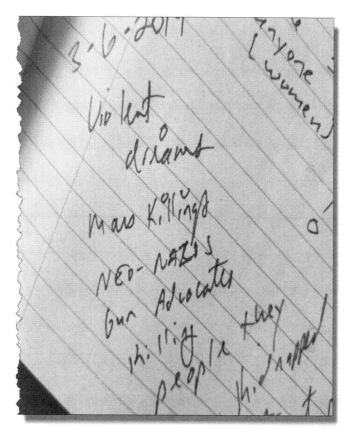

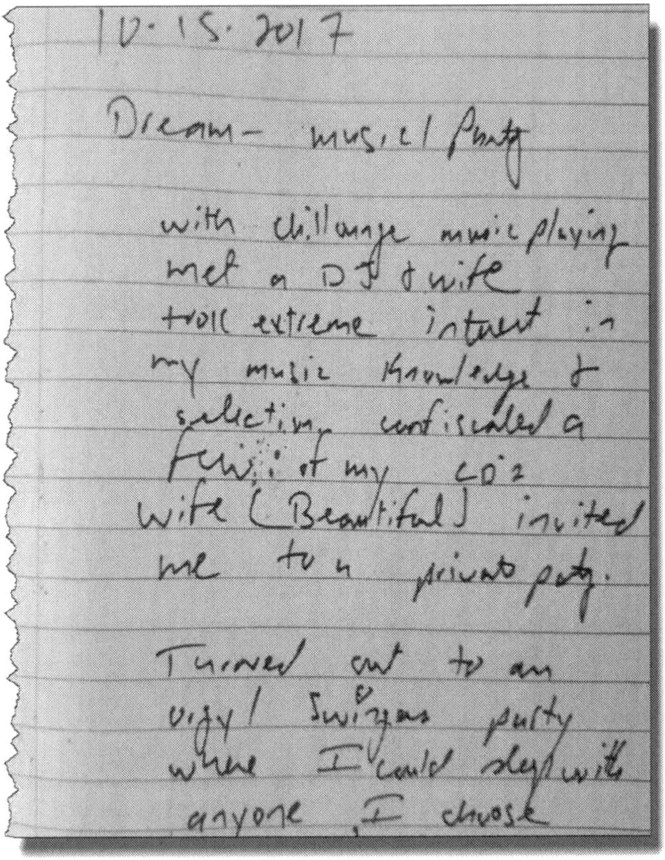

10-15-2017
Dream – Music / Party
With Chillounge music playing
Met a DJ and wife
Took extreme interests in my music knowledge
and selection. Confiscated a few of my CDs
Wife beautiful invited me to a private party
Turned out to be an orgy / swinger's party
Where I could sleep with anyone I choose (women)?

10·15·2017
Dream– music/ Party
with Chillounge music playing
met a DJ & wife
took extreme intrest in
my music knowledge &
selection, confiscated a
few of my CD's
wife (Beautiful) invited
me to a private party.
Turned out to an
orgy / Swingers party
where I could sleep with
anyone, I chose

October 12th, 2018
3:04 AM
Felt warm breath over me
Nostril breathing
Huge bed indentation
Something crawled over me
Warm / something breathed into me

3:03 AM
Sci/Fi
Nightmare
Family conflicts
Couldn't Sleep after darted away
Weird hums – unknown!!
Heartbeats
****
4:06 AM October 13th
Dream of me & long-lost best friend (he doesn't drive)
Friend having drinks at a bar
Floor covered with snakes

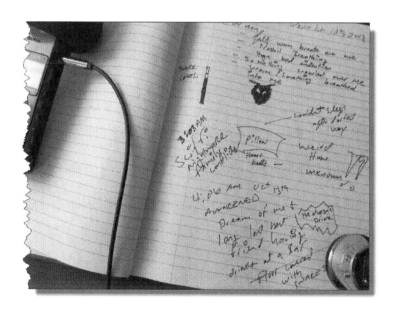

4-17-2019
1:36 AM

Woke up shivering and quivering
Something told me to wake up. Was having a bad dream.
Dreamed I had a BIG gash in my head.
Was bleeding profusely. My mom and a stranger was
present. Mom looked shocked and dumb founded. She was
trying to stop the bleeding. Massive blood loss. That's
when I realized I was dreaming. Woke up shaking &
quivering. Blood pressure 160/100
Turned on heater. Put on sweatpants
2:19am blood pressure is now 117/83. Goes way down
What was this? I felt a quiver and euphoria moment?
*Visit to doctors office that day revealed nothing wrong.

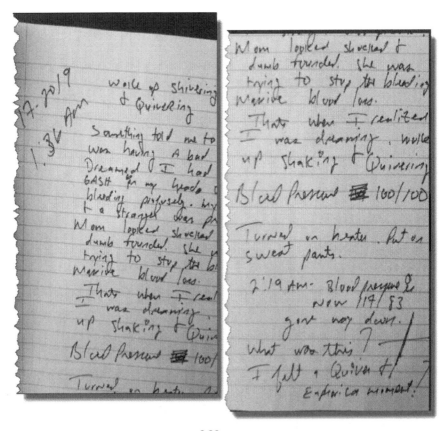

4-6-2019
5:00 AM
Raspy Seduction
Voice (Telepathy)
Whispers in my dreams to turn over. I felt an entering. A swoosh / swoon
She sounded desperate like she needed to bond with me. (Euphoria) Sexually?
Said "please turn over......" I was too tired to oblige.
What would have happened?

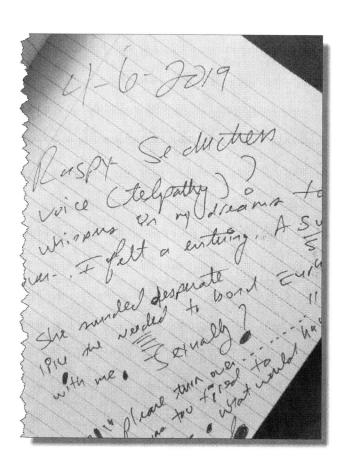

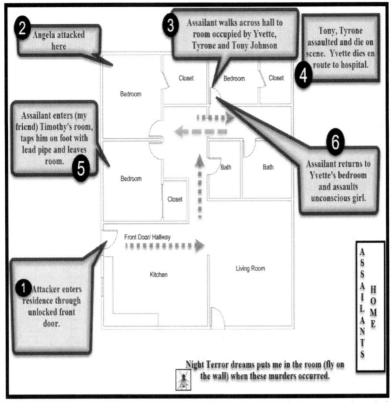

May 2016, I started having repeated nightmares / night terrors involving my old friend. **I can't explain why. I'm the fly on the wall observing the path** the murderer took (as revealed in the *Austin American Statesman* 1984).

" I LOOKED INTO his eyes and they had a demon look **in** them."
Survivor – Angela

"...At night, when the streets of your cities and villages shall be silent, and you think them deserted, they will throng with the returning hosts that once filled and still love this beautiful land. The white man will never be alone. Let him be just and deal kindly with my people, for the dead are not altogether powerless."

Chief Seattle

Bothell, 1909 Courtesy UW Special Collections

Illustration – A minion traversing easily between both locations. Bothell house and where I live now. While the Gray Lady looks on. Forever trapped.

Made in the USA
Lexington, KY
12 November 2019